P9-CCR-925

THE EDUCATION OF A YANKEE

Also by Judson Hale

INSIDE NEW ENGLAND

JUDSON HALE

The Education of a Yankee

AN AMERICAN MEMOIR

1817

HARPER & ROW, PUBLISHERS, New York

Cambridge, Philadelphia, San Francisco, Washington

London, Mexico City, São Paulo, Singapore, Sydney

THE EDUCATION OF A YANKEE. Copyright © 1987 by Judson D. Hale, Sr. All rights reserved. Printed in the United States of America. No part of this book may be used or reproduced in any manner whatsoever without written permission except in the case of brief quotations embodied in critical articles and reviews. For information address Harper & Row, Publishers, Inc., 10 East 53rd Street, New York, N.Y. 10022. Published simultaneously in Canada by Fitzhenry & Whiteside Limited, Toronto.

FIRST EDITION

Designer: Sidney Feinberg

Copy editor: Katherine G. Ness

Library of Congress Cataloging-in-Publication Data

Hale, Judson D.

  The education of a Yankee.

  1. Hale, Judson D. 2. Journalists—United States—Biography.
3. Yankee (Dublin, N.H.) I. Title.
PN4874.H216A3 1987   070'.92'4 [B]   86–46069
ISBN 0–06–015752–6

87 88 89 90 91 HC 10 9 8 7 6 5 4 3 2 1

To my brother,
Roger Drake Hale, Jr.,
who made all the difference

Contents

Photographs follow pages 54, 150, and 198

Acknowledgments

Thanks and thanks and ever thanks . . .

. . . to Abe Collier, Richard Meryman, Geraldine Mathews, Ann Friedl, Burgess Ayres, Prof. Jere Daniell, Austin Stevens, Richard Heckman, Lawrence Willard, Annabelle Dupree, Allan Fox, Kenison Smith, Fred Huberlie, Reta Huberlie, Esther Fitts, and Mel Allen for helpful advice and/or specific recollections.

. . . to all the good people who sent me *Yankee*-related anecdotes that, as it turned out, I couldn't use. (I'll save them, though!)

. . . to Mr. and Mrs. ("Dickie") Howland Vibber, Sheila (Nichols) Williams, Mrs. Alfred ("Fia") Jetter, Jim and Ruth Hansen, John MacDuffie III, and Paul and Viola Susee for spending so much time sharing their memories with me.

. . . to all the Gardners, Trowbridges, Kaupis, Germonds, Whitcombs, Huberlies, Dows, Hales, and Sagendorphs for participating, knowingly or unknowingly, in this story. (There may be a few of you who would rather some of it had remained untold. But please know it is *all* written with love and respect.)

. . . to my sons, J.D., Dan, and Chris and to Frank Gardner, Eloise Gardner, Lorna Trowbridge, Rob Trowbridge, Marjory Gardner, and Jane Kaupi for their specific and very meaningful help.

. . . to Susan Mahnke Peery for her encouragement, expert copyediting, and unflagging enthusiasm for the project; to Ann Grow for

ix

many "after hours" at the *Yankee* office typing and retyping the manuscript; and to Sallie Coolidge, my editor at Harper & Row, who steered me in the right direction from the beginning.

. . . to my sister, Patsy (and husband, Whit, too), who remembered with me for so many hours on tape. (Patsy, I hope you feel I've done our story justice.)

. . . to my mother, Marian, who knew from the start I'd be covering sensitive family matters but who remained, as always, supportive to the hilt.

. . . and, finally, to my wife, Sally, who was the only person to whom I offered "veto power" over certain of the contents related to her—for reasons that are obvious in the reading. The fact she did not once exercise this power, in spite of moments of misgiving, is a tribute to her courage and strength of character. The potential help her part in this story would have for others in similar circumstances out-weighed her powerful instinct for anonymity and privacy.

Prologue

A s we marched into the dining hall, accompanied by an orchestra
playing patriotic music, I was thinking how unusual it was not
to have had a cocktail hour. I'd expected that drinks would be served
in the area outside, where we'd gathered a half hour previously. But
no, there'd just been a general milling about while I, the only stranger in this group of more than three hundred members of the New
England Society of South Carolina, was introduced to one after
another. It was one of those rare times in my life when I felt I had
a strange accent. But I was looking forward to presenting the talk
I'd carefully prepared for the occasion. Its title: "In Search of the
Yankee."

The orchestra stopped playing while we stood behind our designated places to recite the Pledge of Allegiance and hear a short
prayer. Then the music began again with "Old Cape Cod" followed
by "Moonlight in Vermont." The place settings were beautifully
elegant, each place card was engraved like a wedding invitation, the
smell of fresh flowers on the tables permeated the air, and everyone
was dressed in formal attire.

"Be prepared for anything and bring your tuxedo," the previous
year's speaker, Abe Collier, retired chairman of the New England
Mutual Life Insurance Company, had called to tell me just before I
left for Logan Airport that morning. I didn't know what he meant
by that, but I did haul out my father's old black suit from the back
of my closet—it would do as a tuxedo—and now had it on. It was
the very suit my father is wearing in the photograph on my office

wall—the one of my wife, my mother, him, and me, all beaming happily at the Copacabana nightclub in New York in March of 1963, one month before he ended his life in the kitchen of his Marblehead, Massachusetts, home. I wished he could see me now, the guest of honor about to address a distinguished group of Charleston Southerners on the subject of the word "Yankee" and his beloved New England.

A moment later, the door to the kitchen opened and out streamed about thirty black men in immaculate white uniforms. Some of the men carried pitchers of clear liquid. The others held a small jar in each hand.

"Would you prefer an olive or an onion in your martini, sir?" asked one of the jar men who'd arrived behind my chair.

My heart fell a little. The occasion was so festive and grand that cocktails at this point seemed inappropriate. But, what the heck, one small martini might just add to the flow.

"I'll have an olive," I said. After taking a few sips, I turned to my host, a soft-spoken retired army general with whom I'd spent the afternoon touring Charleston. To my surprise, he'd already downed his martini—in one smooth, rapid motion.

"I'd better just drink half of this," I said to him, "so I can be sure I don't go to sleep during my speech."

"There's no such thing as 'half' tonight," he replied with a smile. I looked back at my glass and understood. It was again filled to the brim. Then I noticed that throughout the hall there were groups of waiters hovering around each table like hawks. The second any glass was set down following a sip, a pitcher swooped down to bring it back to full.

Much later, after many sips, almost as many toasts (including three or four to "the President of these United States"), and a lovely chicken dinner, dessert dishes were cleared, coffee cups replaced the martini glasses, and it was time for me to be introduced.

My quiet, soft-spoken host, the General, who now rose while clanging on a small bell with a fork, had become silent during the previous fifteen minutes.

"Judson Hale . . ." he began. The hall quieted down. "Judson Hale . . ." he said again, staring unsteadily at the long typewritten introduction he held. He was having difficulty. "Judson Hale is a real Yankee. No." Pause. "He's better than that." He began to smile at his audience, then down at me. His confidence returned in a surge. As he flipped the typed introduction sheet onto the table, he spread his arms wide and with an exuberance that lifted everyone into one of the loudest and most heartwarming ovations I've heard, he shouted, "He's a DAMN Yankee!"

From then on, I could have read from the telephone book and received an equally friendly response.

To start I opened a tattered 1855 edition of *The Old Farmer's Almanac* and read George R. Russell's definition of a Yankee. "Ice and granite, it is said, are the chief products of New England," I read, "and they fitly symbolize the hearty character of her sons."

"How 'bout the sons that *left?*" This from an old gentleman at a table toward the back of the room. He'd told me earlier that his ancestors, like the ancestors of many of the men present, had left New England and settled in Charleston around the time of the American Revolution.

"They were probably more intolerant of those tough winters and the rocky soil, they may have been more ambitious, more restless, or perhaps of the wrong political persuasion for the times. . . ." I began seriously and then paused, nodding to a waving hand at the table directly in front of me.

"Not as complicated as all that, son," the waving man said, half rising from his chair. "The ones that left just weren't as goddamn *stubborn,*" and the hall erupted in renewed laughter in which I joined.

And so it went, back and forth, more a dialogue than a speech. My prepared notes mingled with my host's rejected introduction on the table.

Much later, after dozens of the men had come up to me individually to shake my hand (with both of theirs) and say "Y'all come back *soon,* hear?" the General and I walked out onto the pier in front of the club building for a breath of the warm, moist evening air. The harbor was calm, and in the distance, its lights faintly reflected upon the dark waters, was Fort Sumter, where the first shots of the Civil War were fired in 1861. We looked across at it together, deep in our own thoughts, until the General interrupted our friendly silence with "My great-granduncle was in the war on the Northern side— originally hailed from Sullivan, Maine. That's where the stream in 'Down by the Old Mill Stream' is located. He had his own definition of a real Yankee. I mean a *damn* Yankee." We both laughed, remembering his introduction and the hilarity it engendered.

"What's that?" I asked.

"A Yankee is a man who ain't leanin' on nothin'," he said. Has a nice, simple ring to it, I thought. Fits the image like a glove. I stored it away for future banquets.

After a pause, the General went on. "They loved you in there tonight because you were exactly what they thought a true Yankee ought to be." He said it as a compliment. So I took it as a compliment. But as we wandered back off the pier to the parking lot, I contemplated some of the "Yankee traits" we'd identified over the course of the evening. Stubborn, frugal, audacious, snobby, practical, prudent, contrary, shrewd, tenacious, and most certainly "not leanin' on nothin'." Is that, God forbid, what I've become over the past fifty-three years? I wondered. . . .

Chapter 1

———◆———

Ingenuity

BOSTON was a good place to start. But not for my brother, Drake. He started in the same three-storey Victorian house I did, next to the library on Heath Street in Chestnut Hill (part of greater Boston), in 1926. Seven years later, when I was born, he'd already been living in Switzerland for three years, never to return home. I would first meet my brother during the summer after my sophomore year at Dartmouth College. And yet when Drake was only three years old, he became responsible for a radical change in the lives of my mother and father that, in turn, changed the course of the lives of both myself and my sister, Patsy, born three years before me.

The circumstances that precipitated this upheaval in the Hale family were not known to me until later. In a sense, my first memory of Drake was how he ate bananas.

"This is how poor Drakie-boy liked his bananas," my mother would say. It was never "Drake" (named after my father, Roger Drake Hale), always "poor Drakie-boy." And she would mash a combination of peeled banana and brown sugar on my plate with a fork until it became a layer of goo covering the entire surface like a pancake. I would eat out a "room" from the center, then a hall, perhaps several bedrooms, a living room, and a kitchen. Just as "poor Drakie-boy" used to do.

Because of Drake, Patsy and I probably received extra attention not only from our parents but also from the entire gang of household maids, the cook, and our special nurse, Frieda, a young lady with a

heavy German accent who lived in a room on the third floor with
her husband, the chauffeur and handyman. Patsy and I called her Fia.
Of course, being the son—and now, with Drake five thousand miles
away, the *only* son—I was the happy recipient of the larger portion
of that extra care and attention. Both of us, however, were treated
exactly according to the rules, instructions, and advice contained in
Dr. Richard M. Smith's little maroon book entitled *From Infancy to
Childhood.* Dr. Smith was upper-class Boston's own "Dr. Spock" of
the 1930s. Raising children, advised Dr. Smith to every "Doctor,
Mother, and Nurse," requires "more than native instinct."

It seemed to me that far more than native instinct was utilized
in Dr. Smith's apparent obsession with constipation, for instance.
Not only were we forced to eat exactly three stewed prunes before
breakfast, an ordeal seldom accomplished without at least one gag,
but a good portion of the morning had to be spent sitting on our
special little toilet, low enough, per Dr. Smith's instructions, to allow
our feet to touch the floor.

"Tell me when you're finished," Fia would invariably instruct,
and then a few minutes, a half hour, or maybe even an hour later,
when we'd screamed "Finished!" we'd be allowed to begin our
morning play. But if Fia decided after a careful inspection that our
performance was inadequate, we were either sentenced to an additional term on our bowl or given two tablespoons of milk of magnesia. Strangely, I liked milk of magnesia. But only a masochist could
have liked the procedure initiated the following morning if results
were again, two days in a row, judged to be unsatisfactory. It was
a fate worse than eating prunes.

An enema.

"Secure an infant's syringe, which consists of a soft-rubber bulb
with a hard-rubber nozzle," instructed Dr. Smith. "The syringe
should be filled with warm soapsuds and water. The tip should be
greased and inserted into the rectum, and contents should then be
expelled slowly. The syringe may be withdrawn and the process
repeated two or three times."

Patsy and I received hundreds of enemas during our early years
of life here on earth. In fact, when I recently returned to the house
on Heath Street, owned now by former State Representative Jon
Rotenberg and family, and wandered through the rooms to determine if anything familiar would jog my memory, one of the most

vivid recollections that came surging back was the enemas.

But there are pleasant memories, too. Like pure olive oil baths. According to Fia, now a widowed grandmother living alone in Wellesley Hills, Massachusetts, it was "quite a vhile before you vere given a bath in vater." We also had daily glasses of fresh beef juice, prepared by the cook, Johnnie, a very large woman with, like Fia, a foreign accent and a fascinating (to me) paralysis on one side of her face. She would cook an entire roast beef for the sole purpose of squeezing the juice out of it.

"It vas the thing to do for, shall ve say, the better-class children in Boston in those days," Fia recalls now, "but I could never understand vy anyvun vould vant their children to drink blood." However, for Patsy and me the thought of big glasses of warm beef juice almost cancels out the prune and enema memories.

Dr. Smith was also big on afternoon naps. To us, naps represented a vast, endless sea of excruciating boredom.

Wrote Dr. Smith: "The children should take off their clothes— or at least the outside clothes—and lie down in a room alone, with the windows open and the shades drawn. During the nap time they should not be read to or have any toys." The pitiless doctor conceded the obvious, particularly true as the years progressed, when he admitted that "toward the latter part of this two-hour period, children frequently begin to have difficulty in going to sleep." Oh really, Dr. Smith? But then he turned downright mean: "If this is the case, the rest period should be continued even though the children do not go to sleep."

No toys, no talking, no reading or being read to, no sleep—in a dark, cold room for two hours every day. If Patsy and I had known at the time who was responsible for this, we might have been able to strangle Dr. Smith when he showed up, as he occasionally did, for one of the many formal dinner parties my parents hosted while we were living in Chestnut Hill.

As it was, I endured my naps by acting out stories about two little four-legged creatures with long skinny heads that walked about on my bed and occasionally wrestled. They were my hands. Also, I smuggled elastic bands into naptime and became skillful at shooting them up so as to strike a certain star on my star-covered ceiling. (The target later on in Vanceboro, Maine, was a specific knot in the wood.) After hitting the star, the idea was to have the elastic fall in such a way that it landed within a small circle I'd drawn on my chest with a crayon.

This little pastime, my first lesson in Yankee ingenuity, served me well some twenty years later when a case of tuberculosis forced me to take a year-long "nap" in an army hospital. We were forbidden to "do" anything for hours on end there, too.

There was one particular nap at Chestnut Hill in which I was *not* bored. It was the only time in my life when I actually, no fooling, saw a ghost with my own eyes. It was a warm spring afternoon in 1936. I was just beginning my two hours in my large star-covered second-floor bedroom and of course I wasn't even *slightly* sleepy. She silently emerged from the wall opposite my bed, dressed in long, flowing red and blue robes, the way the Madonna is usually pictured. I sat bolt upright as she glided over to within three feet of my bed and stared at me. Her pretty face appeared to be that of someone in her mid-twenties.

"What do you want?" I said calmly, at the same time feeling a sharp drop in the room's temperature. She remained silent, staring, but in a kindly rather than a menacing manner.

"Who are you talking to, Juddie?" Fia called in from the sitting room across the hall. She always called me "Juddie," and today, when someone starts a letter or phone conversation that way, I know it's someone who has known me for more than forty years.

"Oh, nobody," I replied. For some reason, I felt that was what the apparition wanted me to say. But she communicated nothing other than her kindly look. Then, slowly, she glided backwards across my room, all the while facing me, and disappeared through the same wall.

I continued sitting upright on the bed, staring at the spot where she'd vanished. Perhaps a minute later, another figure slowly emerged halfway from the wall at the same place, paused for a long moment, and then glided back out of sight. The temperature in the room became warmer. The second figure was also dressed in long robes but was a man with a white beard. He wore a king's crown.

Fia came into my room after the king had left, but I again denied having spoken with anyone—and I've never described the incident to anyone since. My silence was, and always has been, my secret, conspiratorial communication with whoever they were—and are. Particularly her.

Bedtime didn't follow naps by much, but it was more fun. Together, Patsy and I prayed mindlessly, giggled uncontrollably, and listened to a story. Then after Fia tucked us in and I was in my room alone, my mother would come to sing to me.

"Twinkle, Twinkle, Little Star" was a regular. Also George Gershwin's "Summertime" from *Porgy and Bess.* For years I thought it was a song my mother had made up herself. "Your daddy's rich and your mother's good lookin'," she'd sing in her warm, professional-sounding soprano voice, and that's just the way it was! "Your beautiful mother" was how everyone always seemed to refer to her. And she was. Thirty years old at the time of my birth, with piles of red hair, a good figure—which grew to be more substantial during her opera-singing days later on—a lovely face (on which she always applied a stage-size portion of makeup, much to the astonishment and, expressed to me years later, the irritation of her Boston friends), she truly looked the part of the stage personality she wished someday to be.

Another favorite was Nevin's "Mighty Lak' a Rose," a song she later often included in her concert programs. I can see her now, elegantly dressed for dinner in a black low-necked evening gown with thousands of sparkling sequins on it, leaning over my bed, looking at me tucked beneath the covers, and singing every word as if it were written for me alone . . .

> *Sweetest lil' fella,*
> *Ever body knows*
> *Dunno what to call him*
> *But he's mighty lak' a rose.*
> *Lookin' at his mammy,*
> *Wid eyes so shiny blue,*
> *Mek you think that heav'n*
> *Is a-comin' clost ter you!*

In later years, particularly the teenage ones, I'd be embarrassed when she spontaneously sang at dinner parties or private gatherings of any sort. But before I learned to be embarrassed, it was a bedtime ritual that came "clost ter heav'n."

"Your mother was always partial to you, and your dad particularly loved Patsy," recalled Fia during my visit at her house in

Wellesley Hills in August of 1985, when we met again for the first time in nearly fifty years. We sat on lawn chairs outside, eating a piece of her chewy homemade cake, which, even after all the years, she said I *had* to eat. (It was not a chore.) She still spoke with the German accent I had grown to associate always with care, protection, and adoration.

"I probably paid *too* much attention to you, Juddie," she said as she leafed through a thick old diary devoted exclusively to her daily care of me from March 16, 1933, when I was born, to 1937. It's written entirely in German. A typical entry, translated, reads: "February 19, 1934. He has five teeth and weighs 20 pounds and 15 ounces. Likes to eat and is very lively and he climbs up on tables and chairs." I showed her an album I'd brought with me, filled with photographs taken by my father during the Chestnut Hill years, including picture after picture of me as an infant. "Look at all my lovely Juddies," she said softly to herself as she turned the pages.

During the summers, the same general schedule was maintained at a cottage out on Marblehead Neck, Massachusetts, except that the beach was an added ingredient in the day's activities. There, always fully protected from the sun by umbrellas, huge floppy hats, and bathrobes, we children would conduct afternoon "tea parties," complete with tables, chairs, place settings—the works—much as we'd observed grown-up tea parties. Sometimes, when Patsy and the children of my parents' friends were occupied elsewhere and Fia was given a rare afternoon off, I'd conduct a tea party by myself. This would amuse Johnnie, and she'd prepare little cakes and sandwiches along with a pot of hot water in which milk and sugar were added but no tea. We called it "Cambridge" (for cambric) tea. Her daughter, Ingrid, one of the maids, would carry everything out to the beach and with exaggerated motions and great good humor ceremoniously serve it. It was Ingrid who taught me the little tea-party poem that is so ingrained in my memory today.

> *I had a little tea party one afternoon at three.*
> *T'was very small, three guests in all*
> *Just I, myself, and me.*
> *Myself ate up the sandwiches, while I drank up the tea.*
> *T'was also I who ate the pie and passed the cake to me.*

Meals at Marblehead Neck and Chestnut Hill were not eaten together as a family. At the Chestnut Hill house, Patsy and I, along with Fia, were served earlier, in a sunroom off the main "grown-up" dining room. (Occasionally Fia would eat a second meal with my parents so that my mother could "practice her German" with her.) There were many weeks when my parents were away, usually visiting Drake in Switzerland, but even when they were home, contact with my father was reserved for the brief interval between my supper and bedtime.

"I understand you've been naughty today," my father said to me one evening when I greeted him on my way to bed, as he was sipping one of his evening cocktails. He was, as usual, dressed in a dark suit, white shirt, and tie. I had poured a jar of honey on my head during breakfast that morning.

"If it happens again, there'll be a spanking," he added sternly. Although we grew closer later on, in those days my father was a formidable, distant creature from the alien "grown-up" world. At six foot two, slender but with a strong, wiry body, wavy dark brown hair, and a strong nose along with other facial features that somehow combined to create a both delicate and rugged appearance, he was always described to me as "very handsome." At my birth, he was thirty-three.

I'd never been spanked, nor ever was, but those two short sentences that evening sent me quaking as if threatened with death. As I went up the great winding staircase to my bedroom, all the while being comforted by Fia, who knew me better than anyone, I committed myself to being "a good boy" forever. Of course, not even little golden boy me could be a good boy *forever*. At any rate, I'm sure my father forgot the incident before he and my mother sat down to dinner that evening. I, on the other hand, still remember it fifty years later.

There was one regular exception to the strict separation of parents and children at mealtime. Every other Sunday, dressed in our best (for me, short pants, jacket, and tie, with metal garters holding up my long stockings), we drove in any one of a number of wonderful shiny cars to my father's parents' house in nearby West Newton for a "grown-up" Sunday dinner. "Grandpop," as we called Frank Judson Hale, my paternal grandfather, was a tall, straight, handsome, but severe-looking old man with a small white mustache, a fringe of white hair around his bald head, and a decided air of authority. He was used to giving orders and having them obeyed. Grandma, née Grace Herrick, on the other hand, was a silent, meek little lady whose cheeks were so soft you had to be careful not to suck her skin into your mouth with the obligatory kiss of greeting. They lived in the largest house in West Newton. Stucco-covered, with a red tile roof and one two-storey wing for the servants' living quarters, it was surrounded by seven acres of meticulously manicured grounds. Not long after Grandpop's death at age ninety-one in 1954, the house was torn down and the seven acres divided into a half dozen "estates."

We *always* arrived at 11:30 a.m. Grandpop and Grandma *always* were standing together on their spacious veranda, waiting for us. Grandpop was *always* irritated with anything less than precise orderliness and punctuality. And everyone was afraid of Grandpop, except my mother, who wasn't afraid of anyone. (Grandpop, curiously, particularly liked her.) It was my mother, for instance, who sternly calmed him down one Sunday when we arrived twenty minutes late. Patsy, sitting in the back seat, had thrown up on my father's neck on the way over (both Patsy and I used to do a lot of throwing up in cars), and we'd had to turn back so he could change his clothes. Two weeks later, as we arrived for the next Sunday dinner at Grandpop's, there was a brand-new tricycle waiting for Patsy on the veranda. She recalls the moment today as one of her most exciting childhood memories—and the *only* one in which she came out better than "Juddie."

My memories of these Sunday happenings consist of a canary, grandfather-clock bongs, goldfish, and increasingly desperate attempts to control restlessness as the day wore on. The canary cage in the living room was where Patsy and I headed first, and then, after trying to make him chirp, it was outside to the formal gardens containing a fountain and a pool of goldfish. If the weather was fair, Grandpop and the other grown-ups would slowly follow us out (grown-ups moved excruciatingly slowly), and Grandpop would pull down on an ingeniously contrived handle connected to a valve in the center of the fountain. This would turn the water on. So we'd watch the fountain. And watch the goldfish. At that point, before the visit had hardly begun, Patsy and I were coming very close to running out of things to do.

The grown-ups would then stroll down a gravel walk, and we'd follow, running in zigzag patterns and circles, past various flower gardens with birdbaths, past a tennis court, through a small orchard, and on up to a ledge on which was a marker indicating that the spot was the highest in the city of Newton. Grandpop had had a stone bench put there and liked to point it out as the place where Aunt Mard's beau had asked Grandpop for her hand in marriage. Aunt Mard (Marjory) was my father's older sister, but until I was in my early twenties, I thought her name was Aunt Mod.

"Right here, sitting on that bench," Grandpop would say, as if it had been an occasion of historic significance. For Aunt Mard, no doubt, it was. My mother referred to her as "poor Aunt Mahdie"— similar to "poor Drakie-boy" but for different reasons. The label was a reference to the fact that Aunt Mard's husband eventually left her and she reared their two sons, Cousin Robert and Cousin Frank, alone. And to the fact that Cousin Robert died of polio while still in his early twenties, two years after Cousin Frank's legs were crippled by the same disease. Both Cousin Frank and Aunt Mard—who is now well into her nineties—have been living happy, productive lives over the years but my mother, at eighty-four, still refers to her as "poor Aunt Mahdie."

If Patsy and I could manage to break away unnoticed from the grown-ups up there at the highest point in the city of Newton, we'd race back to the house for the last entertaining thing to do during the biweekly visit: to search under the dining room table for the button or some other clue to indicate how Grandma noiselessly summoned waitresses from the adjoining kitchen at various times during the meal. Patsy was convinced it was a foot pedal connected to the kitchen buzzer, but we never found it. As with most forms of Yankee ingenuity I've encountered since, I couldn't begin to fathom how it worked.

As soon as we'd hear the grown-ups coming in from outside, we'd dash out from under the table and sit ourselves on the living room chairs (but not on Grandpop's special chair), resigned to the fact that the long Sunday dinner ritual was about to begin.

One cocktail apiece (just fruit juice for Patsy and me), mixed by Grandpop from a silver tray of ingredients brought in by a waitress dressed in a black uniform with a white ruffled apron, was the opening scene. Then a slow procession into the dining room and our special places, designated by silver napkin rings with our names engraved on them.

"Love you," Grandpop would invariably say to Grandma, giving her a hasty peck on the cheek while he helped her be seated at one end of the table. Years later I'd learn about the irony of that particular ritual. But at the time, Patsy and I had no inkling of Grandpop's regular Monday afternoon liaisons with the mysterious "Mrs. Kennard." We were, as it turns out, the only two people seated at the table who *didn't* know!

Of far more immediate importance to Patsy and me were the bread sticks, buttered and toasted—in that order. "That's enough. You'll spoil your appetite," one grown-up or another would say, and we'd turn our attention to the silver dish of mixed nuts, with an "H" on it, in front of every place. Butter balls, each about the size of a marble, would be passed in a silver bowl from one person to the next (I was allowed two), and then Grandpop, sitting at the opposite end of the table from Grandma, would imperceptibly nod his head. At that she would, either electrically or psychically, but without the slightest sound or movement, summon the black-uniformed waitress from the kitchen. She'd be bearing a tureen of creamed tomato soup that she'd methodically, silently, ladle out into our individual bowls. When all the bowls were filled, she'd return to the kitchen, re-emerge with a bowl of croutons, and daintily spoon several of these onto the surface of every soup.

One gathered a spoonful of soup by moving one's spoon from the side of the bowl closest to one in the direction of the side farthest away. And although it was allowable to gently blow upon a spoonful, there were to be no slurping sounds. Consuming soup at Grandpop's was a chore.

Eventually there'd be another nod from Grandpop, another mysterious signal from Grandma to the kitchen, and the soup dishes would be cleared and a huge roast beef, always cooked rare, would be set in front of Grandpop. He would stand, sharpen his knife with long easy strokes on a skinny-handled sharpening steel, and then begin to "caaave" (as everyone present pronounced it) slices from the roast, placing one or two on the single plate held by the waitress, who would carry it to the designated person, ladies first, exchange it for his or her empty plate, and return to Grandpop for the next serving.

It took *forever!*

Three separate bowls of vegetables and a bowl of mashed potatoes, plus a gravy boat, all had to be individually passed around by the waitress before Grandma lifted her fork as a signal to begin. There was never a salad.

Fingerbowls on round lace doilies along with Grandpop's finger-bowl story occupied the time between clearing the main-course dishes and serving dessert. Grandpop preferred to tell tried-and-true humor stories over and over rather than tackle new ones. His finger-bowl favorite concerned a local carpenter who had been doing extensive renovating work in Grandpop's house a few years after he bought it in 1898. After he'd finished the work, Grandpop had, rather uncharacteristically for the times, invited him and his wife for Sunday dinner. When the fingerbowl on the lace doily was set before him, the carpenter bluntly asked Grandpop what it was for. Grandpop explained, after which the carpenter retorted, "Mr. Hale, at our house we usually wash our hands *before* dinner."

Much laughter all around, loudest from Grandpop.

Whereas Grandpop was the central figure in the grand and elegant *caaaving* ceremony of the main course, Grandma took center stage at dessert time. It was Grandma who *caaaved* a gigantic, perfectly molded half-circle of homemade vanilla ice cream that the waitress set before her on a silver platter every bit as large and beautiful as the one for the beef. Pretty exciting. But then the methodical, silent, interminable serving-and-passing-empty-plates-back-one-at-a-time procedure would once again commence, followed by the ladling out of the steamy-hot chocolate sauce.

The final act was the slow-motion move back to the living room for after-dinner coffee, brightened considerably by the ever-present platter of plain white peppermints.

Some of the manners learned at these "grown-up" meals have remained with me, but the greatest lesson of all was patience. The fact that I have never experienced true boredom since my early childhood—even during five-hour airport delays—I credit fully to those long-ago afternoon naps, the hour-long sessions on our little toilet bowls, and Sunday dinner at Grandpop's.

And so my early days as an adored little Boston boy drifted along in routine fashion. In my possession today is an old yellowed clip-

ping from the *Boston Transcript*, dated November 10, 1935. Somehow it captures the image I have of my young life back then. The
headline reads "Brookline Brother and Sister at Play," with the large
photograph below showing Patsy on the tricycle Grandpop had
given her, dressed in a Best & Company double-breasted hounds-
tooth overcoat with velvet collar, white knee-high stockings, Stride
Rite oxford shoes, and felt hat with a feather in it. I am beside Patsy,
standing, dressed in an overcoat exactly matching hers and the same
long white stockings, but with a classic newsboy cap. Beside me, on
the lawn, is a stuffed pig.

The caption reads: "Caught at play by the cameraman were Miss
Patricia Hale and her brother, Master Judson Hale, young children
of Mr. and Mrs. Roger D. Hale of Heath Street, Brookline [Chestnut
Hill is part of Brookline]. Their mother, Mrs. Hale, is the former
Miss Marian Sagendorph, daughter of Mr. and Mrs. George Adam
Sagendorph of Louisburg Square. She will honor her debutante
sister, Miss Joan Sagendorph, with a dinner and theatre party the
night after Thanksgiving."

Aunt Joan, one of my mother's two much-younger sisters, the
one my mother would "honor" with a dinner and theater party the
night of Thanksgiving 1935, was to be the unlucky recipient of a
lobotomy a couple of years later. Lobotomies were a briefly popular
medical procedure of the '30s in which one or more nerves attached
to lobes of the brain, those having to do with emotions in Aunt Joan's
case, were surgically severed. It was performed because of her emotionally overwrought state of mind (she threw a flowerpot at my
maternal grandmother) after being stood up at her church wedding
by a man who was already married. The operation rendered her
incapable of leading a normal life outside of an institution. We
referred to her always as "poor Aunt Joan."

I've often thought of Joan's case as being a simple matter of bad
timing. Because she was unfortunate enough to have been deceived
by a married man and to have heaved a flowerpot at her mother at
the precise time this particular medical fad was being practiced in the
medical capital of the world, where she lived, Aunt Joan became, for
the rest of her life, "poor Aunt Joan."

My guardian angel, perhaps the silent one in the flowing blue and
red robes, would never allow anything bad to alter the life's course
of little Juddie, "the most beautiful child in Chestnut Hill," as Fia

remembers me now. The direction of my life's journey seemed apparent at the time of the *Boston Transcript* photograph of Patsy, my stuffed pig, and me.

There I am, the apple of everyone's eye, dressed in my Sunday best for dinner at Grandpop's, already approaching my third birthday without anything horrible happening, as it had with Drake. I was finally the son who would hunt and fish with my father in Canada. I would go to Milton and Harvard, as he had, enter the family textile business or perhaps "the world of finance," marry a wealthy Radcliffe debutante, make additional millions of dollars, play tennis, golf, squash, ride horseback, sail down the Maine coast, have lunch at the Somerset and Algonquin clubs, drink wine at St. Botolph's, wear a tuxedo for baked bean stag dinners at the Union Club, have supper at the Brookline Country Club on Thursday (maids' night off), and hate Franklin Roosevelt, even the very memory of him. Eventually, the natural assumption runs, I would retire "on invested funds" north or west of Boston, join a curling league, summer in Little Compton or perhaps, as Grandpop and Grandma once did, at Prout's Neck, Maine, give a huge chunk of money to Harvard, perhaps Milton too, serve on many corporate boards, set up trusts for the children and grandchildren, and hate Florida for anything beyond a three-month stay in the winter.

Well, I *did*, as it turns out, go hunting and fishing with my father in Canada. "Poor Drakie-boy" wasn't quite able to change *everything* . . .

Chapter 2

Frugality

IT HAPPENED to Drake suddenly, without warning, one morning in Chestnut Hill as my father was working at his desk. Drake was less than a month past his third birthday. The date was October 6, 1929.

"I looked up to speak to Drake as he came into my study," my father recalled years later, "and then I noticed his eyes looked strange. As though he was seeing something unseen that terrified him. He began to scream in an abnormal way. The sound would be as loud when he sucked in his breath as when he'd scream it out. A continuous, loud, crowing screech. I couldn't believe such a horrible sound was coming from our beautiful little red-haired boy. There'd never been even a hint of anything wrong before that morning."

Patsy and I think today that there may have been a hint. During Thanksgiving 1985, we unearthed a trunkful of my father's old 16mm movies. They'd been in Patsy's attic at her farm in northern Vermont, unopened, since my father's death in 1963. Although many date back to the early 1920s, the majority are in perfect condition. We borrowed a projector from the local high school and set about to have an evening of old memories. The first reel we decided to see was meticulously labeled "Drake—1½ years old" in my father's handwriting. It flashed on the screen—clear, sharp, steady, black and white. There he was, being wheeled down the sidewalk outside the Chestnut Hill house. He's coming directly toward the camera. The nurse pushing him, dressed in a fur hat and coat with huge fur collar, is smiling. It's not Fia. Must be the nurse referred to in my mother's diaries as "Fraulein." The carriage stops within three feet of my father and, although there were no zoom lenses in those days, Drake's little face, wrapped in a hood, becomes the central focus. He looks so chubby, cute, and normal. He smiles. Then the smile is wiped away as if by a hidden shadow. For an instant, his eyes widen and the pupils disappear. His eyes are solid white. A split second later, the shadow passes, the eyes return to normal, and his smile returns. Patsy and I agreed we'd just witnessed an ominous hint of what was to come in full force a year and a half later.

The circumstances of Drake's birth were significant also, in hindsight. He was two weeks late, weighed almost twelve pounds, and was pulled from my mother, a "mere sylph of a girl in those days," as she says, by metal forceps that so contorted and bruised his head that the doctor had to mold it back into shape. After consulting recently with a doctor friend of mine, there's little doubt in my mind that a bilateral subdural hematoma (a swelling containing blood) was the result, causing irreversible brain damage that would become apparent only after the passage of time as calcification occurred—in Drake's case, exactly three years. The Hale family destiny was forever changed on September 17, 1926, by a pair of long-handled metal forceps.

Dr. Smith's book, *From Infancy to Childhood,* provided no help on that terrifying morning in my father's study. "Put the child into a tub of warm water" was his remedy for convulsions, perhaps the closest thing that could conceivably account for Drake's behavior. My mother tried it. It had no effect. Drake not only continued his screeching with both the intake and outgo of his breath but began to hit his face with his clenched fists and bang his head violently against a wall.

Years later, when my mother became an undergraduate at Emerson College following my father's death, she wrote a paper on the experience for her freshman writing class. "It was a wild, terrifying noise," she said, describing that first morning, "which never ceased that day. It never ceased for days—and weeks and months. Our beautiful boy had become very ill, suddenly, out of the blue. We took him to many doctors and psychiatrists in Boston with no relief. It was an unknown strange case and they told me to put him away in an institution. I could not bring myself to do such a thing. At the tender age of twenty-six, I had a faith that could move mountains."

* * *

There was no extraordinary need for the strength Drake's condition would require of her when my mother, Marian Bradford Sagendorph (her Boston friends called her "Mannie"), was growing up in Newton Center, Massachusetts. There were early signs of her spunk and adventurous spirit, however, a spirit that continues into her mid-eighties today.

From the diary of Grandma Jane, my mother's mother, Jane Hansell Sagendorph, dated August 20, 1905: *Marian followed the balloon man today and we thought she was lost. Frightened us dreadfully. We had to telephone the police but soon afterwards found her.*

Another, dated November 3, 1905: *Marian had a terrible fit of sneezing today and when I reached her, she was covered almost a half inch thick with powder—the work of her brother. That afternoon she was choking and I found her mouth full of graham crackers. Same reason as the powder.*

Her brother was Robb Sagendorph, three years older, destined to be the founder of *Yankee* magazine thirty years later, editor of *The Old Farmer's Almanac* before me, and the "Uncle Robb" I'd meet on only two occasions before I began working for him at *Yankee* in 1958.

My mother and Uncle Robb never really saw eye to eye. She called him "a funny duck," and he always accused her of being "stage struck," which she would consider a compliment. He didn't. (Neither would the majority of their peers in and around Boston.) The powder and graham cracker episodes, as described in Grandma Jane's diary, set the tone for their relationship forever.

There were to be two more children, sisters, born to the Sagendorphs about ten years after my mother and Uncle Robb. We were always told these two "late children"—one named Betty, the other "poor Aunt Joan," who had the lobotomy—were brought into the world in order to save the Sagendorph marriage. Maybe they did, for a while . . .

My mother's father, George Adam Sagendorph, "G.A." to everyone except Patsy and me, to whom he was "Da," came from a long line of Sagendorfs/Sagendorphs/Segendorfs reaching back to Johann Adam Segendorf and his wife, Margaretha, who immigrated to this country from the Rhine river valley in Germany, by way of Holland and England, and settled along the Hudson River in 1710.

In the Sagendorf/Sagendorph/Segendorf genealogy, a 700-page book of mind-boggling detail, is the family motto: *Ich hatte kleine Ruhe, bis ich es heraus gefunden hatte.* ("I had a little peace, until I found it.") I used to think that was the stupidest family motto in existence. Today I tend to think it's the most profound.

Among the ancestors included in the book are Sagendorfs/Sagendorphs/Segendorfs who fought in every United States war, including those against Indians, since 1710; a Sagendorph gored to death by a bull in 1827; a Sagendorf with tuberculosis who traveled across the Plains in a covered wagon in 1858, carrying the boards for his coffin; a Sagendorph who was the first captain to leave New York for the Pacific in command of a ship powered by steam (talk about obscure trivia questions!); a Sagendorf who drew the "Popeye" comic strip for many years; a Segendorf who had triplets in 1802; a famous aerial-photographer Sagendorph; several Harvard professor Sagendorphs/Sagendorfs; and a Sagendorf who adopted a daughter whose sister was Mary Todd, who became the wife of Abraham Lincoln. Uncle Robb loved that last one. Deliberately ignoring logic, he'd facetiously say maybe that was the reason why he looked so much like Abraham Lincoln (which he did).

Today lots of Sagendorph/Sagendorf families have lived in Massachusetts for many generations, but George Adam Sagendorph, our Da, began life in Philadelphia, attended the University of Pennsylvania (at least that's better than Yale!), and then took over the reins of Penn Metal Company, a steel-manufacturing plant in Parkersburg, West Virginia, with corporate offices in Boston. Hanging on my office wall today is a large gold-framed oval photograph of Penn Metal's founder, my great-grandfather, Longley Lewis Sagendorph. He appears surprisingly young, sensitive, almost "pretty." My youngest son, Christopher, aged twenty-one at this writing, says he looks like a "fruitcake."

Sociologist E. Digby Baltzell in his book *Puritan Boston and Quaker Philadelphia* says that in his view, upper-class Philadelphians value *noblesse* while their Boston counterparts stress *oblige.* "The people in Boston all want to be chiefs while in Philadelphia they are all content to be Indians," he says.

I think it's safe to say, however, that if you were living in Boston but came from somewhere else, Philadelphia was as good a place to have "come from" as any. Da and Grandma Jane made the transition easily, before my mother and Uncle Robb were born, and Da, having succeeded his father as president of Penn Metal, was already a "chief" and would remain one.

Before he sold the company to the Keene Corporation in the early 1970s, I attended several Penn Metal stockholders' meetings as a representative of my mother's few shares. Da was still Chairman of the Board and President, though past ninety years of age. His treasurer, secretary, and various vice-presidents were younger men. Most were in their mid to late eighties.

Da conducted the meetings with an iron fist, brooking no questioning of his policies. If anyone hinted of disagreement, he'd launch into a long dissertation regarding how *some* people were intelligent enough to be grateful for the progress Penn Metal had made under his leadership over the past sixty-plus years and how *some* people (at this point he'd stare balefully at whoever had had the audacity to raise a simple question) were not *intelligent* enough to be grateful.

There was another side to Da—the fun-loving, charming, debonair side. The side that had everyone in stitches with his latest jokes, told with the appropriate accents. He dressed stylishly, with a fresh flower in his lapel, he moved among people with an easy, elegant grace, and as my mother remembers, he was constantly "surrounded by beautiful women." Doubtless this latter point contributed to the fact that my mother always described her parents' marriage as "strained."

Grandma Jane, my mother's mother, led her own life, separate and seemingly oblivious of her dashing husband. She was interested in "spiritual research," attended seances in which mediums spoke messages from other worlds, and studied various ancient and modern philosophies, including one begun around 1900 by an Austrian scientist named Rudolf Steiner, a name that was to become an integral part of my own childhood. She cared for "poor Aunt Joan" over the years, she was an accomplished oil painter, she always had plenty of dogs and parrots, and sometime in the 1920s she bought a one-acre island on Palfry Lake, part of Spednic Lake, ten miles of water from the little Maine town of Vanceboro. There she would isolate herself for a month or more every summer, without Da, to meditate, study, and paint. She called the island "Star Island," another name that would have great significance to me and to my family.

So it was that my mother and Uncle Robb grew up in a psychologically divided household, although they both did all the usual Boston things common to the times. They moved to Chestnut Hill, summered in a little southern New Hampshire town called Peterborough, attended the proper private schools early on, and learned their *please*s and *thank you*s, how to dress, and how to dance at Miss Marguerite Souther's Eliot Hall Dance Classes at Jamaica Plain where, as noted in Grandma Jane's diary, "Cabot Lodge [was] always poised and delightful." Later Uncle Robb, like everyone, attended Milton before entering Harvard while my mother "giggled [her] way through Westover" School in Middlebury, Connecticut, the "in" finishing school for wealthy young Boston and New York City ladies prior to matrimony. (Young ladies were *not* encouraged to attend college.) All very predictable. After that, Da and Grandma Jane moved to 12 Louisburg Square on Beacon Hill, where, according to commentator Rod MacLeish, you needed "a backlog of distinguished ancestors, a broad Cambridge 'a' in [your] speech, and a running acquaintance with the . . . achievements of Ellery Sedgwick, Thomas Bailey Aldrich, and Margaret Fuller."

Afternoon tea at 12 Louisburg Square with Grandma Jane—Da hardly ever seemed to be there—was an occasional family obligation throughout my growing-up years. It was a dreary affair, far different from the lavish Sunday dinners at Grandpop Hale's. At Grandma Jane's, a small pot of tea plus a plate with an inadequate number of plain cookies would be presented by an ancient servant dressed in everyday plain clothes and summoned by Grandma Jane with a simple "You can bring in the tea now, Mrs. Browning." Grandma Jane would pour tea for two or three of those present, add the sugar and lemon or cream, and then run out of tea. The antique pot held only about a pint of liquid. So Mrs. Browning would limp slowly back to the kitchen to fetch more. By the time she returned with another full pot, those served tea on the first round would have finished and be waiting for seconds. Grandma Jane was as likely to serve them a second cup as someone who had as yet received none. Overall, the entire afternoon was just one long replenishing ceremony. The plate of plain cookies, devoured within the first five minutes, was never replenished. Grandma Jane may have come from Philadelphia, but she certainly had all the right instincts for conducting a properly frugal afternoon tea party on Beacon Hill.

When both were in their eighties, after over sixty years of marriage, Da and Grandma Jane divorced. "It just wasn't working out the way they'd hoped it would," Uncle Robb said to me at the time, but there was a sad part of it too. Da remarried immediately, to a charming middle-aged woman who was heiress to the Underwood deviled ham fortune. A couple of years later Grandma Jane lay dying. She'd been living alone with her dogs, parrots, Mrs. Browning, her painting, and her gardens in a large house next to the reservoir in Lincoln, Massachusetts. Her last words, according to both Uncle Robb and my mother, who were present at her bedside, were "Is she pretty?"

Da seldom visited the *Yankee* magazine offices, at least not after my arrival there in 1958. I recall only one instance, in 1959, at the birth of my firstborn, Judson, Jr. He came alone and looked grand in a bright blue herringbone tweed jacket, which Uncle Robb complimented him on. "Oh this," Da responded with a casual shrug, "I bought this at a rummage sale years ago." Like Grandma Jane and her tea parties, he had all the correct Boston attitudes of upper-class gentility.

Grandpop Hale, on the other hand, was a different type of old Yankee altogether. Although he acquired far more money during his lifetime than Da did during his, Grandpop did not represent upper-class gentility. When he wore a tweed jacket, it was from Brooks Brothers and he'd be proud to tell you so. Grandpop was a farmer's boy. The "shabby gentility" of Boston's aristocracy was simply "shabby" to him.

For Da, the appearance of New England frugality served to mask his true financial circumstances. "Rich," even "wealthy," were dirty words. "Well-to-do" was tolerated, perhaps, but only when absolutely necessary. For Grandpop, frugality was an essential tool for achieving and maintaining financial security. To be recognized as "wealthy" was a compliment. To hide it wouldn't occur to him. Accordingly, Grandpop retired early in life, about the time my father was at Harvard, and did virtually nothing except feed the canary and listen to Gabriel Heatter give the six o'clock news for the last forty years of his life. He'd earned it. Da never retired, remaining on the job into his nineties. "Taking it easy," for any reason, ran counter to his basic Puritan instincts.

The combination of Grandpop's frugality coupled with his luxu-

rious surroundings and comforts was a source of family amusement. For instance, he owned the fanciest, most expensive cars of the day —Grandpop was the first in Newton to have a Stanley Steamer— and had "stolen" his company's best mechanic to be his full-time live-in chauffeur. And yet he insisted his chauffeur buy gasoline in the early morning. "Gasoline expands with heat," he'd explain during Sunday dinner, "so a gallon of gas in your tank in the cool morning will become more than a gallon in the warm afternoon."

Grandpop would carefully fold and save used paper napkins. He'd turn off all the lights in the living room before we'd ceremoniously troop into the grand dining room for Sunday dinner. "Gotta save the bulbs," he'd say. He had elaborate fountains and birdbaths around his property but would turn on the water only when someone was actually standing in front of one of them. In short, old-fashioned New England frugality was in Grandpop's blood, despite his newly acquired wealth.

Frank Judson Hale—Grandpop—was born on his father's farm in Newton Upper Falls, Massachusetts. I have a large photograph of his father, Amos Hale, hanging on my office wall at *Yankee*. With a short white beard, dressed in a fancy dark suit and ribbon tie of the post–Civil War style, he has the rugged, hardworking look of the farmer he was. I learned only recently why he is holding his left arm behind his back.

"He was ashamed to show his hand in a photograph because he'd lost some fingers in a farming accident," Aunt Mard, his granddaughter, now living in a home for the elderly in Boston, told me during one of my visits in 1985. "My mother told me never to look at his hand, so of course I looked at it all the time."

"Amos" is a common first name, as is "Judson," in the Hale genealogy, which dates back in America to one Thomas Hale, who immigrated to Newbury, Massachusetts, from England in 1637. Lots of Hales remained in Newbury; others went on to settle in places like Compton, New Hampshire, and Winchendon, Massachusetts. Although, to my knowledge, no official Hale genealogy has been compiled, genealogical tidbits I've acquired over the years include the facts that there were many farmers and ministers, that the Herrick family was closely intertwined with the Hales over several generations (Grandpop's wife, Grace, was a Herrick), and that one line extends all the way back to the famous Englishman Sir Alfred

Drake—who never married! Unfortunately there is no evidence to indicate that any one of *my* Hales was ever put into the position of being able to say he regretted he had but one life to give for his country.

The original Thomas Hale's wife, Thomasina, was born in Scotland, and perhaps therein lies the origin of the Hale family tradition of frugality that passed through the generations to my great-grandfather, Amos, on to his son, Frank (Grandpop), and, sad to say, came to a screeching halt with my father. "Use it up, wear it out, make do, or do without" might well have been the family motto.

For instance, great-grandmother Tamsen, Amos's wife, would empty all the coffee cups of the farmhands and boarders each morning and then scrape the sugar that clung to the bottoms into a bowl she kept for the purpose. On Saturday mornings, she'd use the sugar in a large cake served for Sunday dessert.

Great-grandfather Amos would chew his tobacco in the morning, leave the quid to dry on a fence post at noon, and then, later in the afternoon, smoke it in his pipe.

Great-grandfather Amos was frugal with his words, too. He was sort of a "Cal Coolidge" before Cal Coolidge was born. My favorite family story illustrating that characteristic concerns the evening Amos, an active Baptist, invited a Boston Baptist minister to dinner before the visitor was to deliver a guest sermon at the Newton Upper Falls Baptist Church. Great-grandmother Tamsen prepared a hearty farm dinner, but the visiting minister ate hardly any of it. He just picked at his food, explaining to his hosts, "I never eat before I preach."

After the meal, while Tamsen remained at home to clean the dishes and put Grandpop, then a boy, and his two brothers to bed, Amos took the visiting minister in a carriage to the church. Following the service, the minister caught a late train back to Boston. When Amos returned home, Tamsen asked, "Well, how was the sermon?" Great-grandfather Amos's six-word reply was as thorough and informative a critique as anyone could ask for. He said simply, "He might just as well et."

Nearby to the Hale farm in Newton Upper Falls was a small company that made factory machinery for manufacturing textiles. It was called the Pettee Machine Works, and it was here that Grandpop began his career. By day he served as office boy. By night, as the family story goes, he "gathered" scrap from behind the plant, then sold it back to the company the next morning.

From there he rose rapidly to various positions of responsibility. One day about 1882 he approached the president of the company to ask for another promotion. It was a period when Pettee Machine Works was falling on hard times. Years later, my father told me the gist of the conversation.

"The only vacancy for you now, Frank," said the harried and discouraged president, who only wanted to retire and be free of his business burdens, "is *my* job."

"That's a tough job," Grandpop supposedly replied. "How much does it pay?"

"You can have $8,000 a year if you'll take over my worries," replied the president.

"Where is the $8,000 coming from?" said Grandpop, who by this time was knowledgeable in all aspects of the business.

"That, Frank," said the president, "is your first worry."

And so Grandpop took over the top job at Pettee Machine Works. By recognizing that textile industry fortunes were no longer to be made in New England and by establishing sales offices in Charlotte, Greensboro, Greenville, and Atlanta, he began to build it back to prosperity. He once told Aunt Mard's son, Cousin Frank, that he never in his life took more than $60,000 in salary. His investments, however, even during the 1930s, long after he'd retired, were shrewd. By the time he was thirty, in 1893, he was worth $4 million.

He was also shrewd in his choice of people around him. Grandpop was well aware of the drawbacks to his poor farming background in the world of "old money" Boston. So he brought in as his partner a Boston Brahmin by the name of R. Paul Snelling. Mr. Snelling had all the proper social connections. Grandpop was "Mr. Inside," arriving at work at 5:30 a.m. or earlier, just as he would have on the farm (much to the exasperation of his managers, who felt obliged to do the same). Mr. Snelling was "Mr. Outside," hobnobbing with all the right people who could help with sales and raising capital at Boston's exclusive luncheon and dinner clubs.

Together they expanded the company which, after a series of mergers in 1912, emerged as the Saco-Lowell Shops, Incorporated, with large manufacturing plants in both Biddeford and Saco, Maine, as well as in Sanford, North Carolina. Today, like Da's Penn Metal Company, Saco-Lowell has become part of a conglomerate.

I never met Grandpop's "social arm," R. Paul Snelling, but as *Yankee* editor I have, of course, read stories about the lovely, stuffy little world in which Snelling operated in behalf of Saco-Lowell. A favorite, mentioned in Cleveland Amory's *The Proper Bostonians*, occurred at one of R. Paul Snelling's clubs, the Somerset. It seems that during one of the monthly (all-male) dinners, at which Snelling may well have been present, a fire started in the flue of the charcoal broiler in the kitchen, extended to other parts of the club, and took all of four hours to fully extinguish. The conduct of Joseph, the club's famous manager and head waiter, has been held up as the epitome of proper Boston behavior under harrowing circumstances.

When the firemen arrived at the front entrance at 42 Beacon Street, Joseph refused to allow them in, telling them to use the service entrance at the rear of the building. Thirty-one club members were dining at the time, and Joseph made certain all were allowed to complete the main course without interruption. Then, and only then, he went from table to table with the solemn, quietly spoken announcement still remembered by those present. "There will be no dessert this evening, gentlemen," he said. "The club is on fire."

By the time my father came along in 1900, seven years after my Aunt Mard, Grandpop had established his fortune and his reputation in the textile industry as "one of the great machinery salesmen of all time," according to an industry newsletter obituary written following his death in 1954 at the age of ninety-one. It goes on to say that most of the great textile mills in the South today—and Grandpop at one time served on the boards of twenty of them—"owe their early existence to the financial and technical assistance extended by Mr. Hale and his associates at Saco-Lowell." Great-grandfather Amos's boy had made it big. No Hale, all the way back to Thomas Hale in 1637, had ever made so much money. As for his son, my dear father, well, no Hale would ever *lose* so much money.

The arrival of my father into the luxurious Hale household caused peculiar and drastic changes in the private lives of Grandpop and Grandma Hale.

On a warm evening in August of 1985, I talked about this aspect of our family history with Cousin Frank, my father's nephew, as I sat with him and his wife, Eloise, on the front porch of their summer home, an old restored farmhouse in Woodstock, Vermont (they'd been neighborhood companions since childhood, husband and wife for almost forty years). Cousin Frank, a tall, vigorous, handsome man, now in his sixties and a grandfather many times over, wears heavy braces on his legs (paralyzed from the polio he suffered in 1951) and walks with metal canes but lives a normal, active life nonetheless. As far as I can see, the only adjustment he has made to his disability is that he has had to rig all of his antique cars with hand brakes and hand accelerator levers. Because Cousin Frank's father had deserted his mother (my Aunt Mard) when he was still a boy, he became very close to Grandpop.

"From the time your father was born, I believe our Grandpop was banished from Grandma's bedroom," said Cousin Frank as Eloise passed around some crackers and cheese to go with the cocktails we were sipping.

" 'Banished'?" I responded—this was something my father had never told me. Besides, the word had a pleasingly dramatic ring to it which I felt bore repeating.

"Yes, banished," said Cousin Frank. "Between the births of my mother and your father I believe there were several miscarriages, so that when your father finally came into the world, Grandma developed an obsessive fixation on him."

"What sort of fixation? And what's that to do with Grandpa being banished from Grandma's bedroom?" I asked, fascinated.

"It was a germ fixation," said Cousin Frank. "Grandma became obsessed with keeping your father free of germs. She wouldn't allow anyone to touch him, except herself. She wouldn't allow anyone in his bedroom, except herself."

"So I suppose if she were the only one to touch my father," I returned, "then she felt she should keep herself from being touched?"

"Something like that, I think," said Cousin Frank. "Anyway, it wasn't long after all this occurred that Mrs. Kennard came into the picture."

"Mrs. Kennard?"

"Yes. Grandpa's partner, Mr. Snelling, introduced Grandpop to Mrs. Kennard, a 'grass widow'—that's a divorced woman, versus a 'sod widow,' who is widowed by the death of her husband. Anyway, she was a little older than Grandpop but very handsome and well connected. One of her sons was a famous Harvard football player whose name you'd recognize. But we'd better not get into names."

I agreed. Cousin Frank went on to describe how Grandpop would, from then on, take the 1 p.m. train into Boston every Monday, returning precisely at 5:30 p.m., and how everyone in the house, including Grandma, knew this was his scheduled time to visit Mrs. Kennard. He said his mother, Aunt Mard, occasionally accompanied Grandpop on this Monday afternoon ritual and would be taken for a meal or an afternoon matinee.

"Did she know the true nature of the relationship between her father and this Mrs. Kennard?" I asked.

"Not initially," said Cousin Frank, "but later on everyone knew. She has told me you could set a clock by the sound of Grandpop's footsteps leaving the house on Monday afternoon and returning before supper. He was that punctual and predictable."

According to Cousin Frank and Eloise, Aunt Mard, now ninety-two, looks back on the Mrs. Kennard episode in the family history as simply a fact of life. A highly moral, straight, upright, strong Yankee lady if ever there was one, she recalls it as unacceptable behavior, but behavior that had to be accepted.

Cousin Frank and I, by this time well into our second cocktail on the porch that August evening, agreed this was not an atypical New England reaction to "such matters," providing the circumstances can be interpreted as justification—like the proverbial story of the man rumored to be sleeping with his housekeeper. He was excused by the fact that "his wife's an invalid, you know." Eloise informed us we were not being quite as profound—or amusing—as we thought. (Of course she was right.)

Grandma apparently accepted Mrs. Kennard, too. At least the family thought so until like Grandma Jane on my mother's side, she opened a small window onto her true feelings as she lay on her deathbed. It was January 1944, by then at least twenty years since Grandpop had had his last Monday afternoon with Mrs. Kennard. ("When they got older," Cousin Frank told me, "the relationship just sort of petered out.")

My parents and several other family members were with Grandma as she lay dying that winter afternoon, but she wished to speak only to my mother. Her fixation about germs had long since faded into history, but perhaps, in her semiconscious state, she somehow felt my mother would now be taking over as the official protector of her precious son, my father, Roger.

"I can see all my relatives waiting for me, Mannie," she said weakly, barely above a whisper, looking directly at my mother and using her nickname. Then she turned surprisingly feisty. "God, I was hoping I was rid of those dopes once and for all!" she said with a smile. Everyone laughed.

"Mr. Hale would like to come in for a few minutes," said a nurse who'd just spoken with Grandpop as he stood, uninvited, outside Grandma's bedroom door. Grandma didn't respond. The nurse repeated Grandpop's request. Again Grandma was silent. Then, in a voice suddenly strong and distinct, she turned to my mother and said, "Mannie, will you please go out and tell that old goat he can stay where he is. I've had enough of his orders. I'm going to die in peace!"

Grandpop never came in. And Grandma slipped away moments later.

My father survived Grandma's germ fixation during his early years, went on to attend Pheasanton and Milton and then Harvard, where he belonged to the Banjo Club and the prestigious Fox Club, played polo, drove Grandpop's fancy cars to football games, and dressed in a raccoon coat. He developed his love of sailing during summers at Prout's Neck, Maine, and his love for the Maine woods during his camping trips down the Allagash River with Grandpop.

I have an album of old photos taken on one of these early Allagash trips, and it's fun to see how "roughing it" was for wealthy New Englanders in the early days. There are scores of guides doing all the cooking, canoe carrying, wood chopping, and such. There are huge tents set up just for dining, another for the "kitchen," as well as sleeping tents. Grandpop and his grown-up friends are always dressed in suits and ties. There's even a photo of my father—he looks to be about twelve years old—sitting on a dead deer with a rifle across the antlers. The handwritten caption reads, "My first deer." Another photo next to it shows one of the guides cleaning it out. In later years my father had nothing but contempt for anyone who could not or would not gut his own deer.

According to Aunt Mard, Grandpop attempted to teach my father the ways of true Yankee frugality all through these growing-up years. He instructed him about buying gas in the early morning, about turning off lights, about not throwing away things that can be used again, like paper napkins, and all that sort of thing.

"I don't think your father learned *any* of these lessons very well," Aunt Mard recalls today. "He was given everything a boy could ever want whenever he wanted it—so he no doubt couldn't see the point!"

She remembers he would sometimes borrow money from her—ten cents here, fifteen cents there. "Borrowing" from Aunt Mard was a little habit that was to crop up again in later years. But by then, unfortunately, it wasn't so little.

My father proposed marriage to my mother in one of the carriage sheds behind a hostelry known as The Tavern, now long since replaced by a bank, in Peterborough, New Hampshire, where the Sagendorphs had their summer house. They'd run in there to take shelter from a thunderstorm, and suddenly, my mother says, he just "popped the question." She was ready for it. Although she had many suitors at the time, Grandma Jane had already strongly advised her to accept a proposal from my father, should it come. "Roger is a good, steady boy," she'd told her daughter, "and he'll take good care of you." So my mother accepted. They were married in Chestnut Hill, June 25, 1923, the week my father graduated from Harvard. He was twenty-three, she was twenty.

"It was a very busy week," my father once told Cousin Frank. "I graduated from college, got married, and sailed for Europe all in five days!"

My mother wrote in her diary, "I went into marriage totally ignorant of sex. Roger, too." She goes on to say, "We traveled all over Europe for a three-month honeymoon—with lots of money."

The photo album of their European trip in 1923 shows them in three-quarter-length bathing suits on the beach at Biarritz; watching a bullfight in San Sebastian; posing on a wall of Carcassonne Castle; strolling down a sidewalk in Monte Carlo; making comic faces at "our swimming hole, Villa d'Este," wherever that was; holding a glass of wine up to the camera at a mountaintop restaurant with a view of the Matterhorn in the distance; and on and on and on. Three solid months of it.

When they finally returned, they settled in Billerica, Massachusetts, for a short time, then Cambridge, and finally, along with a host of household servants, into the big house on Heath Street, Chestnut Hill, for "the best seven years of our marriage," as my mother recalls them now. The 16mm movies my father took during that seven-year period show picnic after picnic out on various rocky beaches or on board lovely big sailing boats. The women, laughing, clowning, making faces, are in calf-length woolen dresses with dropped waistlines and are wearing cloche hats that cover their entire heads. The men, posing more sedately, are in suits and ties. Life was one big, long picnic.

"Didn't Dad have to go to work in those days?" I asked my mother recently.

"Oh, no," she said, "he never even thought of it. His whole life was me. He was always giving me jewelry and spoiling me beyond measure. If I just mentioned casually that I liked the look of, say, a fur coat one of our friends was wearing, Rog would go out the next day and buy me one like it—or better."

"Didn't you ever think he was overdoing it a bit?" I asked, because my mother today is as frugal and careful with her money as any old Yankee could be.

"No. I just enjoyed it," she replied with a shrug.

I asked her how my father occupied himself during a typical weekday in Chestnut Hill, and she didn't seem to know. After thinking about it for a few minutes, she came up with, "Well, he used to go to the bank a lot."

Cousin Frank says my father worked briefly at Saco-Lowell and may even have formed an organization in Boston, funded by Grandpop of course, called Eastern Machinery Corporation, but if so, it was short-lived and had no particular impact on his young life. His passions were sailing his 42-foot yawl, named the *Marianette* after my mother, compiling a book on ocean navigation that was never published, riding horseback, playing polo with some of his Harvard friends, making little things in the elaborate workshop he had built next to the house (he was a fine craftsman when he applied himself), taking periodic trips to exotic places with my mother, and participating in all the regular Boston social functions of the day.

Drake's arrival on September 17, 1926, was, in spite of the difficult delivery, just another happy occasion in the uninterrupted flow of picnics, parties, trips, and general good times with friends in similar circumstances. He didn't cramp their style a whit. After all, there were nurses to take care of everything.

And Drake was a beautiful, healthy baby (seemingly), who grew ever more so in his first three years. A framed photograph among my mother's possessions today shows Drake at about two years old. He's at the helm of the *Marianette,* clutching the spokes with both little hands. A nautical "captain's hat" is jauntily set back upon his head, allowing his hair to fall over his forehead. The tip of his tongue is just visible as he happily and mightily concentrates on steering his father's boat.

Chapter 3

Idealism

THE FOLLOWING are excerpts from my mother's handwritten diary, beginning in the fall of 1929 and continuing until November 14, 1932, the date of her last entry . . .

October 11, 1929: Discussion with Dr. Garfield and Dr. Worcester —conclusion reached that we could ignore noise, keep Drake away from all excitement and people, have positive thoughts continually, plenty of air, exercise and sleep—no medicines.

November 8: Improved somewhat. He ran ahead of me to the post office—did not crow at all on street, seemed very natural and happy. Said "Lettybox daddy" and carried the letter to the box without throwing it away. Took his supper quietly with no noises and went to sleep early. Had worst night of all. Wakened at three and screamed louder than I have ever heard him for hours. Simply shrieked. Fraulein changed him and found nothing physically wrong.

November 11: My room seems to upset him constantly. Fraulein thinks my influence disturbs him so we are going to try not having him see me at all for a few days.

November 19: He seems happier—I hear his merry laughter much more often. He plays better with Rog and responds better. . . . Saw him again this morning by accident. He looked at me, gargled with his hand to his mouth and wide eyes, cried and ran back to his room fast. I don't quite understand that.

December 1: I leave my door open in the morning. He walks right by and does not wish to have a thing to do with me.

December 10: When he returned from his walk I was sewing in the baby's [my sister Patsy's] room. I called him. . . . He cried and would not come. I went into his room, took hold of him gently and told him everything was all right, that I loved him and not to cry. He quieted down and looked at me very sweetly. He was just going to kiss me, an unusual act, when he looked behind him, screamed, crowed, slapped me hard . . . then banging each side of his head with his fists . . . he kept this up incessantly until bedtime.

December 16: Drake has been better this week. Very normal, quiet, happy and responsive. I went to see him Friday PM. He seemed glad to see me and did not make the usual fuss or noise.

December 25: Drake has kept up his good improvement for two weeks which is the longest time without a setback this fall. We all feel very encouraged and, on this Christmas day, I feel that the root of the trouble is cured and that now the old habits just have to gradually and slowly disappear.

January 29, 1930: He is talking more and tries so hard to express himself. He runs into dark rooms joyfully now and plays hide and go seek. . . . We have been able to do away with the harness, all except the hands and now it seems a question of keeping up the same quiet routine with perfect understanding and sympathy which we have all acquired and praying that he is cured.

March 18: Drake went into another spell today. Needless to say it shocked and surprised us very much as we had considered him completely cured. He started all of a sudden downstairs with Rog . . . to whine and hold his mouth open and drool. Then he started to make the noise in his throat. He bumped his head against things and banged his hands against his face. He asked to have his hands tied back of him . . . then he grew worse as he banged his face so hard that it bled, his nose bled and his teeth and lips were all cut.

April 4: Now Drake is almost out of it. He has been steadily improving all week. . . . He is talking much better than before. He said

"Put blue blanket on please. . . ." He is very close to me now . . . when he does the bad habits he slaps his hands and says "no no" and puts them in back of him.

June 27: He has been shrieking for three days. We are exhausted. We cannot find any physical disorder.

July 17: How can such a child face the world? Should I separate my children on account of imitation? How to educate him? Should I send him away for the day to be helped? Wouldn't a special nurse be bad for his progress? He would not do things for himself which he needs so, yet *one* nurse finds it too much. . . . Fraulein, who has been so splendid all winter, seems to have lost her power with Drake. . . . She is very tired and therefore I feel she must leave.

August 21: Drake has been in a bad spell for almost three weeks. It has taken the form of bumping his head unbelievably hard. . . . He seems to feel that a chair is his one haven of safety and rushes to one in an uncontrollable way and sits up on it and then seems to calm down, but as soon as his feet touch the ground he either has to hold our hands or he loses complete control of himself. . . . I am truly worried this time.

September 5: Things have taken a decided turn and our whole life is being changed. . . . Drake persists in his bad spells and it seems to grow worse every day. . . . He is pale, hollow-eyed, weak and completely exhausted. He cannot stop bumping his head and feet and seems utterly gone.

September 6: I felt I must do something urgently. I went to Dr. Thom and told him all I could about Drake. He said that school was the only alternative but that he must see Drake first. I could not get an appointment for a week so I put Fraulein in the back of the house exclusively for Drake and I took entire charge of Patsy.

I know I must do one of two things:
1. A house in the country with Fraulein or,
2. an institution.

I have begun to look at houses all around here. . . . Drake improving under Fraulein's constant attention. He still cannot control the bumping though.

September 7: Mother arrived today with news of the Rudolf Steiner School in Dornach, Switzerland. . . . We learned it was very near Fraulein's home in Mulheim, Germany, and that Fraulein had been there and taken courses there. It is on a spiritual basis with music and everything, an important feature in the cure of many afflicted children. The thought greatly interests me.

September 12: I took Drake to Dr. Thom. He told me that Drake would always be very abnormal and backward and that as far as he could see part of his brain cells were dead and would never grow again. He said it made no difference what I did with him. He advised me strongly to send him away from home on account of the depressing influence of such a child around. When I mentioned the Dr. Rudolf Steiner School in Switzerland he approved highly and so I decided right then and there I would take Drake over there. . . . It is the right thing to do.

My father was not convinced at first that the Rudolf Steiner School in Switzerland was the right place. He felt it might be "too occult," not scientific enough. But something had to be done. And so he, my mother, and Drake set sail on the SS *Cleveland* on September 21, 1930. Patsy, seven months old, was left in the care of Fraulein. While the *Cleveland* took a small number of passengers, it was primarily a freighter—my mother remembers even cattle aboard. It was felt Drake's inevitable screams and violent behavior would be too objectionable to the passengers on a luxury ocean liner.

"It took us fourteen days to reach Le Havre," my mother remembers, "and poor Drakie-boy screamed the whole way over. Any slight ship noise would set him off. And he continued to scream in the rented car from Le Havre to Switzerland. It was a nightmare trip."

But when they finally arrived at the Rudolf Steiner School in Arlesheim, just outside Basel-on-the-Rhine, they witnessed what they later referred to as a "sign" that this was the right place for Drake. My mother described the moment in her paper for Emerson College, written thirty-five years later . . .

We arrived at a small house called the *Sonnenhof,* which means "Sunshine House." A small young woman with black hair pulled back into a tight bun opened the door for us. She introduced herself as Dr. Julia

Bort. Immediately Drake, who was following several yards behind me holding my husband's hand, broke away from him and ran straight up the steps toward Dr. Bort. When he reached her he threw his arms around her and silently hugged her closely—a loving gesture I had never seen him make before with me or anyone. Although no one spoke English and neither my husband nor I knew any German, it was not difficult to understand that Drake belonged in the *Sonnenhof!*

The next day, accompanied by someone who knew a little English, they visited the eight-storey molded concrete edifice known as the Goetheanum, located high on a nearby hill overlooking the valley of Dornach. When I first set eyes on it twenty-four years later, during the summer of 1954, I was appalled at its massiveness. Built as if from a single concrete form of immense proportions, it looks at first like an igloo for giants. I doubt if there's another structure anything like it in the world. Yet when you get used to it a little, the contoured, flowing, rounded forms begin to take on a certain majestic beauty.

The Goetheanum, completed just two years prior to my parents' first visit, was—and is—the center of a philosophical, religious, artistic, medical, educational, architectural, and agricultural movement known as "anthroposophy," derived from the Greek words for "man" (*anthropos*) and "wisdom" (*sophia*). Begun by Austrian scientist and philosopher Rudolf Steiner, it essentially teaches that true wisdom is possible for man only when he is able to perceive spiritual truths equally as well as material truths. In the realm of ultimate truth, said Steiner, there can be no conflict between science and religion.

"Anthroposophy" was a word that was to become an integral part of my early life and education.

Rudolf Steiner had been dead for five years when my parents were first introduced to his philosophies at the Goetheanum that morning after arriving with Drake. The anthroposophical movement, however, was still being carried forth by his followers in Switzerland, Holland, Germany, and the Scandinavian countries. (Today there are approximately 25,000 members of the Anthroposophical Society. And the anthroposophical homes for the mentally retarded, such as Drake's *Sonnenhof*, number about two hundred in twenty countries.)

My father was impressed with the loving atmosphere immediately apparent in Drake's little "Sunshine House," but everything else seemed bizarre to him. Here he was in a building that looked like some sort of giant concrete monument to a mushroom, being presented in broken, barely understandable English with something called "anthroposophy," which apparently dealt with everything in the world, including spiritualism. It made him decidedly uneasy. He thought of himself as a realist, a man handy with carpentry tools, someone who could disassemble and assemble a high-powered rifle, find a buoy in a fog bank, remove the carburetor in his Buick roadster, hit a tiny ball with a stick from a horse at full gallop, and twirl a lady around a ballroom floor until everyone else stood back and watched.

Now he was being told that each person possesses, besides the physical body, an "etheric" body by which we live and grow, an "astral" body by which we sense, think, and feel, and finally, an "ego," or "higher self," that is an actual spirit unifying the other three. I wish I could have been there that morning just to see my father's expression as these very serious Swiss people—and anthroposophists, I've noticed, tend to be on the serious side—tried to convince him of the notion that one is alternately "born" into the spiritual as well as the physical world and that each person experiences many lives in both worlds on the long road to his final destiny of perfection and wisdom. I'm sure he was wondering what in blazes he, a regular upper-crust Harvard lad from Boston, Hub of the Universe, was doing there listening to these people discussing "occult science," "higher knowledge," "universal spirituality," and "spiritual research."

My mother, on the other hand, immediately began to absorb the Steiner philosophy with an enthusiasm born of desperation. After a year of witnessing her firstborn abuse himself, and after a year of alternating between a euphoric feeling of faith that he'd get well and dread that he never would, she was ready for some *hope*.

Perhaps Drake would improve here in Switzerland, she thought. Perhaps in time he'd be well enough to come home to Chestnut Hill and resume a normal life. But even if that was not in the cards, there was hope. Even if Dr. Thom had been right about his having dead brain cells that would never grow and even if he remained in this foreign home throughout his entire life and never came home again, there was hope. The philosophy called anthroposophy, she began to realize from the day they arrived, refuted Dr. Thom's statement that "it would make no difference what was done with him." It *would* make a difference. If not in this life, then in the next, or the one thereafter.

Drake would be exposed every day to music, art, and literature. Whether he screamed or not, he'd be taken to concerts, plays, and special art exhibits. (Over a period of years, he would actually memorize the passages from Goethe that were read to him every day.) Along with other retarded children, he would be taken to a beautiful Swiss mountain house owned by the Anthroposophical Society for "summer vacations." He often enjoyed excursions on steamboats down the Rhine, accompanied by a bevy of nurses. He would be loved by the other children and by generations of young student nurses and teachers who'd spend several months or a year at the *Sonnenhof* as part of their education in the Steiner approach to mental retardation.

My mother and father remained in Switzerland with Drake for six weeks on that first trip. My mother's enthusiasm was, I'm sure, a strong influence on my father, but what began to turn him around during that period was his realization that so many anthroposophists were scientists—realists like him! That was a surprise, after his impressions of the first few days. Rudolf Steiner himself had been a physicist, born in 1861 in Kraljevec, then part of the Austro-Hungarian Empire and now in Yugoslavia. My father was pleased to be told that at no place in any of Steiner's hundreds of published books or lectures does he attempt to communicate a so-called spiritual discovery until it could be understood by means of the ordinary, everyday human consciousness. Sort of the Missouri "show me" approach to the occult!

My father explained to me years later a simple example of what might be termed a "spiritual" discovery. "Go outside and observe exactly how the sky looks at a given time," he said, "and memorize what you see—the cloud formations, wind, temperature, everything. Do the same on the following day, at the same time, exactly recalling the conditions of the first day. Same for the third day, recalling the first two days. And so on until your mind has developed to the point where it can remember the conditions on hundreds of individual days in succession. Sometime in the process, you'll begin to see weather conditions coming up in the *future* as easily as those in the past. Or so Steiner maintained—and evidently he did it."

"You ever try it?" I had to ask.

"I memorized about fifteen days one time," he said, "but then I decided I didn't *want* to see into the future."

I recently asked Dr. Richard Head, former chief scientist for NASA during the Mercury program of the 1960s, about this anthroposophical method of "seeing" the weather and climate of the future. Since 1970 Dr. Head has worked full-time for us compiling all the scientific data used in making the long-range weather forecasts in *The Old Farmer's Almanac*. He stared at me for several moments before returning to the sun cycle information he was studying on the screen of his computer monitor. I decided not to pursue the matter.

During those initial six weeks in Switzerland, my father met anthroposophists with medical degrees and degrees in education, chemistry, and physics. He talked (almost always through an interpreter) with agricultural experts about soil treatment, crop rotation, fruit tree management, and the proper care and breeding of cattle. He visited the biochemical research laboratory at the Goetheanum and observed the results of "biodynamic" farming and gardening. Slowly but surely, it all began to make some down-to-earth practical sense to him.

During the days my mother, along with a nurse, would take long walks with Drake. She'd sing songs to gatherings of the children, accompanying herself on a gold soprano lyre she'd purchased in Basel (Patsy occasionally plays it nowadays). She learned about the natural remedies for medical ailments—minerals, metals, and herbs —and she struggled with the language difficulties in assimilating the Rudolf Steiner approach to education, known as a "Waldorf" education today. (Like that of the salad, the name originates with the Waldorf-Astoria cigarette factory in Stuttgart, Germany, prior to World War I. Rudolf Steiner developed an educational system for the children of the factory workers back then, and through the years the word evolved to mean a Steiner school or Steiner-type education.) In the evenings, my mother and father would attend concerts or an occasional English lecture at the Goetheanum. They'd watch demonstrations of "eurythmy," too, a form of expressive dancing through which, some six years later, I would learn the letters of the alphabet!

By the time they left Drake and set sail for home just before Thanksgiving of 1930, both my mother and my father were convinced that the late Rudolf Steiner's "anthroposophy" was pretty much the solution to *all* the world's problems. It was the wave of the future. They were converts, with all the enthusiasm and zeal of converts.

My mother's diary took on a radically different tone. One shipboard entry, written on the way home, begins as follows . . .

November 14: It has come about through the evolution of man that art, science and morality have developed separately and we have not realized that there must be harmony between them in order to reach the necessary knowledge for man's progress.

They arrived in Chestnut Hill to greet nine-month-old Patsy and the houseful of servants. It seemed quiet and tranquil after the experience of Drake's last year there. Nurse Fraulein, exhausted from her part in the ordeal, was planning to return to Germany. She'd soon be replaced by Nurse Fia, but the rest of the regular cast of Boston servants, relatives, and friends were carrying on—"business as usual." Of course nobody, with the exception of Grandma Jane, had the vaguest notion of what my mother and father had been up to in Switzerland except that it was somehow connected with the fact that "something had gone wrong" with their son, Drake. Insanity, the rather terrifying word used to cover any mental aberration, wasn't discussed in those days. In most everyone's mind it was too closely connected with the word "heredity."

"We thought your parents would be crazy to have any more children," an old family friend, now in his mid-eighties, told me recently. My mother says that particular consideration never entered her mind for an instant. Thank goodness. (I was but a year and a half from conception!)

As to both my parents' sudden enthusiasm for anthroposophy, well, everyone chalked that up to a temporary reaction to the Drake tragedy. It was something that would soon pass once they again became immersed in their normal Boston social life.

It did not pass. There was nothing temporary about it. Within a few weeks of their return, they rented public rooms in downtown Boston and began to give evening lectures on the teachings of Rudolf Steiner. My father emphasized the subjects of agriculture, education, and medicine. My mother leaned more toward religion and the role of painting, sculpture, dancing, and music. Initially a few of their society friends attended these lectures out of loyalty. However, they were soon turned off by the mental exercise required for an appreciation of Steiner and, frankly, by pure, unadulterated boredom! Anthroposophy can be, as they say, "pretty heavy going." Even the translations of Steiner's actual lectures and writings are sleep-inducing unless one is motivated sufficiently to penetrate the long, hazy, convoluted sentences to find what is essentially a fascinating, challenging approach to life.

Their friends were also turned off by the bearded, "creepy-looking" Arabs who began coming to the lectures in increasing numbers. The occult aspects of the philosophy seemed to be the attraction for "an Eastern element," as my mother puts it, then living somewhere around Boston. She adds, "We didn't know how to get rid of them!"

A year later, in the fall of 1931, my parents returned to Switzerland to visit Drake. Here is how my mother described, in her diary, the first glimpse of him after a year . . .

Friday A.M., October 17, 1931: Peeked in at Drake doing eurythmy. Beautiful face. Greeted us in the hall. He recognized us immediately and asked for Baby Sister. "Mommie and Daddie" he said, putting out his hands. No emotion. Beautiful voice. He was pale but healthy-looking, tall and saint-like. Most impressed by spiritual quality. Felt like kneeling before him. . . . He led me up the stairs to his sunny room and put my hand all around his crib. He sat down at his own little table and chair and drank his milk and ate his crackers. . . . "Mommie and Daddie kommen heute" etc. . . .

Saturday, October 18: Glad to see me—ran and took my hand and we went for a walk. He talked a lot of German which I did not understand. Asked me if he could throw his hat in the pond. Not understanding, I said "Ja." In it went. Was delighted when Daddie had to fish it out with a stick.

Monday, October 20: Went to Sonnenhof to find Drake weaving. Ran to me the minute . . . I opened the door. A bit aggravated at my coming and going for a while and then he settled down.

Another year later, now pregnant with me, she returned again, this time with Grandma Jane but without my father . . .

November 4, 1932: Drake remembered me immediately and felt very deeply. . . . Indrawing noise has changed to more human outgoing noise . . . the mouth still poor, uncontrolled as yet, hangs it open. . . . The Ego is not down in his body yet, but he thinks a great deal and one has the feeling he knows all. . . . Hits himself with his hands and at times has to have them tied.

November 13: Drake spoke about the sun and moon the whole walk —"Auf Wiedersehen grosser Sonnen und Auf Wiedersehen Kleiner Mund" etc.—and seemed troubled about something. I think he can feel our trip is coming to a close.

November 14: Last day before I sail home. I watched him have lunch. Drake said grace very sweetly, then he ate very nicely by himself. . . . He listened to everything that Maya, his present nurse, and I said. Then we prayed together at his bedside—he put his head toward me to kiss for the first time. I sang a German song which he loved and said "wieder" [again]. He drew close to me and seemed to understand the whole situation. Then, in German, he said, "The sun comes and goes, the moon comes and goes—and Mommie comes and goes."

Although my mother, often accompanied by my father, was to return to Switzerland every year until World War II, the remaining 108 pages of her diary about Drake are blank.

I came into the world the following March 16. "You got a good one *this* time," said Da, my mother's debonair father.

Also into our Boston world came the anthroposophists from Switzerland. My father began financing the voyages and initial living expenses of three officials of the Steiner movement who came to study the possibility of organizing Waldorf schools, biodynamic farms, and Steiner laboratories in America.

One was huge, jovial (rare for an anthroposophist!) Dr. Ehren-fried Pfeiffer, who would, a few years later, scare me half to death by throwing me in the air in time to some German poem he was reciting. He would come to Vanceboro, Maine, many times to help my father set up the Steiner laboratory there, where blood would be crystallized on little round glass plates for the purpose of identifying the existence of cancers and other diseases. (More on that in the next chapter.)

There was Dr. Hermann Von Baravalli, the mathematical genius who, with his Swiss wife, Ruth, would move for years from one Waldorf school to another all over New England. I could never fathom the reason for so many moves, though I suspect he was a rather volatile, quick-tempered man. I do know that trailing after the Baravallis was always a little group of children belonging to the same American followers of the Steiner education philosophy. Patsy and I were, of course, to be in that number. My parents were convinced that whatever school the Baravallis happened to be teaching in in a given year was the right school for us.

Finally there was Dr. Gunther Wachsmuth, Steiner's biographer and then treasurer of the Anthroposophical Society, who was natu-rally pleased to have found a wealthy young American couple anx-ious to part with money on behalf of Steiner's work. As my father reflected years later, "Financing those people was probably the first time Grandpop's money went to a charitable cause in any meaning-ful amount." Grandpop was generous to a fault to any relative, no matter how distant, but not outside the family. His largest annual contribution in that area was five dollars to the Red Cross.

Shown in one of the many family albums I have today are two photographs of these three anthroposophists dressed in dark suits with vests, having just arrived from Switzerland. They're standing together on the back lawn of our Heath Street house along with, in one photo, my father, who was looking so young, innocent, and proud, and in the other, my mother, who could be taken for a 1930s movie star. They're laughing, probably about something to do with attempting to understand each other's language, and the Swiss doc-tors are holding their cigarettes in the inverted way Europeans do.

When people today are leafing through this old photo album, they invariably pause when they come to these two pictures. The photos on the preceding pages show people sailing, picnicking, and posing on holiday around the world. The photos after it begin, page by page, to look different, more serious, less frivolous, eventually showing scenes that I and other participants alive today find all but unbelievable. "Who in the world are these fancy foreign-looking men with your mother and father?" is the inevitable question, to which I can only say, "Well, it's a long story . . ."

I should add that anthroposophy never caused my parents to totally lose their zest for "the good life" and all the luxuries Grandpop's money could buy. It never came to *that*. (At about the time of my father's graduation from Harvard, Grandpop gave something on the order of a million dollars each to him and Aunt Mard.) But as reflected in the photographs, their interests had changed.

"Our old life of society, parties, and cocktails seemed to have no more meaning," my mother wrote about this period more than thirty years later, "and I felt the important thing was to dedicate myself to the work of Rudolf Steiner."

They replaced their standard wedding rings with thick gold rings imbedded with rubies and small diamond stars, especially designed to symbolize various facets of the anthroposophical philosophy. For many years, even after things turned sour, these rings represented their bond to each other and to the new philosophy they shared.

Both of them studied translations of Steiner books and lectures for hours every day, and my mother kept notebooks in which she wrote down her thoughts and philosophical discoveries. "Knowledge leads through art to the heights of the supersensible life," she wrote in one. "Art, science, religion, morality, and knowledge must *harmonize*," with the last word underlined several times.

Emerging through much of her early interpretation of Rudolf Steiner's philosophy is, over and over again, an emphasis on the arts. The arts were the element of the Steiner work in which she began to feel she, herself, might best make a "contribution." To be sure, unlike her mother, Grandma Jane, she couldn't paint. She wasn't particularly interested in ballet or sculpture. She wrote well enough, yet felt no desire in the area of literature. But she could *sing!* She loved to sing. Even before it was trained, her soprano singing voice, already put to good use at Westover School, was rich and beautiful.

So she began taking singing lessons, and gave informal concerts for friends at Marblehead Neck the next summer. Cousin Frank remembers accompanying family members on several occasions to a studio in Boston to "watch" her sing on a local radio program.

She looked the part of a singer, too. To the horror of everyone except my father, for whom she could do no wrong, she began to enhance her natural beauty with theatrical makeup and hairstyles. She even decorated several rooms of the Heath Street house in dramatic patterns of lavender, pink, and rose, the likes of which, as Uncle Robb, her "cruel" brother, once said to me, "no one in Boston had ever seen outside the Old Howard" (a famous Boston theater, featuring strippers in its later years).

As I've mentioned, Uncle Robb had always accused her of being "star struck," but now the thought of a singing career was becoming a serious mission, a mission that "harmonized" with her newfound philosophy of life.

My father was supportive. He encouraged her to pursue every avenue toward a successful career even though some of those avenues, such as voice lessons in New York City, took her away from home for weeks at a time. He was proud of her always. The notion of a beautiful, talented wife who might well be famous someday had a strong appeal for him.

On an entirely different level it was painful.

"He joined us for lunch quite often," recalled my nurse, Fia, when I visited her in 1985, "and he seemed tense during those times when your mother was off in New York taking singing lessons. She was so beautiful, you know, and he was so devoted to her."

By early spring 1936, I'd passed my third birthday without any horrendous problem; it appeared Drake would not be coming home in the foreseeable future; Patsy was ready for school, but there were no Waldorf schools in the area; although the Steiner lectures in the city had come to a stop, the philosophy of anthroposophy remained the central focus of my parents' young lives; my mother was seriously contemplating a full-fledged singing career; Boston social life, such fun in earlier times, now seemed meaningless; and my father, at the age of thirty-six, had virtually nothing to do.

Furthermore, aside from providing financial support to the Anthroposophical Society and "the three wise men," my father and mother had nothing to do *together* on behalf of furthering Rudolf

Steiner's philosophy in America. *That* they considered their highest priority and the only way to justify the tragedy of "poor Drakie-boy."

Thus, it was time for a major decision.

In order to make it, they decided to drop everything for a couple of months, leave Patsy and me with Fia and the others of the ménage, buy a trailer, and, just the two of them, drive across the country to San Francisco! (My mother and father never did anything in a small way.)

It was one of the first trailers to cross the country. Maybe *the* first. They left Boston on May 10, 1936, making Worcester the first night, Stafford Springs, Connecticut, the second, Bear Mountain overlooking the Hudson on the third, and then on through Pennsylvania, west to St. Louis, Kansas City, Wichita, and over to Santa Fe, Flagstaff, Las Vegas (then a small western town), Los Angeles, and San Francisco. People were curious all along the line. At night they had no trouble obtaining permission to stop at private homes and farms, and they'd almost always join their hosts for breakfast the next morning.

In McPherson, Kansas, my father caught a gas station operator putting gasoline into the trailer's drinking-water tank. The man had never seen a trailer before and didn't know any better. He could tell something was wrong, however, by the look on my father's face as he suddenly leaped out of the car and charged back toward him, yelling. The poor man dropped the hose and ran out into the field behind the station. My father chased him for more than a quarter of a mile but wasn't able to catch him. Their drinking water smelled of gasoline for the remainder of the trip.

Flat tires were a daily occurrence on both the two-door Ford convertible and the large four-sleeper trailer. On one hot afternoon outside Delhi, Colorado, the jack holding up the trailer for a tire change gave way. At the time, my mother was sitting on the little toilet situated directly in front of the side door. The sudden downward lurch propelled her out through the door and all the way across the road into the ditch on the other side. Even years later, my mother never really forgave my father for that. It wasn't so much the actual episode that bothered her. She was unhurt, though a bit shaken. Rather it was the fact my father laughed for such a long time. He continued to chuckle about it occasionally for the rest of his life. "I just wish I'd had my camera ready the second she came flying out," he'd say.

They traveled 5,024 miles, sold both car and trailer in San Francisco, headed east by train, and arrived home at Chestnut Hill on July 3 . . . with the decision made!

Later, they said the future course of their life together was determined as they sat on the edge of the Grand Canyon, their feet hanging over the side. It sounds unbelievably dramatic, but knowing my mother and father, I think it's probably true. For them, momentous decisions were to be made in monumental, inspirational settings.

Within days after their return, furniture was being taken from our Heath Street house, huge trunks were being packed with clothes and belongings and taken away for temporary storage, and the servants, including beloved Fia, were being told their services were no longer needed. Unless, that is, any of them would be willing to live in a tiny backwoods Maine town on the Canadian border, called Vanceboro. That's where the Hales were going to live! (Fia did spend a summer in Maine taking care of Patsy and me one year later —but we never saw cook Johnnie, her daughter, Ingrid, or any of the others again.)

The decision was to establish an anthroposophical center, something like the one in Switzerland, in a wilderness part of America, free of the influences of Boston or any populated area. They'd build a Waldorf school for pre–high school children, including Patsy and me, naturally. There would be a medical laboratory in which to conduct research on Steiner's theories of disease identification. A working farm would demonstrate the advantages of Steiner's "bio-dynamic" gardening and his suggested methods of animal care. A cultural center, including a theater, would attract, through my mother's contacts in the theater world, singers, musicians, writers, and painters from all over the country to do their creative work in undisturbed, beautiful surroundings. Finally, to finance these anthroposophical undertakings, there would be a large hardwood lumber business, including two lumber mills for the cutting and finishing of the harvested logs.

Why Vanceboro? Well, it fit the "wilderness" requirement, and both my mother and father were familiar with the town through

Grandma Jane. During the 1920s and early 1930s, it was from Vance-boro that Grandma Jane had been taken in a motorboat each summer the ten miles to her wilderness retreat called Star Island. Since she hadn't been making that long trek for several summers, she was happy to sell the place to my father. We would live in Grandma Jane's log cabin that first summer (and, for that matter, every summer thereafter until 1947) while a year-round house in Vanceboro would be hastily erected, the first of what would eventually be fifty or more separate structures of all varieties.

The dream, the incredibly idealistic and wonderful dream from which, years later, my poor father would never recover, was under way.

Chapter 4

---◆---

Audacity

V̲ANCEBORO, Maine, was such a remote town that, as the saying
goes, everyone living there had to keep his own tomcat. "Is it
very far to Vanceboro?" I asked a gas station attendant in Topsfield
on my brief trip back in 1974. "No, it's not far from here," said the
attendant, and then he added, "but when you get there you might
wish it was a sight further." (The "thickly settled" sign outside town
was followed by three or four houses within the next mile.) In the
summer of 1936, however, Vanceboro was "surviving" better than
it is today. Located at the headwaters of the St. Croix River (which
separates Maine from Canada), 110 miles northeast of Bangor, it had
a population of around 800. Today it's about 350.

The main source of employment in 1936 was the active railroad
center. During the winter, more than thirty freight trains passed
through Vanceboro daily, many carrying potatoes (kept from freezing by charcoal stoves in each car) from Aroostook County in the
north, traveling east and south through New Brunswick, crossing
the border again to Vanceboro, and then on to Boston and New
York. There were always several daily passenger trains, too, from
both Boston and Montreal on their way to Fredericton and Saint
John. I can hear in my mind today the slow, heavy puffing sounds
of two laboring steam engines attempting to get a long line of loaded
cars moving out of the Vanceboro station area and then suddenly
collapsing into a rapid-fire series of puffs as their big wheels began
simultaneously to spin on the tracks. Somewhere stored away inside
me forever, too, are their distant wails as they approached the cross-

ing outside McAdam, Canada, faintly audible to us even up on Star Island during calm summer nights.

Besides railroad jobs, residents found work with the Eastern Pulpwood Company, which was sometimes cutting in the area, and with the U.S. government W.P.A. projects. Active from late spring through fall were a few "sporting camps," too, located on Spednic Lake, which began at the dam in Vanceboro and extended north, partly in Canada, for some thirty miles. Certainly the most permanent, steady jobs were at the Canadian and American customs buildings located at the Canadian end of the bridge crossing the St. Croix. Vanceboro residents passed back and forth across this international boundary with little more than a nod from whoever was on duty. Strangers, however, were thoroughly searched for dynamite. Vanceboro customs officials had an obsession about the possibility of their bridge being blown up. The railroad bridge just a few hundred yards down the river had been blown up by a German spy during World War I, and no one intended to take any chances of that happening again.

A few years later, when World War II began, both bridges were guarded twenty-four hours a day by a group of twenty black soldiers, probably the only blacks ever seen by anyone in Vanceboro up to that time. I grew up believing all black people were ardent nature lovers. When I chatted with one of the men on duty near the railroad bridge one day, he told me he was "watching the trees grow."

Although there were these jobs in Vanceboro, it was nonetheless a two-class society: poor and dirt poor. Aside from the sporting camps "up lake," there were no inns, hotels, motels, or tourist cabins. So there were no tourists. There were very few outsiders in town either, so I don't recall any expressions like "flatlanders" or debates as to who was and who was not a "native." Everyone was a native.

The one and only doctor was Dr. McLean in McAdam, who covered all the small towns on both sides of the border for a radius of thirty miles on mostly dirt roads. The nearest movie theater was in McAdam, too. There was no drugstore, no golf course, no tennis courts, no swimming pools, no summer people, no library, and no organizations like Lions, Rotary, Women's Club, Historical Society, or anything remotely similar. People cut ice on the lake during the winter for their icehouses and iceboxes; probably less than half the population had indoor plumbing; deer meat was a large part of everyone's diet, often mixed with rice, beans, or noodles to stretch it out; many families kept a cow and a few chickens; if you didn't have a car, and many didn't, you walked even if the trip took most of a day; and everyone knew everything about everybody at all times. Any deviation from normal routine was noticed: "Where's *she* goin' at this time of the mornin'?"

A lifelong lesson in country living, learned early on, was never to say anything bad about anyone to anyone. Chances were pretty good that the person you were talking with was related to the person you were talking about.

One might also add that there was no fear of economic disaster in Vanceboro. Everyone was already about as poor as they could get. Accordingly, there was no "keeping up with the neighbors," no false illusions about something another world called "success." To get along from day to day one needed only to be self-reliant, innovative, and practical.

Mr. Teague, the owner of the general store in town, gave me an early inkling of the merits of practical thinking. Although he owned a glass eye, he seldom put it in. So the gunky-looking hole in his face was something right out of a horror movie, and of course I was fascinated and revolted at the same time. My father said the lemon extract he nipped on all day placed him on a mental level where he couldn't care less about his personal appearance. Mr. Teague told me the *real* reason, however. "Ain't no use wearin' my glass eye, Jud," he said to me one day when he noticed me staring at his face. "I can't see *nothin'* with it!"

I've occasionally written about Vanceboro over the twenty-eight years I've been with *Yankee* magazine and have therefore received letters from several subscribers who once lived there too. One, a Mrs. R. Carr from Providence, Rhode Island, sent me what she said was a verbatim account of a conversation she once heard between Mr. Teague and a lady customer who walked seven miles to and from the store every week.

Customer: "Y'aint got no eggs today, has yuh?"

Mr. Teague: "I ain't said I ain't, did I?"

Customer: "I ain't asked yuh is y'aint—I asked yuh ain't yuh is, is yuh?"

Mr. Teague: "Ayuh."

My brother, Drake, had already been living in Switzerland for three years, never to return, when I came into the world on March 16, 1933. Because I appeared normal in every way (although so had Drake for his first three years), I was welcomed into the world with as much joy, love, and, I'm sure, relief as any little boy could be. That's me, with my mother, ABOVE. She'd already begun her singing career by then. At LEFT, I'm on the lap of my beloved nurse, Fia, outside our Chestnut Hill house. My sister, Patsy, is beside us. BELOW: During my first summer on earth, my father introduces me to his 30.30-caliber rifle during a visit to Star Island, my grandmother's wilderness retreat in Canada, ten miles from Vanceboro, Maine.

Hanging on my office wall today are photographs of my two great-grandfathers, Longley Lewis Sagendorph, LEFT, and Amos Hale, BELOW. The former, always described as "sensitive-looking—almost pretty," was the founder of Penn Metal, a steel-manufacturing company in Parkersburg, West Virginia, whose executive offices were eventually moved from Philadelphia to Boston, where his successor, his son George (my mother's father—a.k.a. Da), remained president until he was well into his nineties. Amos Hale made his living as a farmer in Newton Upper Falls, Massachusetts. My father liked to tell me Amos was so frugal he'd chew tobacco in the morning, leave the quid to dry on a fence post at noon, and then smoke it in his pipe later in the day. Unfortunately, Amos didn't live long enough to know about or share in the great wealth rather suddenly acquired by one of his three sons, Frank, my father's father, just prior to 1900.

ABOVE: That's my mother's debonair father, George Sagendorph—my Da—in the center, at about age eighty-five, a few days after (or before) his marriage to the lady on his right (Lorna Underwood). On Da's left is "Uncle" Charley Purdey of Boston, a lifelong hunting pal of my father's. BELOW: Amos's son Frank Judson Hale—a.k.a. Grandpop—with his wife, Grace. It was only recently that I learned how sadly unnatural their relationship had been.

Before Drake's nightmare changed the course of my family's life forever (beginning on October 6, 1929, when he was three), my mother and father, shown ABOVE in their 42-foot yawl, the *Marianette*, out of Marblehead, devoted themselves to parties, trips, and general good times with Boston friends in similar circumstances and social standing. Grandpop's gift to my father upon his Harvard graduation was such that, according to my mother today, my father "didn't even think of going to work" upon returning to a houseful of servants after a three-month honeymoon in Europe. Drake's arrival in 1926 was another happy event and didn't cramp their style in the least. As the photo of him at RIGHT shows, Drake was sometimes taken aboard the *Marianette*, where he happily wore his father's yachting cap and even struggled mightily to steer.

At LEFT, Grandpop holds my sister, Patsy, as we arrive for "Sunday dinner at Grandpop's," in West Newton—*the* longest, fanciest, slowest-moving, most boring weekly culinary ritual of Patsy's and my young lives. (Patsy is very happy here, though—Grandpop has just presented her with a new tricycle, an event she vividly remembers to this day.) The two over-stuffed people shown at RIGHT on March 15, 1933 (the day before I was born) are my mother and Da, her father, with a sympathy pillow inside his coat. As to the photo BELOW, well, it's difficult for me to realize that the happy little one-year-old boy on my mother's lap is, indeed, Drake. Who could have guessed then what fate soon had in store for him?

ABOVE LEFT: My father proudly poses with three members of the Anthroposophical Society, none of whom spoke English, newly arrived (and financed by my father) in Chestnut Hill from Switzerland, where Drake had been left a month before. (From left to right: Dr. Gunther Wachsmuth, Dr. Ehrenfried Pfeiffer, and Dr. Hermann Von Baravalli.) The photo of my mother and Drake, ABOVE RIGHT, was taken in Switzerland the following year. BELOW: The Goetheanum, designed by Rudolf Steiner (1861–1925).

ABOVE: Looking toward the barn, later much enlarged, in the mid-1930s, when my parents' grandiose dream in Vanceboro, Maine, was just getting started. The school, theater, laboratory, mills, etc., were still to come. BELOW: Sheila dances her "butterfly dance" in *Cinderella* out on Alice May Point, one of many plays my mother wrote, choreographed, directed, produced, and you-name-it during the Vanceboro years. That's me with arm outstretched, supposedly a prince but feeling like a jerk.

ABOVE LEFT: My father on Star Island with Metropolitan Opera star Friedrich Schorr, considered one of the greatest baritones of all time. That's his wife, Upie, with them. She was also a famous Wagnerian singer but had retired except for singing arias to the loons. ABOVE RIGHT: Frankie Smith, my father's teamster, dressed as the coachman for my mother's production of *Cinderella*, complete with my father's formal opera hat. (He was apt to refer to the extensive vocalizing the singers-in-residence at Vanceboro did each morning as "hollerin'.") BELOW: Teatime for Patsy and me.

When I received that letter from Mrs. Carr, I couldn't help visualizing my mother walking into Mr. Teague's store the morning they arrived on the overnight sleeper train from Boston. She could very well have been wearing her "Brünnhilde hat," as we called it, with two real eagle wings on either side, and she probably asked Mr. Teague if he carried the S.S. Pierce line of canned goods and cheeses. The town was never to be the same from that moment on. For the next eleven years, the Hales would bring out the best in Vanceboro and then, toward the end, the worst.

The first step was to purchase a piece of land. For several seasons prior to 1936, my father and three or four of his Harvard buddies had gone deer hunting from a little log cabin on a lake called Eastbrook, a mile inland from the shore opposite Grandma Jane's Star Island. They'd had to purchase their supplies and arrange for a boat and guides in Vanceboro, so my father was already familiar in town as a "sport," as outside hunters and fishermen were called. In other words, he had sufficient contacts to make immediate inquiries the morning they arrived. "We're going to live here permanently and start a farm," he said brightly to one old-timer at the store. "Do you know of any land around here for sale?" To that he received the stock country answer, which he loved to repeat to me years later: "Don't know of any that ain't."

Within several days, after making deals with a half dozen property owners as well as with the Eastern Pulpwood Company, he had his "piece of land." He bought twelve thousand acres. I have searched the family records in vain to ascertain the price. It was undoubtedly not as good a deal as the two cents an acre the United States paid for Alaska in 1867, but I'll bet the per-acre price was only a few dollars.

At any rate, Hale land now surrounded the town of Vanceboro on three sides. Across the lake and river on the fourth side was Canada. Lake and river frontage totaled more than ten miles. Trains coming to Vanceboro from either Bangor or Montreal traveled six miles through Hale property. The only highway into town, Route 16 from Topsfield, wound through Hale property for the last ten minutes of the bumpy "thank you ma'am" drive from Bangor.

It was a good beginning. Now all that was left to be done was to build a rambling one-storey, seventeen-room house with six bathrooms on a hill overlooking a ten-acre pond; a barn with sufficient space for thirty-five or forty milking cows, six riding horses, and twenty-two workhorses; a poultry house for five hundred chickens; a shed and pen for some pigs; a house in which some of the farm-hands could live; a two-storey fifty-by-one-hundred-foot wood-working shop with concrete floor; a long two-storey building con-nected to the main barn, the top floor to house offices, two apartments, and an auditorium for plays and square dances, while beneath would be the slaughtering area and storage garages for all the farm machinery and the big red fire truck my father was to purchase upon discovering Vanceboro had no fire department; not one but two hardwood lumber mills with associated sheds; a bunk-house and cookhouse for mill and other workers, to be called "Tim-ber Village"; a laboratory in which to conduct anthroposophical experiments with plants, cow urine, and human blood; a fifty-foot-long greenhouse connected to the laboratory; and a little red Wal-dorf school with bell and bell tower.

That would about do it. Well, in addition there would have to be lumber camps, veritable wilderness villages built of logs and tar paper whose locations would shift from winter to winter as the lumbering operation moved from one cutting area to another. And, oh yes, there'd be the little cabins and lean-tos on beautiful picnic spots, usually points of land overlooking the lake. (Couldn't give up picnics altogether!) Finally, ten miles up the lake, the Star Island accommodations would have to be expanded to include a large com-fortable main summer house built of logs, a guest house, a guides' cabin, a workshop, an icehouse, and sufficient docks and floats for all the canoes and motorboats we'd need.

All of it together, excluding Star Island, would be called Sunrise Farm, with a red, blue, and yellow logo showing the name over a half-risen sun. The Sunrise Farm logo would appear on trucks, tractors, cars, carriages, sleighs, stationery, milk bottles, egg crates, and on my father's tin fishing-tackle box. Of all these, only the tackle box remains in my family's possession today. I sometimes look at it to remind myself that Sunrise Farm really happened.

The farm buildings, school, laboratory, offices, and various living quarters, including our own new house, would be spread out over some hills and open fields between two "duck ponds," as we called them, at the end of a two-mile dirt road running next to the lake north of the village. The two mills, located within a quarter mile of each other, would be on the lakeshore close to town, right above the dam marking the beginning of the St. Croix River. Timber Village, or "the logging headquarters," as auction brochures would call it after the eventual collapse of everything, would be on another hill in the southwestern part of town, above the railroad station and close by the public school and Mr. Teague's general store.

Work began on the home, farm, school, and laboratory right away, with the mills, Timber Village, and the first lumber camps following close behind. In my father's mind there was no reason to delay. It never occurred to him (until it was too late) that perhaps a more prudent approach would be to consolidate one stage of the undertaking before proceeding to the next. At last he had a mission, a purpose to his life, something meaningful to occupy every minute of his every day. He intended to make the most of it without dillydallying about following a "prudent" pace of development. As a result, most of Sunrise Farm was up and going within a couple of years, although additional construction continued almost to the end.

Now, practically overnight, just about every Vanceboro resident who didn't have a year-round job with the railroad or customs found himself or herself working for Roger Hale!

"It was as if someone trucked in a couple tons of ten-dollar bills and told everyone to go get 'em," recalls Jim Hansen today. Jim (now retired and living in Newburgh, New York, with his wife, Ruth, who was the daughter of Bessie, our Vanceboro family cook) was a teenager in Vanceboro during the late 1930s. He was hired on to help with the milking and the clearing of fields. His father, Carl, a blacksmith by profession, had been working on government public works projects as far away as Danforth and even Lincoln but now had the opportunity to practice his profession full-time right in his hometown. There would be a veritable *herd* of horses for him to keep in shoes for the next decade.

"We'd clear one big field of rocks and stumps and then we'd tackle another," Jim told me recently when I went to New York to visit him and Ruth. "There was always plenty of well-paying work for everyone and their brothers once your father came to town." He showed me a photograph of himself and two other men we couldn't identify posing in front of some horses. "That's Nip and Tuck, your father's first two workhorses," he said. "Pretty soon after that we got

Jack and Jill and a couple of other teams to help pull out those stumps. We drilled and dynamited the rocks." He recalled how one of the men had his fingers blown off before they "learned to be more cautious about the way we drilled rocks." He remembered, too, the difficulties of bringing the necessary dynamite through customs from McAdam. "Dynamite really spooked 'em," he said.

The first time many of the townspeople saw my mother was at a church business meeting following the regular Sunday service the fall after we all arrived in Vanceboro. The majority had already *heard* her, however. You couldn't help it. Within a couple of days after we'd moved into the first section of our new house, her strong, vibrant, mature soprano voice was very audible above all the construction noises throughout the farm area. When the wind was right and the house windows were open, it carried across the pond below the house to the outskirts of Vanceboro village. But nobody heard songs per se, or for that matter, anything resembling music very often. Rather, they were hearing vocalizing—my mother conducting her daily two-hour voice exercises.

There'd be a single loud note on the piano (shipped up from the Chestnut Hill house early on) followed by my mother's voice singing *aahhh* on the same note. Then there'd be three additional *aahhh*'s rising up the scale and three more down to the original note followed by another bang on the piano, one note higher. Three *aahhh*'s up, three down, and another bang—and so forth all the way up the scale. At the highest note her voice would be required to gather real power in order to hit the three *aahhh*'s that were even higher. *That* part often carried as far as the village. After completing a full scale of *aahhh*'s, she'd begin one exclusively of *oooo*'s, then *eeeee*'s, and back to her favorite, the *aahhh*'s.

At the end of the session she'd launch into an operatic aria of some sort, often the wild, dramatic *"yo ho to ho eeaaoeew!"* battle cry of Richard Wagner's Brünnhilde and the *Die Walküre* maidens, which, because of its vocal difficulty, was one of her usual final "exercises." As far as Vanceboro people were concerned, it was all, to say the least, pretty startling. "I thought at first she was hollerin' for help," one of the farmhands told my father, who chuckled about it with me years later. (I don't believe he ever informed my mother, however, that her singing was once taken for "hollerin'.")

"Most of us were a little in awe of your mother," Jim Hansen remembers. "We couldn't figure out what a person like her was *doing* in Vanceboro." Then he adds quickly, "But she was always very gracious."

The reason my mother decided to attend the church business meeting in town that first fall was not because she was interested in joining the church—we never belonged to any church after my mother and father became anthroposophists. She attended in order to suggest that the church members consider putting on, with her help, some sort of theatrical production. If they agreed, it would be a first step in bringing "culture" and "the arts" to Vanceboro and Sunrise Farm. She never doubted they'd jump at the idea. It would even be a fund-raiser.

There were almost a hundred townspeople present at the meeting, and shortly after it began my mother found what she considered to be the perfect moment to rise from her chair and address the assemblage. The subject being discussed was how to raise sufficient money to purchase a bell for the then-empty belfry tower. An absolutely ideal circumstance!

"I'd like to recommend we put on a variety show," my mother began in her cultured Boston accent, confidently utilizing "we" as if she'd been in town for years. "We'd charge admission, of course, and if we performed here as well as in some of the other little country villages nearby [my mother always had a storybook vision of things like "little country villages," "hardworking country people," and "darling little churches"], we could easily realize enough money to buy our bell." She paused. The silence was deafening.

"I would be happy to organize it, direct it, and participate in it," she added, looking around the room for even one flicker of approval from anyone present. There was none. The silence continued. No one as much as moved.

She sat down. There was nothing else she could do. The meeting hung suspended in a sort of catatonic state for perhaps two or three minutes. Maybe longer. Finally an old-time resident named Frank Ray, one of my father's newly hired carpenters, rose to his feet.

"I think," he said very slowly and very quietly, "Mrs. Hale may have a pretty good idea. Why don't we give it a try?"

To this day my mother is grateful to Frank Ray, who lived to the age of ninety-nine and died only ten years ago. He broke the ice. The show was on!

My most vivid memory of the actual performance at the town hall two months later consists of sitting in the third row watching everyone on stage throwing flowers to the audience, and my mother specifically aiming and throwing one flower that landed directly on my lap. (I was four, too young to participate.) Except for a skit and singing in a chorus line, Patsy doesn't remember much of anything about it. "I hated it so much," she says, "I think I've blocked a lot of it out of my mind."

The skit she recalls was typical of several my mother devised to take place in front of a backdrop hand-painted to resemble Mr. Teague's general store. "Do you have frogs' legs?" Patsy had to ask someone dressed to look like Mr. Teague (who refused to play himself in the show). "No," was the response, "guess it's probably just my arthritis." That sort of thing.

My mother's most vivid memory of the entire effort was the problem of determining how much beer to have on hand during each rehearsal. No beer or not enough beer and nobody wanted to do anything. Too much and everyone wanted to do everything for too long! It was a fine line. Sometimes, after a particularly wild rehearsal, she'd purchase sufficient beer for just one apiece the next time and find half the men in the cast almost falling-down drunk just the same. Her new friend, Frank Ray, advised her that the cure for this was to keep everyone at rehearsal "real busy all the time." That way there'd be less opportunity to slip outside for a nip or two from the bottles stashed in the pickup trucks.

But there *was* talent, she remembers. A housepainter with a huge beer belly, named George Ketch, had an excellent tenor voice and played the accordion. His favorite song was "The Umbrella Man," which he performed superbly when the alcohol content of his blood was somewhere between small and moderate. The railroad station-master was a skillful magician, particularly with a deck of cards. One of my father's office workers, a man named Louis Hansen (no relation to Jim), delivered skit lines with such a fine sense of reality and timing (even stone sober) that my mother urged him to leave Vanceboro and become a professional actor! (He didn't, of course. But over the years he told a lot of people what she'd said.) A woman named

Esther, with two small, snuffling, raggedy children constantly at her feet, painted the backdrop of Mr. Teague's store and displayed the skills of a true artist. Frank Ray himself, as it turned out, could do a very lively and acrobatic Irish jig.

The final performance went well, all things considered. To be sure, George Ketch wouldn't stop singing "The Umbrella Man" and eventually had to be escorted offstage, where he then insisted on continuing his act as "background music." Also, at one point my mother had to hurry out to take the place of one of the skit performers who froze and was unable to continue. In addition, she sang "Indian Summer," "Annie Laurie," and "Come to the Fair" (the show's theme song) and functioned as prompter, curtain-puller, lighting director, costume arranger, trouble-shooter, and mother hen. No emergency was too great for her to handle, although she does recall one moment that particularly tested her mettle. That was when Frank Ray sidled up to her seconds before going on to do his Irish jig and handed her his false teeth. He asked her to hold them until he could complete his act since they'd popped out of his mouth during the dress rehearsal. There was nothing she could do but comply.

The applause at the end of each act or individual performance was long and enthusiastic. No jokes were too corny, all problems were overlooked—it was a great triumph.

"It made us realize we were fortunate to have a lady like your mother in town," Jim Hansen says, "though we still couldn't figure out why she'd *want* to be there!"

So, as my mother had planned, Vanceboro's "Come-to-the-Fair All Star Variety Show," as it was billed, went on a one-week tour to "other little country villages nearby": McAdam, Topsfield, and Calais, which is thirty miles downriver from Vanceboro. And it raised more than enough money for a church bell.

About a month after the variety show, Vanceboro residents were invited to Sunrise Farm for a free Nativity play on Christmas Eve in the just-completed school building, the start of an annual tradition throughout our Vanceboro years. It was my first theatrical performance.

My job was to sing four verses of "We Three Kings" all by myself. I did it with no problems the first time through. Didn't feel even a twinge of the stage fright that was to totally incapacitate me in front of hundreds of people during a school play five years later. I say "first time through" because I was called upon to repeat the whole thing during a second showing that followed directly after the first. I hadn't realized there'd be a second performance, and I commenced to cry bitterly when I was so informed. I cried from the beginning of the second performance right through to the end. Yes, I bravely sang the four verses of "We Three Kings" again, but this time it was more of a wailing of them than a musical rendition and tears were streaming down my face throughout. No one could comfort me, not even my mother backstage, and I refused to explain my problem. Ever. But, well, this was it: (1) The second performance would occur after the time I was ordinarily expected to be in bed for the night, (2) Santa Claus would come and I wouldn't be there, (3) Santa would think I must still live on Heath Street in Chestnut Hill, and therefore (4) Santa would leave no present for Juddie in Vanceboro. Despair!

It was a tremendous relief, therefore, after Patsy and I were finally tucked into our beds much later that evening, to hear Fritz and the other dogs begin to bark at Santa's sleigh flying in from the north, and with an ever-increasing sound of bells, the sleigh land on the roof above us with a great clatter of reindeer hoofs. We were there in time for him after all. "Ho! ho! ho!" Santa bellowed in a deep voice amid much foot stomping. Then there was a loud *thump* followed by a veritable stream of rapid-fire curse words in a voice suddenly familiar. Patsy and I popped out from the bottom of our beds where we'd been huddling under the covers in exquisite terror and peered out the window that overlooked the roof. There was my father. He had a broomstick in one hand (to make reindeer hoof sounds) and a string of sleigh bells in the other. He was lying prone on the roof but was twisting the upper part of his body to look at his backside and the new rip in his best riding pants.

It was, you might say, an educational sight, and one that would forever obliterate my worries about having to be in bed early on Christmas Eve. From then on we could repeat the Nativity play *three* times over for all it mattered.

Solid, down-to-earth, no-nonsense blasphemy was a memorable part of the following year's Christmas Eve as well. That was the year Primo, the tough little boy from town whom my mother hoped to cure of using blue language by making him an angel in the Nativity play, was heard to bellow in his hoarse, screechy voice during the silence just before the curtain rose, "Some son-of-a-bitch stole my goddamned wings!" Of course the roar of laughter from the audience destroyed the quiet, reflective religious atmosphere my mother was hoping to create, but it was a moment never to be forgotten by anyone present.

I wrote about Primo in the December 1979 issue of *Yankee* ("The Imperfect Little Angel"), ending with "God bless you, Primo, wherever in the world or Great Beyond you may be today . . ." Two weeks after the issue was sent to subscribers I received a letter from his sister. She said Primo was living just "beyond" Machias, Maine, retired from a thirty-year army career, and that although my mother may not have cured his "cussin'" she did something for him "no one else could ever do. She made him an angel and he's never forgotten it."

The most elaborate theatrical production my mother produced was *Cinderella*. Our entire Waldorf school, called the Mainewoods School, participated. She decided it should be performed outdoors with real horses and a real coach, so a large wooden stage on a stone foundation was built a mile from the farm, on a lakeside field where we'd already had picnics and erected a lean-to. It was called Alice May Point. Wooden benches for the audience were constructed on the gently sloping hill above the stage, my mother's grand piano was brought from the house and placed on a lower platform like an orchestra pit, and one of the farm wagons was transformed into an elegant golden coach, complete with high seats front and back for coachman and horn-blowers, golden wheels, and an enclosed compartment in the middle for Cinderella. It was magnificent.

Cinderella's coachman was old Frankie Smith, my father's main teamster. He had a large handlebar mustache, had lived in Vanceboro all his life, was a virtual genius on all matters equestrian, and was known for his pithy bits of somewhat confusing wisdom in the genre of Yogi Berra. At a town meeting a few years earlier, when some people in Vanceboro had suggested raising a little money to build a decorative fence around the cemetery, old Frankie had crushed the idea flat when he turned to the person sitting next to him and in his raspy voice, loud enough to be heard throughout the hall, said, "Why do they need a fence? Nobody inside can get out and nobody outside wants to get in!" You could never argue with Frankie.

For the *Cinderella* play Frankie drove the coach with Hattie and Harry, two high-strung, fidgety riding horses not accustomed to pulling anything. They'd buck, prance around, and generally create a fuss even after they were strapped into their harnesses, but my mother was adamant that such an elegant golden coach not be pulled by heavy, plodding workhorses. Before one of the rehearsals, Hattie and Harry bolted while Frankie was backing them up to the coach to be hitched. After being dragged for a hundred yards or so, Frankie was finally able to stop them, calm them down, and commence the hitching process again. "Why didn't you just let go of them and let 'em run?" my father asked Frankie after it was over and they were heading for Alice May Point for the rehearsal. "Christ sake, Rog, I *couldn't* let go," Frankie rasped (my father was "Rog" to everyone almost immediately, whereas my mother was never other than "Mrs. Hale"). "I couldn't let go," he said again, shaking his head. "It was all I could do just to hold on!"

For the final performance of *Cinderella,* Frankie was persuaded to wear a three-quarter-length velvet tuxedo coat over a red flannel shirt and blue-striped necktie, brown English-style riding britches, a pair of my mother's fanciest western-style riding boots (which she presented to him as a gift), and my father's black opera hat. It was a rather odd coachman's uniform but he looked good up on the high driver's seat of the golden coach, holding Hattie and Harry under control.

"Them's good-lookin' boots, Frankie," Patsy remembers one of the farmhands remarking the day of the performance while Frankie was getting dressed in the barn.

"Good enough," Frankie returned, "but, darn 'em, they're so tight I'll never get 'em on 'til I've wore 'em a time or two."

One of my father's photo albums has six pages devoted to *Cinderella.* One picture is of Frankie posing in front of the golden coach; another shows us all in elaborate costumes in the pine grove near the stage, a large audience visible on the hill beyond; and a third is a shot of one of my father's secretaries playing the piano with a man next to her blowing on a saxophone. All the others, dozens of them, are of Sheila, the nine-year-old daughter of my father's farm foreman, and me. I played Prince Charming. Dressed in black tights, a cape,

a huge hat with a feather and a wide brim rolled over like D'Arta-
gnan's in *The Three Musketeers*, I'm first on one side of the stage, then
the other, always with one arm extended forward woodenly, the
other behind me. It was supposed to be a graceful gesture of loving
supplication toward Sheila, my butterfly princess. I appear exactly
as I remember feeling—like an idiot.

For Sheila it was quite something else. She was dressed in a long
flowing chiffon gown with yards of material attached to her arms to
resemble wings. For more than ten minutes, with piano and saxophone playing in the background, she twirled, whirled, ran, jumped,
and danced about the stage in a truly outstanding display of grace
and feeling. The audience erupted in applause several times during
her performance and gave her a five-minute ovation at the end. Little
Sheila was the toast of Sunrise Farm that sunny spring afternoon out
on Alice May Point.

In the summer of 1985, through a little trial, error, and luck, I
traced Sheila's whereabouts to Mystic, Connecticut. A grandmother
now, she has raised a family but still holds down two tough jobs to
make ends meet. We met at the Burger King just off the Interstate
at Mystic and instantly recognized each other even though it had
been exactly forty years since we'd last been together. With my tape
recorder on the table between us, we reminisced about the Vanceboro days for over an hour.

"Do you remember *Cinderella* and how you were the star of the
show with your butterfly dance?" I asked.

"There's sure been a lot of years over the dam since then," she
answered, turning to gaze out the window, "but, yes, I remember
every second of it." We were silent for a moment and then, more
to herself than to me, she added, "I just wish I could have danced
forever."

As busy as my mother was with the amateur theatrical produc-
tions, she had no intention of restricting her own singing career to
them. She retained her apartment in New York City, and off and on
during the winter months following the move to Vanceboro, she
began serious preparation for the challenging roles of opera. Her
ambition, growing almost to an obsession in those days, became to
sing the role of Brünnhilde—or Sieglinde or Fricka at the very least
—at the Metropolitan Opera in New York, and I can't remember

having the slightest doubt she would do exactly that. Then, as an opera star like her idol, Kirsten Flagstad, the world-famous Norwegian dramatic soprano of the 1930s, she would be, she hoped, a drawing card for singers, painters, and writers from everywhere who would come to the anthroposophical cultural center at Sunrise Farm for creative work and study.

Encouragement in this lofty pursuit came from everyone who heard her sing; a few, like her friend Edwin McArthur, knew what they were talking about. "Eddie" McArthur was Kirsten Flagstad's American accompanist and one of the finest pianists in the world at the time. A frequent guest of my mother's at Sunrise Farm, he always told her she had what today would be called "the right stuff." (I met Eddie McArthur once again in Rochester, New York, my wife's hometown, many years after my mother had sadly abandoned her singing career. "Your mother could have been as great as Flagstad," he told me then, "if she'd done things differently. It was a great tragedy. . . .")

In the meantime, while maintaining opera as her long-term goal, she began extensive singing tours around the Northeast, featuring lighter material. While recently poring through her folders of newspaper clippings, printed programs, promotional flyers, publicity photos, and letters, I was surprised to discover she sang at many of the same clubs and local organizations around New England where, some forty years later, I've given my little talks on behalf of *Yankee* magazine and *The Old Farmer's Almanac*!

At the Wianno Club on Cape Cod, where I've spoken, she mixed Wagner's "Schmerzen" and an aria from the opera *Mignon* with songs like "Annie Laurie" and "My Lover Is a Fisherman." On Saturday evening, February 21, 1942, she was half of the entertainment for a special Washington's Birthday dinner put on by the Greenwich Village Historical Society at Fraunces Tavern in New York, where George Washington bade farewell to his officers in 1783. After she sang Mendelssohn's "Nocturne" and several numbers from Gounod's *Romeo and Juliet*, one Arnold Christofferson completed the evening's entertainment by relating "his experience of being trapped *nine* decks down on the burning ship *Normandie!*"

The undated program for the "Sunday Evening Concert" at the Oceanside Hotel (which burned down in 1958) in Magnolia, Massachusetts, contains all the words for my mother's final song, "Work for the Night Is Coming," so that the guests could comply with the printed request to "please join in singing Miss Hale's closing number." At a church meeting in Ocean Park, Maine, she shared the platform with Louis M. Lyons, later to be a well-known Boston theater critic. On that particular evening, however, Lyons was billed as "feature writer on the staff of the *Boston Globe,* speaking on America's relation to war in Europe and the kind of world that will come after the war."

A man in Boston named A. H. Handley did many of the bookings for her. A typical letter from him, dated September 1, 1941: "I will keep in touch with the Mayfair until I have some sort of answer from them and I hope you will let me know when you expect to be in Boston so I can arrange for the auditions with Zachareff, Russell Cook, etc. . . . Your definite date in New Bedford is January 8th with our Philharmonic Quintette, one group of songs and the 'Mignon' aria with the Quintette accompaniment."

There are a few old fan letters among her memorabilia. "Last Friday night while driving in my car along a lovely road out of Fredericton [Canada], I turned on the radio and, much to my surprise, found your beautiful concert on," says one. "Your program was well chosen, your voice rich, colorful and expressive. 'Wunderschon' for Wagner's music! . . . Someday I may see you on the concert stage but, until then, au revoir ma petite cherie." He adds a "P.S." under the signature saying, "I am a plain Dutchman here in Canada to recover from the fearful beating the Germans gave us in Rotterdam some months ago. Music like yours should restore sanity to an insane world."

A clipping of an article from the *Boston Herald,* also undated, announces her benefit concert for the Marblehead (Massachusetts) Arts Association at the King Hooper Mansion, saying "Miss Hale returned to her native New England for a series of summer concerts, after appearances on the West Coast and in Canada." I suspect the "West Coast" reference might be promotional "poetic license" by her agent, A. H. Handley, but the "Canada" was Saint Stephens, Saint John, and the radio shows on CFMB, Fredericton.

That same clipping then goes on to mention a name familiar to millions of opera lovers at the time: "Miss Hale," it says, "has been working with Friedrich Schorr, the famous baritone of the Metropolitan Opera Company."

As it turned out, Friedrich Schorr became a major character at Sunrise Farm and Star Island during the first summers we were there. With his large, jolly, blond wife Upie (pronounced "Whoop-ie"), formerly a famous singer in her own right, and Eddie McArthur, who was no longer accompanying Kirsten Flagstad, he arrived at the farm one bright June morning with many trunks crammed with clothes and musical scores. Also in tow were three of his New York students. Two were tenors and the other was a pretty and very buxom young dramatic soprano. (I recall one of the tenors hanging a "Keep Off the Grass" sign on her bosom one playful afternoon.) My mother would be the fourth student under Friedrich Schorr's tutelage that summer. A short, heavy-set, balding man who looked very much like the actor Ed Asner, Friedrich Schorr is still considered, even long after his death, to have been the greatest Wotan (the god of all gods in pagan mythology) to have sung that Wagnerian role.

The very day this flamboyant entourage landed at Sunrise Farm, Vanceboro residents were subjected to a vocalizing session that made my mother's seem positively tame. It must have carried for miles. The buxom soprano and the tenors were doing scales at the same time that my mother and Upie were blasting forth with Brünnhilde's battle song, and if all that wasn't ear-splitting enough, there was the great baritone voice of Friedrich Schorr carrying over everyone's, its mighty thunderous tones shaking the landscape.

Vanceboro was subjected to this vocal pandemonium for only several afternoons, however. Then we all piled into our new 26-foot cabin cruiser, the *Milky Way,* headed seven miles north on Spednic Lake, motored through a narrow passage which we called the "thoroughfare" into a separate three-mile-long wilderness lake called Palfry, and proceeded to what had been Grandma Jane's isolated little one-acre island retreat at the northern end. Grandma Jane had named it Star Island, and it was where I'd spend the next eleven summers.

In residence on Star Island for the first Friedrich Schorr summer, besides his entire musical entourage including pianist Eddie McArthur, were Patsy, myself, and our new summer nurse, Gertrude; Hermann Von Baravalli (the German-speaking anthroposophist and mathematics genius from Switzerland) with his wife and son, Edward, who was about Patsy's age; Gene Tessloff, a Boston portrait painter who'd been commissioned to paint as many portraits of the family as he could complete in the two months; several Canadian guides; and perhaps a few others I don't recall. My father was on Star Island every night and weekends. During the day he'd commute to Sunrise Farm in his speedboat, *Polaris.*

Star Island was oval-shaped, flat, crisscrossed with walking paths connecting the various buildings, with beautiful tall evergreens, birch trees, lovely sandy beaches on both the southeast and northwest ends, and an otherwise rocky shore supported against erosion by log abutments on the south end facing the long open part of the lake.

The main two-storey log cabin had modern plumbing (emptying into the lake) in two bathrooms, as did the guest house on the other end of the island. The guides' cabin did not, however. They used a three-holer built out over the lake behind a thick stand of poplars.

There was, of course, no electricity and no telephone. The plumbing was powered by a gasoline pump, light was provided by dozens of Aladdin kerosene lamps, what heat was needed came from Franklin wood stoves, and the icebox contained large cakes of ice that were cut during the winter and stored in layers beneath sawdust in the icehouse.

Despite the apparent lack of amenities, Star Island living was nonetheless luxurious. The head guide, Sid Robinson, did all the cooking, assisted by several other guides, usually his relatives. They cut, split, and carried in the wood for the kitchen stove as well as all the other stoves (my mother insisted a cheerful fire be set each day, much to Sid's disgust when the summer temperature outside was warm) and took care of the flotilla of motorboats and Old Town canvas canoes of every conceivable length that they'd carry on mainland fishing or exploring expeditions to various other hidden lakes off in the hills around us. In other words, in the grand tradition of my father's trips down the Allagash with his father twenty-five years earlier, the guides took care of everything.

The main log "cabin," expanded considerably from Grandma Jane's time, was luxurious, too. Built entirely of logs cut in winter by Sid and his four sons on the mainland and transported to the island over the ice, it had five spacious bedrooms and a grand living room bedecked with bear skins (bears trapped by Sid, shot by my father), stuffed deer heads, handmade Indian blankets, and coat hooks made of bent moose feet. The kitchen had a wood-fueled cookstove and a hand pump on the soapstone sink with which to draw frigid drinking water from the dug well. A glassed-in dining room off the kitchen looked down the lake toward the south. The dining room table, like the table at the farm in Vanceboro, seated a dozen people comfortably and was usually full at lunch and supper (opera singers and most anthroposophists aren't much for breakfasts). Patsy and I and visiting children usually ate with our nurse at the large guides' table in the kitchen.

As for my own bedroom upstairs, next to Patsy's and separated from the master bedroom and bathroom by a long walk-in closet, I can close my eyes today and see every knot in the ceiling boards. There's the crazy man with the crooked smile. To his right are the running deer, the Big Dipper, the yawning dragon, the tunnel leading to the heavens, the skinny, one-legged goblin, and oh so many other familiar old friends. Those tedious two-hour afternoon naps provided sufficient time for ceiling knots and knot patterns to engrave themselves into my brain forever.

When Friedrich Schorr, Upie, his students, and the rest of the guests first stepped into the large guest cabin on the north end of the island, they found one glaring omission in their otherwise comfortable accommodations. *There was no piano!*

In all the excitement, a piano on Star Island was something my mother had simply forgotten to arrange for. So my father took charge, promising to produce one before sunset the following day. Within the hour he was flying back to Vanceboro in *Polaris*, followed by one of the guides in the slower *Milky Way*. Because the piano in the main house at the farm would be needed there, he decided to send four of his farmhands the 110 miles to Bangor in a truck with instructions to buy and bring back the best grand piano money could buy. In the meantime he arranged with a representative of Eastern Pulpwood Company to have a flat lumber scow delivered to the farm docks. When the men returned the following morning with a magnificent grand piano, it was transferred onto the scow, which was hitched to the *Milky Way* and towed the long, slow ten miles up lake to Star Island.

While still but a white dot, the *Milky Way* was spotted coming through the thoroughfare at the far end of Palfry Lake (an approaching boat at *any* time was a major event), and so when the scow was being maneuvered over to the float connected to our docks a half hour later, it was met with great fanfare by a reception committee made up of everyone on the island. Before the scow was even tied securely, Eddie McArthur hopped aboard, sat down at the new piano, and with great gusto began to play Brünnhilde's triumphant music from the second act of *Die Walküre*. Upie, my mother, and the three opera students happily joined in, singing at the top of their voices—but they stopped when Eddie suddenly switched to the final scene of the third act, the one in which the god, Wotan, bids farewell to his beloved daughter, Brünnhilde, sealing her eyes in sleep and calling upon the fire god, Loge, to protect her forever by a wall of flame.

The emotional aria Wotan sings in this scene is one of the great baritone arias in all of opera, and as Eddie McArthur knew well, Friedrich Schorr sang it better than anyone. At a nod from McArthur, Schorr, who'd been helping to tie the scow to the float, took a deep breath and began to sing: *"Leb'wohl, du kuhnes, herrliches Kind. Du meines Herzens heligster Stolz. Leb'wohl. Leb'wohl. Leb'wohl* (Farewell, thou valiant, glorious child. Thou once the holiest pride of my heart. Farewell. Farewell. Farewell). . . ." His deep, vibrant voice increased in power as he continued through the entire aria until finally, as he struck the wooden float three times with a canoe paddle that by now was surely Wotan's magic spear, it soared across the lake and surrounding hills.

I recall wondering at one point why my mother and several others were wiping away tears. But at the end, I'm quite sure that Friedrich Schorr and Edwin McArthur, two of the world's most talented musical artists, received as enthusiastic an ovation as any they'd ever received at the Metropolitan—right there on an old lumber scow tied to the dock on a little island in a wilderness lake ten miles north of Vanceboro, Maine.

I don't often listen to opera today. However, the music from that scene of *Die Walküre* brings a lump to my throat. I'm not sure if it's the music or the memory. Probably both.

For the remainder of the first Friedrich Schorr summer, Palfry Lake was alive with the music of Wagner, Puccini, and Verdi and with songs from the musical shows of the time like *Show Boat* and

Song of Norway. Palfry's loons were a particularly appreciative audience. During the daily vocalizing sessions, they would drift in close to the island and merge their own "dramatic soprano" voices into the three-notes-up-and-down exercises. Upie loved to stand on the south end of the island, where we kept two sheep tethered, and in her professionally trained voice do a repertoire of happy, mournful, and the "predicting-wind-and-storm" type of loon calls. The loons would answer her, but with considerably less enthusiasm.

Other diversions included putting on rather elaborate skits in which everyone (except the guides) participated, complete with costumes and original music and usually dealing with fairies, wood nymphs, and gods; competing in swimming, diving, and boating events during the weekly "Jim Connor Days" (gymkhana), as we called these day-long athletic competitions, ending with gala "awards dinners" in the evening; drifting silently along in canoes during calm evenings after dark while aiming flashlight beams on the rocky mainland shore to pick up the shiny-bright eyes of deer; piling into the *Milky Way* and, with two, sometimes three, canoes in tow, roaring off for all-day picnics at some pretty shoreline spot where the guides would build a fire and fry iron pans full of S.S. Pierce corned-beef hash in gobs of butter (even today, canned corned-beef hash is my favorite food of all foods!); and posing *interminably* for portraits painted by Gene Tessloff.

My portrait, four feet high and painted in oils, showed me standing on the northwest point of the island, in a sailor's suit, hugging in my arms a two-foot-long boat, the *Queen Mary*, which Sid, the head guide, had made in the island workshop for me. In the background were the lake and beach, but over to one side was an open suitcase showing a pair of red pajamas and a toothbrush. I'd carried it across the island for what I must have thought would be a posing session that might last forever, or at least overnight, and Mr. Tessloff was so amused he included it in the painting. I wish I had that portrait today, but it was destroyed in a New York warehouse fire in 1950, three years after Sunrise Farm and Star Island were auctioned away.

On a couple of occasions that summer we rose at 4 a.m. in order to be at a certain swampy, mosquito-infested little chunk of still water at daybreak. It was called Dead Brook, located four miles of rough going beyond the ridge overlooking the east shore of Palfry.

There, using worms dug the afternoon before in the large vegetable garden (maintained by the guides) on the island, we'd pull eighty to one hundred illegally small brook trout out in less than two hours. Each required merely one mighty jerk that would send it sailing over our heads into the bushes, where the guides would remove it and, if necessary, reworm the hook. After we'd filled the fishing baskets and covered them with layers of wet grass, we'd return to the island, where the guides would gut them all, leaving on the heads and tails, and Sid, after rolling each in flour and cornmeal, would fry them in butter for a feast fit for the main dining room of Boston's Ritz Carlton Hotel!

"Fishy, fishy, in the brook; Daddy catch it with a hook," everyone would recite for my benefit during the meal, even though my father seldom went along on these Dead Brook expeditions, much preferring to fish for bass from a canoe with his beautiful Abercrombie and Fitch fly rods. "Mommy fry it in the pan," the ditty would continue, even though the cook was Sid, "And Juddie eat it like a man," which, indeed, I did.

Dr. Hermann Von Baravalli went on only one Dead Brook expedition, and the following summer Dr. Ehrenfried Pfeiffer, another of the three Swiss officers of the Anthroposophical Society, also felt a single visit to Dead Brook was more than enough. Both men were bitten dozens of times by mosquitos, as were we all. But whereas the rest of us abided mosquitos as a matter of course, Dr. Hermann Von Baravalli and Dr. Ehrenfried Pfeiffer became swollen all over and spent subsequent picnics and outings wearing gloves, long woolen socks over their trousers, and head-nets sewn to their hats. It was a rather ominous sign that perhaps anthroposophy wasn't exactly suited to the north country!

It was after one of the Dead Brook trout feasts that Dr. Von Baravalli's ten-year-old son, Edward, convinced me to be deliberately disobedient for the first time in my life. He said to sneak out of my bedroom after dark by climbing out my window onto the roof, which sloped nearly to the ground. Then I was to run stealthily across the island and join him inside a small area in the dock pilings beneath the high diving board. From this vantage point, he said, we'd observe one of the student tenors and the young buxom soprano swimming stark naked in the moonlight. He said he'd watched them the night before and it was "quite a sight."

I was hesitant. I didn't like the fact that the plan entailed misbehaving, but Edward was insistent and, with trepidation, I finally agreed.

My escape from my bedroom and dash across the island in the dark was accomplished with surprising ease, but then it seemed we sat on sharp rocks inside the cramped interior of the dock pilings forever. More likely it was about ten minutes.

Then we heard footsteps overhead. Barefoot footsteps. Assorted gigglings and murmurings, too. Within minutes there was the sound of two or three big bouncing steps on the diving board overhead and suddenly, incredibly, the completely stark naked body of the dramatic soprano, silver-white in the bright moonlight, was flying past our goggling little eyes. It was, in truth, "quite a sight." Although at the time it lasted but seconds, years later it occupied my adolescent mind for hours!

The remainder of the evening was anticlimactic. After the tenor, also naked, followed his partner into the water, the two of them swam out of our limited line of sight to the ladder on the float and, to our great disappointment, returned immediately to the guest cabin. The following few evenings were cold and windy, so although Edward and I were faithfully at our post, our singers chose not to perform. A week later the Schorr entourage returned to New York and their glittering, sophisticated, professional world of music. I wouldn't see another stark naked member of the opposite sex for another six months . . .

My world, as we headed back from Star Island to the farm that September, would consist of visiting the cow barn, learning to dance the alphabet at our new Waldorf school, torturing frogs, watching bizarre experiments in the new laboratory, and generally observing the frenetic activities going on every day around me. I was an innocent, well-loved little observer—a trusting, sublimely happy being without a single worry or responsibility. Reality was over the horizon.

But it was coming closer.

Chapter 5

The Conscience

IN ONE of my father's 16mm movies, taken at Sunrise Farm the winter following the first Friedrich Schorr summer on Star Island, there's a scene of me feeding a carrot to one of the riding horses in the paddock next to the new barn. There I am, dressed in a snowsuit with pointed hood, holding the carrot through the paddock fence railings for the horse, who bites off the end. Then I pull the carrot back from the horse and take a bite myself. Gobs of horse saliva are plainly visible dripping from its mouth as I offer the horse a second bite. And it's my turn again—and so forth until the carrot is gone.

"Ohhh, how gross!" was the reaction from my nieces and nephew as we watched that reel at Patsy's Vermont farm during Thanksgiving 1985.

The next scene changed their mood from disgust to hilarity and yet it said the same thing about "Juddie" back in the early Vanceboro days. I'm shown skipping down a woodsy road in my snowsuit with snowbanks towering above me on either side. Then, from the right of the screen, comes Fritz, our German shepherd of the time. With a bounding lunge he playfully knocks me into one of the soft snowbanks. Up I rise, covered from head to foot with snow but smiling happily. I resume my skipping. Again Fritz lunges and again he buries me in the snowbank, from which I rise once more to skip down the road. After a third complete cycle of this routine, the picture begins to shake and skew off on an angle. My father had been unable to control his laughter. His little son was unflappable.

So I didn't consider it particularly odd that Grace Nichols, who worked in the laboratory, spent an hour in the cow barn every morning collecting cow urine. As cows relieved themselves, she'd catch it in three brass-handled glass vials.

Grace Nichols was a tall, dark, thin, serious woman of about thirty; her husband, Russell, was handsome, curly-haired, and fun-loving. They had answered my parents' advertisement in the *New York Times* for a "reliable married couple willing to live on a farm in the Maine woods for chauffeuring and kitchen work." However, within a few months of their arrival from Connecticut with their blond eight-year-old daughter, Sheila (later to be the butterfly dancer in *Cinderella*), Russell and Grace had both graduated from chauffeuring and kitchen work to farm foreman and laboratory technician, respectively.

It might be argued that Grace's little morning chore in the barn was a step *down* in her career path. But it had an important purpose, which was to identify potential animal diseases by a special laboratory analysis devised by Dr. Ehrenfried Pfeiffer. Dr. Pfeiffer organized all the laboratory procedures during his frequent visits.

Very early in the morning, just after the men finished their milking (there were no milking machines then), Grace would pace back and forth between the long rows of cow rear ends. She'd be dressed in a white smock and be holding one of the glass vials. Suddenly she'd race toward a cow whose back was humping and tail beginning to rise. If she was quick enough to position the vial correctly, well, she'd be successful.

"I guess I've seen about everything now," I recall hearing one of the new milkers remarking to the others one morning as they watched Grace leaving the barn with three full vials. "Oh no, you ain't," replied another. "You'll see plenty more strange goin's-on around *this* farm!" It was my first clue that Sunrise Farm wasn't like any other.

My sister, Patsy, grew closer to the farmhands than I ever did. While I loved the barn and watched all the activities every day, she participated. She was able to "finish off" a cow down to the last drops, something only people skillful at milking can do. Like some of the farmhands, she was able to squirt a stream of milk from a cow's teat for four or five feet into the open mouth of any one of a half dozen barn kitties that hung around.

Accordingly, my father gave Patsy a cow of her own. She called it Mollycoddle. Before long she was working in the barn every day from "can't see to can't see," as the farmhands described their hours during the dark months of winter, regularly milking six or seven cows in addition to Mollycoddle and doing other barn chores, too.

Today, at her own farm in Vermont, she must comply with strict state and federal regulations on handling milk in a sanitary fashion. But in Vanceboro the only thing the milkers worried about was keeping the milk pails off the barn floor. "There were little metal ledges like half moons on each pail," she recalls, "so that as you sat under the cow, the pail would rest on your knees and off the floor."

The milk was not pasteurized. It was simply bottled in the milk room, capped by a special hand-fed machine, and then distributed around Vanceboro in two wooden-sided beach wagons. Although a few Vanceboro people owned cows of their own, Sunrise Farm "had the milk market pretty well cornered," according to Jim Hansen, who milked as well as delivered. The alternative milk supply, utilized before our arrival in town, was from Bangor via rail.

While my father was proud of Patsy's ability and obvious desire to join in the nitty-gritty of real farm life, my mother had misgivings. She wasn't, for instance, fond of Patsy's habit of laying out all her wet barn clothes to dry on the radiators at night. My mother didn't associate our beautiful new house, complete with fancy silver wallpaper purchased in New York City, original oil paintings throughout, plush wall-to-wall carpeting also from New York, and elegant Victorian furniture brought up from Chestnut Hill, with the smell of cow manure. It hadn't been very long, after all, since her little Brahmin daughter had posed for the *Boston Transcript,* dressed in her white knee-high stockings and tweed coat with little velvet collar and felt hat to match—and here she was rapidly transforming herself into a bona fide, smelly-clothed, backwoods farm girl!

But despite these misgivings about Patsy and farm life in general, my mother was a trouper and did her best to join in. From time to time she'd visit the cow barn, although there were doubtless other places she'd prefer to be. On these occasions she'd always attempt to be cheerful and say something or other to every farmhand working there.

"Milking seems so restful," she mused one afternoon to Miles

Cropley, one of the young farmhands, now in his seventies and still living in Vanceboro.

"Maybe it is, Mrs. Hale," Patsy remembers Miles replying as he rhythmically squeezed the milk out of perhaps the thirtieth cow he'd done that day, "but don't know but what I'd rather go to bed ti-ad!"

Patsy and I were both present the day my father and mother escorted Dr. Ehrenfried Pfeiffer and his wife, Adelheide, on their first visit to the cow barn. Adelheide, a tall, thin, rather severe Swiss lady with hair tightly pulled back, always wore knee-high leather boots over riding pants.

As they strolled down the long corridor between the two rows of cows, my father and Dr. Pfeiffer paused to discuss some aspect of a cow's rump while my mother (dressed casually in western riding garb, including a black suede coat with long fringe hanging from the bottom and the sleeves) and Adelheide strolled ahead arm in arm. Patsy and I were in the hayloft overhead, balancing on one of the hand-hewn beams that crossed an open section through which hay was forked down to the main level.

Suddenly one of the cows below hunched up and exploded with a high-pressure gush of diarrhea that would easily have reached the row of cows on the other side of the corridor. Would have, that is, if the stream hadn't been blocked by my mother and Adelheide, who, as devilish fate would have it, were passing exactly behind that particular sick cow at that particular moment.

They were instantly covered from head to toe. It was a horrendous incident, one that would be a great source of amusement for nearly everyone in later years (*many* years later for my mother—for Adelheide, never). At the time, however, it served as a nasty little reminder that bringing Rudolf Steiner's anthroposophical theories and philosophy to Vanceboro, Maine, for the betterment of America and mankind would have its less than inspirational moments.

My responsibilities as an innocent little observer included other barn activities, too. For instance, I'd watch old Frankie, the teamster. He was always polishing the metalwork on the saddles and bridles in the harness room. Also, I'd invariably be present when he and his silent young hunchbacked helper fed the horses their hay, water, and varying amounts of energy-giving grain (depending on which horse was scheduled to be ridden or worked that day). One time I saw

Harry (one of the two horses that pulled the coach in *Cinderella*) pick up Frankie's helper by the belt and throw him over the half-door into the corridor between the stalls. The poor man was unhurt, but the alarming sight further strengthened my already growing conviction that, unlike everyone else in my family, I would always try to remain an *observer* of horses.

My father, Patsy, and even my mother had their own riding horses. Patsy's, a rather disagreeable English-style roan named Kitty that kicked her in the head almost every time it bucked her off, was purchased locally. But my mother's, a beautiful, dainty black horse with long mane and tail, and my father's, a gigantic, tough bay that no one but my father would ride, were purchased through contacts made at a ranch in Santa Fe, New Mexico. They'd spent a week there during their trailer trip out West. My mother called hers Mañana, while my father's was Ranger. And *their* arrival at Sunrise Farm was observed by half the town of Vanceboro! To transport Mañana and Ranger all the way from Sante Fe by trailer, my father hired a cowboy named Teepee who had never been east of Dodge City, Kansas. Teepee arrived in Vanceboro, Mañana and Ranger in tow, looking every inch the real cowboy he was, complete with chaps, spurs, and ten-gallon hat. No one in town had ever seen anyone like him except in the Gene Autry movies over in McAdam.

After unloading the horses and being introduced to some of the growing crowd of farmhands who'd gathered around, Teepee decided to put on a little show. He asked for a bridle and saddle, which he expertly slapped on Ranger with the sure, casual touch of someone who has saddled and bridled literally thousands of horses. In the next instant he was mounted and, after a dramatic rear, was galloping Ranger up the first hill above the barnyard, past our main house overlooking the duck pond and then on to the top of the second hill, from which one looked down on Spednic Lake and across to Canada. There he stopped, wheeled Ranger around in a circle several times, and waved his cowboy hat to the crowd watching him, transfixed, in the barnyard below. He was Gene Autry, Tom Mix, and Roy Rogers in spades! Then he turned Ranger down the hill and again spurred him up to full speed. My father always advised everyone not to gallop a horse downhill (more likely to stumble), and never to gallop a horse toward the barn unless you were prepared to be scraped off as it charged through the door to its stall. But Teepee

wasn't concerned with those sorts of "English riding school rules."
He was a cowboy and he'd show this crowd of Maine farmers what
a real cowboy from Sante Fe was all about.

As he approached the crowd in front of the barn there was no
slackening of speed. Ranger was flying. Teepee's plan was obviously
to pull him to a dramatic, bouncing stop at the very last second—
and he did. However, he overlooked one relatively small detail. For
the first time in his life, Teepee was riding on an English saddle.
English saddles, as most everyone knows, do not have a pommel,
which cowboys use to attach their ropes and to brace their free arm
against during a sudden stop from a full gallop. So as he pulled up
Ranger with his rein hand, Teepee put his other hand out straight
to brace himself against the pommel that wasn't there. It was at that
point that he flew over Ranger's head and traveled perhaps twenty
or thirty yards in the air, landing with a sickening thump against the
side of the barn.

"If that fellah could sell himself for what he thought he was wuth,
he could buy himself back at quite a bahgain!" old Frankie, the
teamster, was heard to remark as everyone crowded around, administering to Teepee, who was walking with a limp after a few dazed
minutes. He left for Sante Fe within the hour, with hardly a wave
to anyone.

My mother and father called their new Waldorf school the
Mainewoods School and let it be known that anyone in Vanceboro
would be welcome to send their pre–high school children there,
tuition free, in lieu of the public school in the village. There would
be an emphasis on music, painting, and dancing, each child's individual talents and needs would receive special attention, and for the
older children, a single subject like history, English, or mathematics
would constitute the entire daily curriculum for month-long blocks
of time. There would be no grades as such.

Snuggled cosily into a stand of tall pine trees on a winding dirt
road a half mile from the farm, the building was painted a dark
"schoolhouse red," as my mother stipulated, with a large cupola atop
its steep roof and two wings, with gabled roofs, that extended
obliquely into the pines from the rear of the building. The wings
divided the younger children, like me, from the older children, like
Patsy, while the main section served as an assembly room for danc-

ing, the Christmas Nativity, and other plays, concerts, and readings. In the cupola was a Paul Revere–style bell that certainly added to the storybook image my mother had in mind. By pulling on a long rope that hung down in the center of the assembly room, the teachers summoned us in from recess, summoned us back to class after lunch —it seemed as if it bonged most of the day.

In the morning, the sound of the Mainewoods School bell intermingled with the various cling-clanging tones of the heavy Swiss bells hanging on leather straps around the necks of our milking cows. Driven by one of the farmhands, they'd be on their leisurely way to their pasture a few hundred yards down the road from the school. On our daily walk through the farmyard and on up the school road, Patsy and I would join in with them for a half mile as they meandered toward the pasture gate for another day of grass munching. Summoned by the slow, rhythmic bonging of our own bell, we'd continue on to our schoolhouse for another day of painting pictures, playing our wooden flutes, dancing, and frolicking in the pine grove at recess.

My happy memories of recess include watching the older boys tie two or three of the smaller girls (never Patsy) to a tree and tickle them until they cried and screamed in hysterics. Then the bell would summon us all for more painting, music, and dancing. It was, in a word, idyllic.

Many Vanceboro residents weren't so sure the Hales' new school was all that perfect. There was, as would be expected, a general feeling that the emphasis on artistic activities served no useful educational purpose. But the real hostility had to do with what was happening in Europe in 1938. The eve of World War II was not the best of all times, politically speaking, to start an avant-garde school in a remote Maine town (almost as Canadian as it was American), utilizing German-speaking teachers imported directly from "somewhere over there where all the trouble is." Most people were not aware that both the regular teachers and Dr. Hermann Von Baravalli, who taught the older children mathematics for one month during the first year, were from Switzerland, a neutral country whose citizens were appalled at what Hitler was threatening and doing. The problem was they were German-*sounding*.

Once these suspicions were aroused, other "funny" aspects of the school were surreptitiously discussed in some of the local gossip networks. Why, for instance, was there no American flag flying in front of the new school? How come the children didn't recite the Pledge of Allegiance in the morning? The fact of the matter was that, although both my mother and father always considered themselves to be patriotic, they never thought about a flag or "the Pledge." And until several years after the school closed, no one told them that those omissions were considered a problem. For anthroposophists, national symbols were fine but irrelevant to education.

A bit later on, even my mother's maiden name, "Sagendorph," was thrown into the brew. It sounded suspiciously as if her family was full of Germans. (And, prior to 1710, it was!)

None of these murky suspicions surfaced, however, until a year after the school opened in the fall of 1938. Despite everything, there were fifteen students, including Patsy and me.

My contribution to our school magazine, called *The Woodsmen*, written in the fall of 1940, when local hostility to our teachers had become ugly, clearly reflects the fact that my own world remained free of such complicated matters. It was my first published magazine article.

> I went out and the sun was shining very, very bright upon my shoulders so I ran up to the house to get my watch. I got it. Then I went up on Sunset Hill. After I looked around I went down to the duck pond to see some bullfrogs. Then I climbed over the fence and patted some of the cows. Then I patted the pigs and I watched the chickens. I looked around and found a tree and when I got half way up the branch broke and I fell a little. I thought that was a very terrible sort of tree. So I got down and saw some tracks. When I came to the place where they stopped there was a great big hole. Fritz tried to get down the hole and barked. I got a big stick and poked it down but I couldn't touch the bottom. So I threw some pebbles down and went away. Fritz didn't come with me anymore. The End.
>
> *Judson Hale, Age 7*

When I read this composition recently for the first time in forty-five years, the sentence "I went down to the duck pond to see some bullfrogs" released a storehouse of memories I wish I'd forgotten. If the sentence had been truthful, it would have read, "I went down to the duck pond to *terrorize* some bullfrogs."

There is no situation more hopeless for a living creature of this earth than to be a bullfrog in the firm, dirty little hands of a six- or seven-year-old boy. I had no trouble catching them. If I didn't have a fishnet with me, I'd sneak up slowly behind them and with one lightning motion catch their hind legs with my hand.

Then would come the horrible part. I'd carry the poor thing by its legs to an old abandoned tar-paper shack in the woods a few yards in from the shore. There, inspired by the laboratory newly established by my father and Dr. Ehrenfried Pfeiffer for the purposes of conducting experiments on healing and disease identification, I had established my own little "laboratory." But mine was not for healing. And my "experiments" were not designed to help anything. It was, quite frankly, a veritable Buchenwald for bullfrogs.

There were rough wooden shelves in there on which I stored two cracked brass-handled cow urine vials Sheila's mother, Grace, had given me; a few jars containing dead June bugs, moths, and spiders; some rusty tools I'd found in the woods, a few firecrackers, and matches; some flat boards on which there were usually two or three dead frogs in various stages of rot; and several knives. On the floor was a large washtub filled with water—and live bullfrogs.

I'm truly reluctant to describe my "experiments" here, but since it was their very cruelty that seemed eventually to trigger a significant step forward in my progress as a little human being, I'll do so now only in order to help make the point . . .

Experiment A: Place a hollow piece of grass in anus of bullfrog. A common straw will also do. Blow air into grass or straw until bullfrog is approximately three to four times its normal size. Release on pond. Watch the wind blow the bullfrog across the surface of the water like a balloon.

Experiment B: Toss lighted cherry bomb or any brightly colored firecracker so that it lands several inches from bullfrog in pond. Watch bullfrog think it's a bug and grab it in its mouth. See bullfrog blown to smithereens.

Experiment C: Using sharp, clean knife, remove one leg from bullfrog. A dull, rusty knife will serve equally well. Place bullfrog in pond or washtub filled with water. Observe bullfrog swim in circles.

One sunny fall afternoon in my laboratory not long after my article was published in *The Woodsmen*, I was in the midst of Experiment C when, from somewhere out of the blue, I was suddenly overcome by remorse. I ran up to the house for a needle and thread and upon my return removed the bullfrog from the washtub and attempted to sew its leg back on. I cried. I apologized to the bullfrog. I released all my other bullfrog prisoners back into the pond. And I vowed never to be cruel to bullfrogs again.

Many years later, I read in one of Rudolf Steiner's books a passage that explains what may have happened. "What we call 'conscience,' " he wrote, "is nothing else than the outcome of the work of the Ego on the life-body through incarnation after incarnation. When man begins to perceive that he ought not to do this or that, and when this perception makes so strong an impression on him that the impression passes on into his etheric body, 'conscience' arises."

Well, it would appear "conscience" arose that afternoon in my laboratory—thanks to a one-legged bullfrog.

The daily dancing we all did at the Mainewoods School was called "eurythmy," a word instantly recognized by anyone who has had even a nodding acquaintance with Rudolf Steiner and anthroposophy. We wore dark blue tights and cloth shoes that strapped around our ankles. Under the direction of our Swiss teachers, we would hop around in time to flute music. Often there would be no musical accompaniment—we'd just hop around. I learned to write each letter of the alphabet by first dancing out its specific shape and form during our eurythmy sessions.

Part of the eurythmy paraphernalia were three-foot-long copper rods. We'd twirl these rods, integrate them into the shapes we were forming, toss them, balance them during dancing maneuvers, and when the teachers were out of the room, chase girls with them after heating the ends in the wood stove. (As usual, I only *observed* that sort of thing.)

I'm sure former students of Mainewoods School, now grandfathers and grandmothers, sometimes remember those early days and wonder what it was all supposed to mean, particularly the eurythmy. Anthroposophy, as such, is never explained in Waldorf schools: it's practiced. Analysis of the educational philosophy is not part of the philosophy.

It was only recently, in perusing a little yellowed paperback book entitled *The Education of the Child in the Light of Anthroposophy*

(Rudolf Steiner Press, London), written by Rudolf Steiner in 1909, that I stumbled onto his explanation of the purpose of eurythmy. "In eurythmy," he wrote, "not only are color, harmony, form, measure and significance taken from the surrounding world, but out of man himself, because all world secrets are contained in him as a microcosm. The cosmos tells us its more intimate secrets through these human movements."

So *that*'s why we all hopped around in our tights every day.

One afternoon, a certain little ten-year-old girl at the school, who will remain nameless for obvious reasons, attempted to communicate to me, through her own form of human movement, what the cosmos told her regarding its most intimate secrets. As we were leaving the school at the end of the day, she invited me to join her in the large grain-storage shed near the barn. We both had our copper rods, and upon entering the shed, she instructed me to sit up on one of the piles of burlap grain bags and watch what she was about to do. Then she removed every stitch of her clothing, *every stitch*, and proceeded to dance the entire alphabet plus a few other little numbers I'd never seen before. Throughout it all, she held her copper rod in various graceful positions, and a few that I thought were somewhat bizarre.

I watched, fascinated, but as I recall, unmoved. Finally she stopped and instructed me to come down from my observation post atop the burlap grain bags, remove all *my* clothes, and join her in continuing this little private eurythmy session. I said I wouldn't. I believe I might have been ever so slightly tempted, but it was far too bold a rush forward into unknown territory for me at that tender, innocent moment of my life. After some urging, she accepted my refusal with equanimity, and after she put her clothes back on, we left the grain-storage shed and went about our regular childhood business. I've sometimes wondered what Rudolf Steiner might have had to say about this odd little variation on the "spiritual renewal of the art of movement," as he described eurythmy.

The laboratory (that is, the real laboratory), located at the end of a dirt driveway exactly opposite the school, was a favorite place for me to visit and watch the white-coated technicians bustling about. They'd be putting trays containing up to a dozen little round pieces of glass into small hermetically sealed rooms with thick safe-like doors; or cranking a large stainless-steel centrifuge containing test tubes filled with milk (I later learned this was a cream separator that compared the butterfat content of our Guernsey, Jersey, and Holstein cows); or dropping tiny amounts of blood, urine, and other revolting liquids onto glass slides. Stuff like that. It was a very mysterious and intriguing place to hang around!

In charge of the laboratory was a red-cheeked, jolly young German woman by the name of Mathilda von Fragstein, daughter of a Prussian general during World War I and an expert in Rudolf Steiner's theories to do with agriculture, gardening, and animal/plant/human disease identification. We called her "Dickie."

Besides the laboratory, Dickie also managed the greenhouses and the acres of gardens that stretched along for almost half a mile from the laboratory building. Deer fences made of fifteen-foot hardwood poles lashed together surrounded the gardens, and truck roads separated the vegetables, experimental grains, and even large sections of foxgloves and other flowers. But no weeds. "A weed wouldn't *dare* grow in Dickie's gardens," Patsy remembers. Everything was grown "biodynamically," as anthroposophists called it: following the principles of companion planting, with nothing artificial added at any time for any reason. Today the same general approach is referred to as "organic" gardening.

Dickie's fertilizer came exclusively from her compost heaps. Anthroposophical compost heaps were big piles of animal manure to which were added leaves, weeds, rotten hay, corn stalks, garbage from our dining room table, gunk taken from the duck ponds, parts of the guts from slaughtered animals, and grass cuttings. In other words anything, as far as I could ever determine, that promised to rot! However, compost heap ingredients couldn't just be all dumped in together haphazardly. Dickie insisted upon a precise recipe requiring a layer of certain disgusting things, a layer of normal earth, a thin coating of lime specially treated in the laboratory, followed by another layer of disgusting things, and so forth. Then the whole mixture would be allowed to "cook" for six months to a year before it was ready for use in the gardens.

The compost heap seemed to be the most important part of the biodynamic gardening at Sunrise Farm. Careful crop rotation, weed and insect control (via companion planting), sowing only "healthy" seeds (as determined in the laboratory), taking into account the most effective time of day for certain gardening chores, and so on all involved anthroposophical theories meticulously adhered to. But the compost heap was almost a religion.

For instance, compost heaps were the only things we children were not allowed to jump around on. It was as if they were sacred ground. When Dr. Ehrenfried Pfeiffer and his wife, Adelheide, were visiting, the subject of compost heaps dominated the dinner table conversation. Constant laboratory testing of the "process" of various individual compost heaps, performed with much of the reverence often associated with the testing of fine wines, was a weekly ritual. It seemed to me that my father, Dickie, Grace Nichols, and the Pfeiffers spent a lot of time staring at compost heaps.

Compost heaps were not to be joked about, either. I remember my father breaking that unspoken rule just once. Several days after the horrendous incident when my mother and Adelheide were sprayed from head to toe with cow diarrhea, my father laughingly remarked at the dinner table that about all either of them was good for after that was to be "thrown into one of Dickie's compost heaps." No one thought that was the least bit funny.

My mother and father had been introduced to Dickie in 1938 by Dr. Pfeiffer. They were in Berlin on a side trip during one of their visits to Drake, visits that continued annually until the United States entered the war in 1941. Dr. Pfeiffer recommended Dickie as someone with Steiner training who could come to the United States and take over the new laboratory and gardens at Sunrise Farm. So it was arranged that they all meet at a well-known restaurant just off Berlin's beautiful Unter den Linden Avenue, later destroyed in wartime bombing.

The meeting almost didn't take place due to the fact that my mother came within a whisker of being arrested by the Gestapo while she and my father were waiting for Dr. Pfeiffer and Dickie to join them. Pointing to a photograph of Adolf Hitler hanging on the wall, she'd said to my father, "I'm so sick of seeing photographs of that silly ass, Adolf Hitler, everywhere I look around this city," and instantly two English-speaking Gestapo agents were at their table demanding to see her passport. As usual, she was able to talk her way out of a difficult situation. She pointed out to them that in the part of America known as New England it was common to insult anyone you really liked and respected, a rather shaky argument under the circumstances. However, after talking to each other in rapid German for a few minutes, the Gestapo agents returned her passport and walked away.

Dickie arrived with Dr. Pfeiffer minutes later, and although she could not speak a word of English at the time, her future was settled within minutes. She would come to America and Sunrise Farm.

"Your mother and father were so enthusiastic, so idealistic, and they were doing something I just had to be a part of," Dickie, now in her eighties, said to me when I visited her at her home in Spring Valley, New York, during the summer of 1985. She remembers, too, that the Berlin papers of that very day featured stories about a small six-state section of America called New England—and described how it had just been devastated by one of the most destructive hurricanes of all time.

My mother and father returned home a week later, much relieved to discover that the no-name hurricane, referred to in the history books now as the "Hurricane of '38," had not traveled up as far as Vanceboro.

Dickie followed shortly thereafter and was met by my father when she got off the boat in New York City. She brought only, as she puts it today, "a change of clothing, a little English/German dictionary, and absolute faith in your father."

The night she and my father arrived in Vanceboro following their two-day drive from New York, my mother arranged to have a party and square dance in the just-completed auditorium on the second floor of the long building connected to the barn. It would be a way of welcoming Dickie to Sunrise Farm.

As it turned out, that party—into which a tired, bewildered, homesick Dickie was thrust before she'd even had a night's rest— was a marvelous beginning to her new life. The townspeople loved her. She was the only bona fide German in the entire bunch of imported anthroposophists, but they loved her! And it all began with the old carpenter, Frank Ray. The very same Frank Ray without whom my mother would never have received community support for her variety show that raised the money for the church bell.

"I get a kick out of you," Dickie said to Frank Ray when they were introduced. It was one of a half dozen English expressions my father had taught her on the trip up from New York. She knew it was something nice to say to someone but she hadn't learned the proper circumstances in which to say it. The result was that Frank

Ray and everyone else within earshot got a great kick out of Dickie! For the remainder of the festive evening, he and his friends proceeded to teach her more and more outlandish English expressions and then collapse in knee-slapping laughter when she'd innocently repeat them to someone they'd designate.

Dickie didn't understand the jokes. However, she knew how to be warm and friendly and was willing to laugh at herself along with everyone else—and that made all the difference. As a result, the growing anti-German feeling within the Vanceboro community against the serious, rather austere *Swiss* anthroposophists was never directed at Dickie, the German. Unlike the others, she was able to stick with us through the war years and until the very end.

To be sure, the U.S. government was suspicious of her. Until after the war, they prohibited her from leaving the country without official permission, which meant that for four years she was never able to go to the movies, see the area doctor at his office, or shop at the local five-and-ten-cents store, all of which were across the river in McAdam, Canada. But as far as the townspeople in Vanceboro were concerned, Dickie would have been all right if she'd been Hitler's sister.

When I visited Dickie in the summer of 1985, we hadn't seen each other in thirty-eight years. After leaving Vanceboro following the tragic end of Sunrise Farm, she had moved to the Threefold Farm and Educational Foundation in Spring Valley and married the executive director of the foundation, Howland Vibber. Dickie had carried on her laboratory and gardening work with Dr. Ehrenfried Pfeiffer, who, with Adelheide, had also permanently settled in Spring Valley, and generally lived a happy, productive life continuing the work of Rudolf Steiner in America. (The well-established and successful Threefold Foundation today is pretty much what Sunrise Farm was all about forty years ago, without, of course, the lumber business and the opera singers.)

About 1982, Dickie and her husband moved into a home for elderly anthroposophists located a quarter mile beyond the Threefold Foundation. It was here, at the door of their comfortable but tiny two-room apartment, that she greeted me. "Hello, Juddie," she said simply, smilingly, as we looked upon each other for the first time since she was a vigorous young woman in her prime and I was a little boy. She was bent over from a severe back problem that I recall started in Vanceboro, but her friendly face, her hair, now gray, still pulled softly into a tiny bun, and her warm, natural manner were all instantly "Dickie." It was an emotional moment for us both.

The paintings on their apartment wall looked familiar to me (anthroposophical paintings all have a certain instantly recognizable, rather mystical look to them), and the lunch consisted of a hearty stew and four or five biodynamically grown vegetables served European-style from large bowls. To top it off, Dickie's German accent was so nostalgic to me that, well, I felt I'd turned the clock back four decades.

After lunch we perused the old photo albums I'd brought. There was Dickie, in a short-sleeved peasant dress cinched at the waist, standing proudly in front of what appeared to be a field of something resembling corn. The individual plants stand a foot higher than Dickie's head. "That's rye," said Dickie. "With the right compost we could grow rye as high as corn." And there in another picture were those magical compost heaps. Tied to a post to the right in the picture are a pair of reins, obviously attached to a grazing Ranger off camera, left for a few moments while my father took the photographs. In the background are Dickie's gardens, larger, more orderly and beautiful than any I've ever seen in the years since—and I've always enjoyed the annual "best garden" contest on public television out of Boston. Farther in the distance are the barn, offices, and buildings in various stages of the ever-continuing construction.

"To have something like that fail was just too cruel for your father," she said, slowly shaking her head.

We leafed through the album pages silently for a few minutes, finally stopping at one that showed Dickie in her laboratory, dressed in a white smock and looking very scientific. She's holding up a small circular piece of what appears to be frosted glass. It was then I asked her the question I'd come all the way down from New Hampshire to ask.

"Dickie," I said, "what in the world were you all *doing* in that laboratory?"

"I get something for you," she said, leaving the table and disappearing into the bedroom. She returned with two circular pieces of glass of the same sort shown in the old photograph. "These were made at Sunrise Farm," she said. They were about four inches in diameter and engraved on each was an intricate pattern like those one sees on a frosted window on a below-zero morning.

"Crystallizations!" I said, and Dickie nodded. I was proud to have remembered what those little circular glass things were called. Then another Sunrise Farm memory came flooding up. One day as I was hanging around watching the laboratory activities, somebody showed me a crystallization made, I was told, from a tiny piece of birchwood. Clearly visible on the glass was a "picture" of an entire, mature birch tree! At the time I didn't think that was particularly remarkable. The world was full of magic back then. But, in the sudden remembering of it some forty years later, I was astounded. "Could that have been true, Dickie?" I asked, after describing my memory to her. "Is *that* what you were doing—creating pictures of mature trees and plants just from tiny borings or from their seeds?"

"Yes," said Dickie. I hadn't expected her to agree so readily. She went on to explain that she and her laboratory helpers would place a crushed seed, one of several from a single plant, or a small boring from a tree, onto glass, along with drops of warm distilled water and varying percentages of copper chloride. The glass was then placed on a vibration-free table in an enclosed room (entered via those safe-like doors) in which the temperature was kept at a steady 28 degrees centigrade (82 degrees Fahrenheit) for fourteen to eighteen hours. During that time, through the gradual evaporation of the water, "a crystallization occurs," said Dickie, "which becomes a research method by the help of which the vitality and biological activity of the organism may be investigated." Spoken like a true anthroposophist.

"What do you mean?" I asked.

"Well, for instance, the seed of what would become a healthy plant—in other words, the seed with the strongest germinating force —produces a more harmonious formation on a crystallization than does the seed from what would eventually be an unhealthy plant." She showed me the two old crystallizations she'd fetched from her bedroom. Both, she said, were taken from the seeds of barley plants. One showed a confusing assortment of lines and formations with no apparent design. Seeds from that plant produced "sick" plants. The second showed a perfectly symmetrical design looking very much like a healthy barley plant which, said Dickie, all plants from that group turned out to be.

Blood and urine crystallizations were made in the Sunrise Farm laboratory in much the same manner, Dickie explained. Through the resulting patterns on the glass, they showed the existence of diseases, such as cancer, in whatever body, be it a cow or a human being, from which the sample was derived. She told me that at the height of her laboratory activities at Vanceboro, human blood was being sent to her for analysis from anthroposophists in New York, Massachusetts, Connecticut, and even from Europe.

Although crystallizations "harmonized" (a favorite word in anthroposophy) perfectly with Rudolf Steiner's philosophy of healing and body/spiritual health, they were not invented by Steiner. Rather, said Dickie, they represented the original work of Dr. Ehrenfried Pfeiffer, one of those "three wise men" my mother and father brought to America. That explained to me why Dr. Pfeiffer and Adelheide were so often visiting during the Vanceboro years. He was checking up on Dickie's work with his crystallizations. It doesn't, of course, explain why he continued, interminably, to throw me up in the air in time to some sort of German limerick he'd recite. But no matter. As I grew older, this once-terrifying little ritual grew more tedious than scary.

It was difficult for me to phrase my last question to Dickie without sounding somehow insulting to the work to which she, Dr. Pfeiffer, and several other anthroposophists had devoted a large portion of their lives.

"Dickie . . . ah . . . has any verification as to the value of this crystallization process come from the scientific world outside the anthroposophical movement?" I hoped that was a diplomatic way to ask whether or not all of this was actually, if not baloney, an outmoded tool in the diagnosing of diseases.

"Two Swiss doctors, neither of them anthroposophists, verified Dr. Pfeiffer's findings in a book they published in 1936," she said. I asked her to write the title of the book on a pad of paper with the idea I might seek out a copy at the Boston Public Library or perhaps the Athenaeum. This is the title she wrote: *Nachprufung der E. Pfeiffer'schen Angaben Uber die Moglichkeit einer Kristallographischen Diagnostik; Versuch einer Hormonoskopie und Schwangerschaftsdiagnose.* Not the sort of title you're apt to find on the *New York Times* best-seller list! And even if it were translated, I had my doubts I'd know what the dickens it meant. I decided to let the matter drop.

"Experiments with crystallizations for disease diagnosis are still being carried forth today, mostly in Europe," said Dickie. As I prepared to leave and we were saying our good-byes, she clasped both my hands in both of hers and said, nodding toward the two forty-year-old crystallizations from the Sunrise Farm laboratory, "Not everyone believes in it, Juddie . . . but you have seen what I have seen."

I promised her we'd correspond, we agreed she and her husband, Howland, must come visit us in New Hampshire very soon, and we said all the usual things one earnestly says in such circumstances. Finally I walked back out to my car with a certain sadness, wondering if, in truth, I would ever see Dickie again.

I waved to her as she stood on the doorstep of the elderly anthroposophists' home, very much bent over but supported by a cane. "I get a kick out of you!" I yelled. *"Ja, Ja, Ja . . ."* she called back, smiling, and waved in return.

During the long drive home, I couldn't seem to remove from my mind that particular long-ago image I'd suddenly remembered while I was talking with Dickie. The one of being in the Sunrise Farm laboratory and being shown a little round piece of glass on which there was the detailed picture of an entire birch tree, created simply from a piece of wood the size of a fingernail, some distilled water, and a drop of copper chloride.

Two events brought my world of happy-go-lucky innocence to an end in Vanceboro. The first involved a mother cat and her seven kittens.

Although my father didn't allow cats in the house (a rule we all eventually forced him to back down on), there were plenty living in the barn. A new set of kittens was a common occurrence. One day my father informed me that a mother cat and her brood of seven would be mine, exclusively mine, to feed, water, and care for. I was thrilled. No doubt my father felt this would instill in me a sense of responsibility. And it did, but the lesson was perhaps more harsh than he expected it would be.

With the help of Miles Cropley, one of the milkers and general farmhands, I put the mother cat and all seven of her kittens in a large cardboard box and transported them from the barn to the grain-storage building, the very one in which I'd been privileged to witness the little girl's version of nude eurythmy. The grain-storage building was more directly on my walk to school than was the barn, and I figured I could easily stop there each morning to replenish their water, food, and milk.

"Seven little Democrats," Miles said as we set them up in their new home, and then, a few days later, he asked me if my kittens had become good Republicans yet. I didn't know what he meant. "I mean have they got their eyes open!" he said, much to the amusement of the other milkers who were well aware that both my mother and my father were enthusiastic Roosevelt Democrats, having made that shocking (to all their Boston friends) conversion at the time of his second term.

That conversation with Miles was the last time those kittens entered my mind for a week. Maybe more than a week. Every morning I continued to happily skip along with the cows past the grain-storage building on my way to school, but I completely forgot about my new responsibility. Then one morning I remembered again. I rushed to the building and I shall never forget the sight when I opened the door. The food and water dishes were dry and empty. All seven kittens and their mother were stretched out next to the door, where they'd spent their last hours attempting to scratch their way out.

I was devastated then, and I cringe at the memory today. The lessons my father wanted me to learn had been introduced with the force of being hit over the head with a two-by-four! There is such a thing as responsibility. There are consequences not only to one's actions but also to one's inactions. Living things count on each other for mutual survival. Of course, I wasn't old enough to consciously articulate all this, but I do recall becoming aware that there was more to life than floating along on a river current like a leaf.

The second event that helped shatter my world of happy-go-lucky innocence was being told I was going to be sent away from home. One evening early in the summer of 1941, as she sat on the edge of my bed, my mother quietly informed me that the Maine-woods School would not open the following September and I would be attending a boarding school called Edgewood in Greenwich, Connecticut. I felt a thousand butterflies in my stomach.

Over the previous two years, the growing hostility of some of the Vanceboro people, many of whom were Canadian, toward our

German-speaking Swiss teachers had become more apparent. Much of it was subtle. Our teachers often mentioned to my father that they could feel resentment when they went to Mr. Teague's store. Sometimes a few of the farmhands spoke to them in what seemed like a surly manner.

Some of it, however, was not subtle.

On a sunny day in February of that year, the student body, along with our teachers and several visiting anthroposophists from Switzerland, had all piled into my father's two Packard convertibles and several other cars and headed out for a picnic on Bald Mountain, where there was a view of Mount Katahdin. Such school outings were commonplace, even in winter. On this occasion some of the farm office workers served as drivers while our teachers and their Swiss friends rode together in the last car. Our little caravan stopped for a few minutes at the store, and then, as we were getting under way again, we noticed quite a crowd of people, mostly teenagers, lining the street on both sides ahead of us. As we drove by them we waved, but no one responded. They were all looking back toward our teachers' car coming along behind.

A few seconds later we heard a resounding roar of voices shouting what sounded ominously like "Heil Hitler!" We looked back and saw that every person in the crowd was holding his or her nose with one hand and extending the other in a mock Nazi salute. "Heil! Heil! Heil Hitler!" they shouted over and over until we were past the railroad station and heading out of town. It was a shocking, brutal moment not only for the teachers but for us all.

A week later, the Mainewoods School had no teachers. They could no longer function in that atmosphere. After many hugs, tears, and downright uncharacteristic displays of emotion, they boarded the night train for Boston and were gone forever. Several of our other visiting anthroposophists, including one of the laboratory workers, left with them.

My father declared a two-week vacation for the school and then consulted with my mother about finding replacements. Because my mother was in New York City at the time, studying voice with Friedrich Schorr between her concert tours around New England, the "consulting" was done over the long-distance party line. They routinely spoke on the telephone every evening when my mother was away, a fact well known to a dozen or more Vanceboro women who enjoyed picking up their own phones and listening in. My mother and father were aware they had a silent audience during these nightly conversations. The line would noticeably weaken each time another telephone came off its hook.

On the night the teachers went away, my father had to yell to my mother at the top of his voice. Vanceboro knew there was a crisis at Sunrise Farm and wanted to be in on it. "Will everyone please get the hell off this line—I can't hear what my wife is saying!" he finally yelled. Several clicks indicated that a few listeners had complied, but then he heard a woman's voice say, "Maybe you ought ta keep your wife ta home, Roger." Lots of clicks followed and the line became strong again. As far as the listeners were concerned, something worthwhile had finally been said.

The next day my mother contacted Dr. Hermann Von Baravalli in Connecticut and asked whether or not he and his wife would take over the Mainewoods School. Both had taught there for a few month-long segments the year before. But they were under contract for the remainder of the year, and for the following year, with the Edgewood School, a private boarding grammar school in Greenwich. (Edgewood was not technically a Waldorf school, although many of its teachers were anthroposophists.) She located other possible candidates through the Anthroposophical Society in New York, but ultimately everyone turned her down. The word was out about teaching at the Hales' new Waldorf school. If you speak English with a German accent, they heard, you're not going to have a happy time in Vanceboro, Maine.

Our unexpected winter vacation was almost over. To have all the Mainewoods School children suddenly arrive one morning at the Vanceboro public school, consisting of two teachers for almost one hundred youngsters, was out of the question as far as my mother was concerned. At the one school meeting she'd sat in on a year earlier, the high dropout rate was being discussed with the final consensus being that about as many students actually graduated from Vanceboro High as "ought to." One father rose to say he thought his own son ought to be working on the highway. "The whole world isn't gonna wait around for him to finish school," he said. My mother was aghast.

It was too late in the year to send Patsy and me to a Waldorf boarding school. And to hire local teachers who would know nothing about anthroposophy or Rudolf Steiner's theories on education made no sense to her either. Which left one alternative for finishing out the school year.

After canceling her concert tours for the remainder of the spring, my mother returned to Vanceboro to take over the Mainewoods School herself. She'd had no teaching experience whatsoever, but she was confident that somehow she could do it. To help her, she drafted another person with no teaching experience—my father. Despite his busy schedule running the farm and the burgeoning lumber business, he agreed to teach mathematics and "shop" to the older children. For the remainder of the year, one could always tell from the outside of the school when my father was on duty within. Ranger would be tied to the split-rail fence next to the school woodshed.

"Until I stood in front of all the children that first morning we reopened," my mother recalls today, "I hadn't realized I had no idea what I was going to do!"

She muddled through the first day by having us all write essays about such things as "The Person I Admire Most," "What I Like to Do Best," and "What I Should Not Do." I recently found mine in one of the old family scrapbooks. The title of my first indicated, I think, an early sign of some talent in diplomacy. I called it "My Mother." The other two consisted of a graphic description entitled "Cooking and Eating Corned-beef Hash" followed by a vague account, with no details, of an experience I called "Watching a Bad Friend Hurt a Bullfrog."

That evening, she recalled, she pored through the many books saved from my father's Harvard days looking for "a theme, something I could focus the children on for the rest of the year." Upon opening to Henry Wadsworth Longfellow's "The Song of Hiawatha" in a book entitled *Three Centuries of American Poetry and Prose*, she knew she'd found it.

> *Should you ask me, whence these stories?*
> *Whence these legends and traditions*
> *With the odors of the forest,*
> *With the dew and damp of meadows,*
> *With the curling smoke of wigwams*
> *With the rushing of great rivers . . .*

"It was perfect," my mother remembers thinking. "It had history, geography, adventure, romance, philosophy, religion, Indians —everything you could ask for!" The next morning, she announced to the school that the remainder of the year would be devoted exclusively to "Hiawatha."

So we drew pictures of Hiawatha *by the alders in the summer | by the white fog in the autumn, | by the black pine in the winter.* We wrote and performed a play including *the deadly conflict, hand to hand, among the mountains,* between Hiawatha and his father, performed with great gusto by the two oldest boys in the school. We erected a wigwam. We built bows strong *with sinews of the reindeer* (except we used common twine) and arrows *tipped with Jasper, winged with feathers.* We *wore magic moccasins made of deerskin* (except they were eurythmy slippers with beads sewn onto them) and imagined that *at each stride a mile* [we] *measured.*

We began a birchbark canoe, but because we couldn't seem to make the seams waterproof, we switched to a wooden rowboat we christened *Hiawatha.* With a crowd of farmhands, kitchen help, and office workers on hand as an audience, we ceremoniously launched it *by the shores of Gitche Gumee, by the shining big sea water* (the duck pond below our house).

Discipline was more lax than it had been under our rather stern Swiss teachers. At the end of recess, my mother would ring the school bell for what seemed an eternity before everyone straggled back to class from various little adventures in the nearby pine grove, including the older boys' routine tying of little *Minnehahas* to trees. *Who shall say what thoughts and visions | Fill the fiery brains of young men?* Combining Indian dances into our eurythmy sessions usually ended in a rather wild free-for-all with everyone banging on things with their copper rods in an attempted simulation of the sound of tom-toms.

The only accident occurred when one of the boys, Lonnie by name, happened down by the chicken yard one recess with his newly made bow and arrows. According to his later account, he was practicing shooting *ten arrows upward . . . with such strength and swiftness | that the tenth had left the bow-string | 'ere the first to earth had fallen!* when three of the chickens became fatally involved with the "falling" missiles. My father was furious—*from his brain the thought of vengeance*—but my mother insisted that Lonnie simply apologize to him and then write an essay about it under the "What I Should Not Do" category.

It was an educational, fun, stimulating, memorable two and a half months. I'd venture that if you ask any former student of the Maine-woods School what he or she remembers best from the three years of its existence, the answer would be "Hiawatha"!

Thus it was that my mother's one and only venture into the world of the educator became a resounding success. But she didn't want to remain a schoolteacher. Her ambition, always enthusiastically supported by my father, was to be an opera star at the Metropolitan, and that had not changed. When her renewed efforts to bring anthroposophical teachers to Vanceboro for the following fall term proved futile once again, she and my father decided to close the school for good. They'd concentrate on the other aspects of their grand adventure.

Thus it was that my mother sat on the edge of my bed that June evening in 1941 and brought to me a thousand butterflies. Patsy and I would go to the boarding school in Greenwich where Dr. Hermann Von Baravalli and his wife were teaching. Patsy would be in the sixth grade. I'd be in the third.

Looking back on it today as the father of three sons, I think I might have made the same decision my mother and father made. The public school in Vanceboro was certainly on the opposite end of the educational spectrum from what they felt was essential for our development. And there were no other schools around, Waldorf or otherwise.

But for me, the thought of leaving my idyllic, safe, loving, happy little world at Sunrise Farm was an unbelievable thing to contemplate. A nightmare.

And that's pretty much what it turned out to be . . .

Chapter 6

———◆———

One-upmanship

I HAD never heard about homesickness. I'd experienced whooping cough and measles. I knew that something called polio swept into Vanceboro every few summers, striking down children so that they couldn't walk. But it wasn't until I arrived on the campus of the Edgewood School in Greenwich, Connecticut, one sunny September afternoon in 1941 that I, at the age of eight, became acquainted with the primary symptom of this new illness—namely, a pronounced lump in the throat. In my case, the lump arrived as my mother and I sat down with a housemother in the small reception area of the four-storey stone dormitory building where I and all the other little boys would be living. My father was with Patsy and her housemother in the girls' dormitory across the campus.

The arrival of the lump seemed to coincide with the realization that my mother would be gone within an hour. Following directly behind this realization—and the lump—came another symptom: water welling up in my eyes. Just before I felt it overflow onto my cheeks, I jumped up and ran from the room, saying I wanted to "see something outside." Once out in the hallway, I hastily wiped the tears away and composed myself enough to return. Within a few minutes I was forced to leave once again, this time saying I needed to go to the bathroom. After my third or fourth exit and return, I knew the housemother had caught on to my problem because she turned to my mother and said in a breezy, casual manner, "He'll be all right in a day or so. It's just a little case of homesickness." It was the first time I'd heard the word.

Then my mother and father were gone. They left me in my room up on the third floor with my new roommate, a dark-haired, handsome little son of a French diplomat living in Washington, D.C. His name was Michel. Michel spoke English perfectly and, while my mother and father were present, possessed all the elegant, courteous manners of European aristocracy. Within a minute of my mother and father's departure, however, he had grabbed my arm, twisted it violently and painfully behind my back, and hissed in my ear, "I get the bed next to the window. Right?"

Michel surely added a great deal to my overall misery, but he had nothing to do with my case of homesickness. To deal with it, my overwhelming instinct was to wallow in it. And my greatest frustration during those first weeks at Edgewood was the fact I was never allowed the time. If I just could be given one solid chunk of time in which to surrender myself totally to homesickness, I felt I'd be cured of it forever! But no such luck. We were hardly allowed as much as a half hour to ourselves, and that was in our rooms before supper, where, in my case, domineering little Michel held reign.

I was therefore forced to content myself with being homesick in bits and snatches throughout each long day. A little private time between morning classes and lunch, for instance, would provide a good opportunity to think about poor Fritz and picture him sniffing around the barnyard feeling lonely. He'd be wondering why I wasn't bicycling to town, with him running close behind in my dust, in order to purchase a *Loony Tunes* comic book at the railroad station and maybe check the steam engines in the roundhouse. (Mercifully, I wasn't informed until Thanksgiving vacation that Fritz had died that fall.)

On several occasions during the evening meal in the school dining room, I'd look out the window and catch a fleeting glimpse of my mother walking by in the dark. Once I saw both my mother and my father standing outside the glass doors of the library, staring in. But of course, it wasn't her, it wasn't them.

Every afternoon I'd talk with Patsy for a few minutes. We'd meet at the Good Humor man's white truck and suck orange Popsicles. Talking with Patsy was almost as good as having a private "wallowing" time alone. I couldn't tell her that, however. Homesickness was not something one discussed, even with one's sister. I did notice she always wanted to talk about Mollycoddle and her other cows at the farm, but this was fine with me. I just wanted to be around her for as many minutes as the tight school schedule would allow.

Twenty-two days after my arrival at Edgewood, I went through an entire morning without a lump in my throat. I detachedly noted the exact number of days as a piece of knowledge I could utilize in the future: after one day over three weeks, homesickness begins to ease off.

Michel never eased off. He would eat all the cookies my mother instructed Bessie to send me, he was constantly locking me out of our bedroom, and he dictated how everything in the room was to be. For instance, the window had to remain wide open even when it was freezing outside and I had one of my innumerable colds. If I didn't respond to one of his orders, I'd receive a punch in the upper part of my arm. After lights out, when everyone was supposed to go to sleep, he'd jabber on about Paris and his trips around the world. When the housemother would come in to admonish us for the noise, he'd blame me. On my bureau I had a concert program illustrated with a dramatic professional photograph of my mother in a black veil. Michel made it into a paper airplane and flew it out a third-floor window.

He was as competitive an individual as any I've encountered, which meant daily footraces down our long corridor to the stairs, arm-wrestling matches, even water-drinking contests—any and all tests of endurance, strength, or speed that entered his frenzied little mind.

Then one evening just before Thanksgiving of that first semester, I challenged Michel to a contest. It was the first time I had ever done so. Turned out to be the last time, too.

The bell was ringing to assemble us all for supper as Michel and I were walking down the corridor toward the two sets of stairs that circled a stairwell, down which one could see all the way to the dining room on the first floor. Obviously we were not supposed to climb on the banister of these stairs, but I had seen Michel do so on several occasions when the housemother wasn't around. He'd carefully slide down from our floor to the next landing, a rather daring feat considering the three-storey height.

Now I'll have to admit that I've sometimes thought back to that evening and wondered whether or not the subsequent tragedy was the result of a shrewd scheme I concocted, utilizing my knowledge of Michel and his combative, competitive nature. I don't recall making such a plan consciously, however.

Be that as it may, the fact remains I turned to Michel as we walked down the corridor and said, "I'll race you to the dining room!"

My, how his eyes lit up! They were on fire. With a quick nod of his head, he instantly bolted toward the stairs at a dead run, with me just a step behind. He went for the left-hand staircase, I the right. When I reached the stairs on my side, I began hurtling down them two at a time as fast as my legs would go. On his side, Michel didn't bother with the stairs. Instead, he vaulted up onto the banister and, in one clean graceful motion, sailed right over it. Down he plummeted to the hardwood floor of the dining room three storeys below. I'll never forget the sickening sound his body made when it hit. It was sort of a combination of a thump and a crunch.

I stopped halfway down the stairs to the second-floor landing, leaned over the banister, and looked down at Michel on the floor below. People were hurrying over to him. He wasn't moving.

For the rest of my time at Edgewood, I had the third-floor room to myself. I rearranged it my way and kept the window closed when it was cold outside. Michel went to the hospital with a broken arm, a concussion, and some internal injuries, and although I heard he was eventually all right, he never returned. Poor Michel. I hope the experience calmed him down just a little and that he has had a happy life. And, yes, I'll admit he won every contest in which he and I competed—including our last race to the dining room.

Instead of going all the way back to the farm for just three days, Patsy and I spent Thanksgiving 1941 at my mother's New York apartment on Central Park South. Throughout our subsequent years of boarding schools in Connecticut, New Hampshire, and New York State, there were many vacation days spent in New York City. It became a short-term home away from home.

Even for us children, New York visits meant evenings at the Skylight Roof atop the St. Regis Hotel, gala dinners at "21" and the Stork Club, nightclub shows at the Copacabana, and Broadway plays like *Oklahoma* and *Show Boat*. My mother felt we should be exposed to a little sophistication and culture to contrast with our farm life in Vanceboro.

Although I found it all pretty exciting, Patsy didn't. She would have much preferred to be milking Mollycoddle, riding her horse, Kitty, or just joking around with the farmhands in the barn. Getting all spiffed up for a night on the town was not her idea of a good time —then or now. Her dominant recollection of our evenings in New York (neither she nor I remember any daytime activities) was the arguing and bickering between my mother and father.

"We'd be at some fancy restaurant and Mom would begin to belabor a point they were arguing about until it was ten miles into the ground," she remembers today, "while Dad would simmer quietly for a long time and then become sarcastic—which would infuriate Mom even more. And so it would go—on and on and on."

My memory is evidently more selective. To me, our gala, glittering nights in the city were like a romantic, highly sophisticated Cary Grant movie. My mother often wore a full evening gown, my father a tuxedo, and before setting out for wherever we were going, they would share a bottle of imported champagne, from which Patsy and I were allowed a sip or two, along with a large jar of Russian caviar they'd spread on buttered toast and sprinkle with lemon juice. (Patsy and I would not even consider sampling those little black soggy-looking fish eggs on toast until, of course, years later when nobody could afford them.) If the evening was warm enough, we'd be out on the apartment balcony facing Central Park.

During this champagne-and-caviar time, my father would present my mother with a corsage, a large bunch of fresh roses, or perhaps a pin or some other gift, always accompanied by a loving note which she'd read aloud. Yes, there was bickering and arguing, but particularly for a little eight-year-old boy like me, there was an awful lot of romantic "mushy talk," too.

During the Thanksgiving of my year at Edgewood, my mother and father exchanged beautiful leather-bound diary books, both of which are in my mother's possession today. "To my darling wife," my father wrote on the inside flap of my mother's book. "No book is good or beautiful enough to hold your thoughts, dear girl, but this one will at least keep them safely recorded." It is signed "Your devoted husband."

In the book she presented to my father, my mother wrote, "To my dear husband, Roger—in hopes that you will feel free to put down some of your most interesting thoughts in this book, for the benefit of our children and others. With my love, always—Marian."

Written mostly in the winter of 1942, my father's book is filled with his thoughts about the Atlantic Charter agreed upon by Churchill and Roosevelt the previous summer. "This war," he wrote, "is not just a fight to destroy evil, but to create good."

My mother's includes quotes and comments about the Bible, William James, Aristotle, Friedrich Nietzsche, Buddha, and particularly Rudolf Steiner. One observation turned out to be especially prophetic: "A man's worst difficulties begin," she wrote, "when he is able to do as he likes."

There was one thing we often did in New York that I, in particular, didn't like. That was going to the opera. As flying in an airplane involves, as they say, hours of boredom interrupted by seconds of stark terror, so operas, at least for me back then, involved hours of excruciating boredom interrupted by a few seconds of tolerably beautiful music. We always attended the afternoon performance of *Parsifal* if we were in New York for Easter. It was, my mother said, our way of going to church. But *Parsifal* required sitting still for five hours of tedious arias sung by a totally confusing array of sopranos, mezzo-sopranos, tenors, baritones, and basses in various stages of despair, sorrow, or, worse still, religious inspiration. As far as I was concerned, that entire five-hour period had to be endured simply for the sake of the last forty-five seconds of the last scene in the last act. However, I must admit that as that stuffed white pigeon descended from the top of the stage on a string and hung over Parsifal holding the Holy Grail, the instrumental music was beautiful, even moving. Sure had to wade through a lot to arrive there, however.

By the time Patsy and I were at Edgewood, my father had grown to be an ardent devotee of Wagnerian and Italian opera, but he nonetheless enjoyed making amusing (if disparaging) little remarks to me when we were sitting together at a performance. "She's gonna bounce!" he'd whisper during the last scene of Verdi's *Tosca*, as Tosca was preparing to jump off a wall and kill herself after discovering her lover was dead. And, sure enough, we'd sometimes catch a glimpse of the soprano coming back up after bouncing off the landing mattress located behind the wall. For the next few minutes our shoulders would be shaking with our slightly audible giggles, often precipitating a few sharp *shhh*'s from my mother and others around us.

Following the first performance of the opera season the year after the first Thanksgiving in New York, my father was descending the wide, ornate stairs of the old Metropolitan Opera House directly behind a large woman wearing a gown with an incredibly low neckline. Nodding to a sculpture of Caruso on a pedestal at the base of the staircase, he turned to my mother and me, and in quite a loud voice said, "Haven't I seen that bust before?" The lady and her escort turned around somewhat angrily, at which point my father, in what the family always referred to as the ultimate in quick thinking, said, "Well, after all, it *is* opening night." The lady and her escort couldn't help smiling—and my father remained pleased with himself about both remarks for the rest of his life.

For reasons Patsy and I could never fathom, my father's remarks to waiters and waitresses in restaurants took on a cutting edge that wasn't so amusing. He'd complain that his steak was tough, the soup was cold. It seemed out of character for a man as gentle with people as my father ordinarily was. Besides, for Patsy and me it was embarrassing.

"Would you tell someone to bring us more water, please? Ours has evaporated." He used that line often to indicate his displeasure with slow service. I recall one headwaiter, to whom he'd given the evaporated-water line, asking my father to point out the waiter who had initially poured the water. "It's been so long since I've seen him," my father replied, "that I can no longer recall what he looks like." He made that sort of repartee into an art form. And how he loved Boston poet David McCord's epitaph for the gravestone of a waiter: "By and by, God caught his eye."

Upon entering the so-called best restaurants in New York, my mother often recognized theater people and other celebrities, and she was not in the least bit reluctant to chat with them. Often wearing dark glasses even indoors and dressed in something rather dramatic, she appeared to be a celebrity herself. "I'm Marian Hale and I just want you to know that all of America wishes you godspeed on your important trip to Europe tomorrow," she said to John Foster Dulles at "21" one evening in 1953 when I was visiting during my sophomore year at Dartmouth. He rose, probably thinking she was somebody he knew or at least ought to know, introduced her to the three other people at his table, and then proceeded to chat about foreign policy with her. Through all the New York years she did fundamentally the same with such as H. V. Kaltenborn, Bette Davis, John Wayne ("My husband, Rog, just loves every picture you make, but aren't you afraid of being typecast?"), and in 1961 on the dock in Palm Beach to which the *Honey Fitz* was tied, with Jack and Jacqueline Kennedy. On ocean crossings to Europe she was "dear friends" with the captain of the ship before they'd steamed more than a few miles out of New York harbor.

During my New York Thanksgiving vacation in 1941, she spotted Wendell Willkie as we followed the headwaiter into the Stork Club dining room. He'd been defeated by Roosevelt in the presidential election the year before. While my father, Patsy, and I were being seated at our table, she went over to him, was greeted cordially as usual, and then motioned for me, just me, to come to his table too. When I did, she introduced me to him as if she'd known Wendell Willkie all her life.

Willkie immediately lifted me onto his lap, signed a menu for me, and told me that anyone who lived in Vanceboro, Maine, must be "a good, solid Republican" (Maine being one of the ten states that went to him in 1940). I think my mother was surprised to hear me suddenly blurt out that that must mean "I had my eyes open" (I was thinking back to Miles Cropley's remark about my "Republican" kittens), but Willkie guffawed for several minutes and slapped his hand on the table. Then, suddenly reflective and serious, he put me down, looked into my eyes, and said, "Don't ever lose faith in this country, son." When we returned to our table, my mother told me to write what he had said on the menu under his signature, which I did. Throughout the Vanceboro years, I kept it in my underwear drawer at the farm, along with several porcupine noses I usually had on hand, ready to turn in for the fifty-cent bounty payments. Somehow in the moving shuffle in 1947, I lost it—the signed menu, that is.

The days between Thanksgiving and Christmas vacation numbered less than twenty-two, too few for homesickness back at Edgewood to ease off, but in 1941 we had the distractions of the Pearl Harbor attack and wondering when we'd see those little slant-eyed devils pictured in *Life* magazine showing up in Connecticut. Also, it was a great help to be able to indulge fully in homesickness in my own room by myself.

Christmas vacation back at the farm made Edgewood disappear for three weeks. An absence of early snowstorms that year enabled us to have evening skating parties, complete with bonfires and Bessie-made oyster stew heated outdoors in a great old-fashioned iron pot. Russell, by now the farm foreman, and several other men took a fire hose and made ice paths on the hill leading down to the frozen pond. Those were the fastest, longest, most wonderfully terrifying sled rides imaginable, especially for us children. Unlike the grownups, we had to fly down those narrow ribbons of ice in the dark cold sober!

A Christmas Eve day snowstorm gave our annual Nativity play the proper atmosphere. With the Mainewoods School closed for good, we held it in the big main barn that year, with Patsy's Mollycoddle, two sheep we named Orient and Are, my father's Ranger, and two pigs by the names of Piglet and Pooh, as part of the cast. Much discussion with my father followed as to whether or not it would be right to ever *eat* any member of the Christmas Nativity play cast. Because we could not spot Piglet among the other pigs several days later, Patsy and I boycotted the roast pork at dinner that evening even though my father attempted to convince us Piglet was not the one involved. We were positive—and we are both positive today—that poor Piglet was indeed involved.

The last-minute snow enabled another Sunrise Farm Christmas Eve tradition, the caroling tour of Vanceboro, to take place. After the Nativity play was over, old Frankie would hitch Nip and Tuck and another workhorse team to a large four-runner sleigh ordinarily used to haul hardwood logs out of the woods. He'd attach some bells to the harnesses, fill the bottom of the sleigh with straw, and throw in a pile of moldy old buffalo robes, the smell of which is described perfectly by writer Philbrook Paine in a recollection of his own childhood contributed to *Yankee* in 1981. "In its damp state," he wrote, "a buffalo robe had all the sweetness and charm of a skunk hit by an automobile."

All of us children spent most of the carol tour running. I can still feel and hear the hard-packed snow beneath my L. L. Bean gummy shoes as I raced behind the runners of the sleigh, my hands sometimes gripping the rear corner post. Occasionally I'd make a wild leap and come back on board to catch my breath. That's when my mother would direct all of us children to look up into the clear, bitter-cold nighttime sky to see Santa Claus flying in *his* sleigh through the stars above us. If one of the children said they couldn't see him, she'd say, "Use a little more imagination. Try harder." I always saw him.

My last month at Edgewood the following spring was a comparatively happy one, thanks to Patsy, who came down with a case of scarlet fever during the spring term. She was very sick and I didn't see her again until she returned to Vanceboro with me in June, still weak and recovering. But that wasn't why my final Edgewood month was happy.

Scarlet fever being contagious, anyone who had close contact with Patsy during the week prior to the diagnosis of her illness was placed in quarantine in a small wing of the infirmary for the remainder of the school year. Five students were quarantined: I (the only boy) and four girls from Patsy's dormitory, all of them three years older than me. We could play outside in the wooded area behind the infirmary but we were not allowed to attend classes or athletic activities, or to mingle with anyone except each other.

Actually, what we did most of the time was lounge around on our beds in our pajamas. It was a worry-free, homesick-free existence. My bed was next to that of a dark-haired, somewhat chubby, very talkative sixth-grader who looked older than she was. Her name was Jackie.

One afternoon the other three girls were outside somewhere and Jackie and I were alone, lounging and chatting on our neighboring beds in our pajamas. At some point our conversation turned to the subject of procreation. Jackie asked me if I was aware of how it was accomplished. I said I was. Although neither my mother nor my father had ever had a "birds and bees" talk with me, and never would (thank goodness), I had witnessed some of the dogs at the farm doing what I assumed she was referring to, although I had never really given it much thought. Procreation, I said smugly, had something to do with a boy's "private part in front" and a girl's "rear end."

Jackie laughed merrily at that. Oh, she seemed to think it was hilarious. Finally, after calming herself, she said, "A boy's private part in front, yes, but procreation has *nothing* to do with a girl's rear end."

That seemed unlikely to me. The dogs' procreating positions

indicated otherwise. So did the photographs of nude women in my mother's art books that some of the Mainewoods School boys and I had perused on occasion at the farm. Those almost always showed the women from the rear, indicating, I pointed out to Jackie, the importance of that area in females. Jackie giggled even more.

Then she proposed a way to help me understand how it really was. She would, she said, show me exactly what *the* part of her body having to do with procreation looked like. But only under one condition. I had to show her exactly what *mine* looked like.

I immediately agreed, knowing I'd never actually expose myself to her but hoping she would anyway. The key to success was to convince her to go first, which, after considerable haggling, promises, hope-to-dies, and so on, she did. Suddenly I was standing at the side of her bed looking down at a triangular patch of dark hair that was revealed when she lowered her pajama bottoms. Interesting. The little girl who'd danced for me in the grain-storage shed had had hair only on her head, where it belonged. This didn't make sense. It didn't prove her argument about procreation, either. (I remained wedded to the rear-end theory for about another year.) But, yes, interesting.

Strange how one can remember a mere minute or less in one's life and yet forget months and months of other times! The minute I stood staring down at Jackie is a case in point. But then up went the pajama bottoms and it was my turn. I'd already formed my little plan. It involved a bit of duplicity, but I felt I would technically be within the terms of our agreement. I would show her exactly what my very private part looked like.

I went over to the table where our drawing paper and pencils were kept and proceeded to create a rather detailed, colored picture. I was pleased with it when I presented it to her. It could, I thought, have come straight from a textbook on anatomy.

Jackie was furious. She accused me of reneging on our agreement and said I was deceitful and conniving. Although I knew there was no way I could bring myself to do anything other than what I did, she caused me to feel a smidgen of guilt. To be sure, maybe I hadn't actually lived up to the spirit of our agreement.

What little guilt had been generated disappeared forever a half hour later when the three other girls came in. The first thing Jackie did was show them my drawing. "This is what Juddie says he looks like," she said, and they all dissolved in gales of laughter. I tried to explain it was the result of an agreement Jackie and I had made but Jackie said that was absurd. There had been no "agreement" or discussion about procreation or *anything!* The drawing later found its way into the hands of one of the nurses, who gently admonished me, and, well, the whole episode was mortifying to say the least.

It did, however, provide me with two lessons. The first is obvious: duplicity can backfire.

The second is that one ought never to put anything down on paper unless one is prepared to have it shown to the world.

Patsy and I would not return to Edgewood the following fall. Patsy, still weak and not fully recovered, would stay home with her horses and cows and temporarily attend the Vanceboro public school. I would follow Dr. Hermann Von Baravalli, Erica Von Baravalli, and several other Edgewood teachers to a new Waldorf school in Wilton, New Hampshire, called High Mowing.

My "summer of '42" was, as all my summers were, a deliriously happy one on Star Island. Present were the usual gang of opera singers, anthroposophists, and visiting friends and relatives from Boston—plus a brand-new Belgian shepherd puppy called Sunny that was all mine. I was to be given a second chance at caring for an animal of my own and I was determined not to botch the opportunity this time around.

Sunny and I slept in a large tent down by the water, and we were inseparable. We caught frogs in a tall-grass area on the east side of the island but we never—well, seldom—harmed any of them. We chased snakes, and when Sunny was able to grab one, she would kill it by shaking it violently from side to side. During these Vanceboro years, everyone killed snakes on sight, perhaps to avoid being "charmed," as our old head guide, Sid Robinson, maintained could happen. (Spiders, on the other hand, were to be protected: "If you want to live and thrive, let the spider run alive.")

We went on "anything alive" hunts, as I liked to call them, along the mainland shore, armed with my homemade bow and arrows, which never did any damage to an "alive" creature beyond startling it. (Sid enjoyed telling me that my bow and arrow shooting would improve somewhat if I simply drew the circle on a target after, rather than before, I shot an arrow.) On stormy south-wind days, with

Sunny sitting upright in the front seat, we challenged the big waves coming down the lake in my own little beamy, canvas-covered rowboat powered by a two-horsepower outboard. On calm, balmy afternoons, Sunny and I would lounge around on the cool, soft moss under a certain birch tree in an area of the island farthest from any of the cabins. I'd play my harmonica for hours, staring straight up through the branches to the sky, and Sunny, lying beside me, would attempt to catch flies. The private, intimate relationship we established that summer was to endure for thirteen years, despite many long separations.

The seeds of doom to Sunrise Farm were no doubt already sown by the summer of 1942. Grandpop and Grandma Hale, now in their late seventies, paid a visit to the farm and Star Island in late August of that year, after most of the other guests had returned to the city, and I have a memory of serious conversations between Grandpop and my father about money. Grandpop seemed concerned. My father didn't. These conversations would occur while they drank "Star Island cocktails" (scotch, water, ice, and sprigs of mint picked along the path to the dock) on the porch of the main cabin before supper. Grandpop had originally given my father and Aunt Mard approximately one million dollars each at the time of my father's graduation from Harvard, but by 1942 my father had pretty much gone through all of that and was in need of operating funds every year. Grandpop remained generous (to a fault, perhaps), but he was appalled at the magnitude of the Sunrise Farm operation in August 1942, and by the speed at which it was growing. Dozens of buildings were still being built; there were almost thirty workhorses, most of them at the lumber camps on my father's forest land as well as on land leased from the Eastern Pulpwood Company. Sunrise Farm was supplying milk, cream, butter, eggs, beef, chickens, and vegetables to virtually everyone in Vanceboro as well as to people in Topsfield and Danforth. A private Sunrise Farm fire department, complete with shiny red truck, was now housed in one of the new buildings near the barn. A fully equipped slaughterhouse was in operation daily, and the two lumber mills were turning out hardwood boards at a clip of more than 20,000 feet per day.

By 1942 and throughout the war years, the finished lumber went to the shipyard in Bath to be used in the construction of the interiors and deckings of ships. When the United States had declared war on

Germany and Japan the previous December, my father had toyed with the notion of applying for a commission in the navy and being given command of a ship of his own. Several of his yachting friends in Boston had already gone that route, despite their lack of military training. The navy was glad to have mature men experienced in navigation, sailing, and the handling of small vessels. But the government people with whom my father spoke told him they'd prefer he continue at Sunrise Farm, producing lumber for the building of ships. They convinced him he couldn't do anything more important for the war effort.

So, with most of his employees now his age (forty-two) or older, my father poured even more money (Grandpop's money!) into expanding the mills, the lumbering operations, and the farm. If a brand-new Caterpillar tractor, the largest made, would be useful for the construction of roads and for plowing snow, it was bought. If a new vehicle-maintenance garage was needed, it was built. If one of the lumber camps could use another fifty old men or boys, they were hired. It was the most exciting, challenging, happy time in my father's life.

Grandpop's concerns made little or no impression. My father and mother expected as much from him. They respectfully allowed him to vent his feelings but remained more convinced than ever that Sunrise Farm and all it represented would eventually justify the tragedy of "poor Drakie-boy," their firstborn. No matter how logical his arguments, Grandpop didn't have a chance. Details like money, red ink, and "good business decisions" were no match for a bona fide *mission.*

When Grandpop and Grandma returned to West Newton just before Labor Day (never to return to Sunrise Farm or Star Island again), my father had received enough money to continue the grand adventure for another year. Aunt Mard, now divorced and living rather frugally in her small West Newton house with her two growing boys, Cousins Frank and Robert, received exactly the same amount. She didn't need it, she didn't know why Grandpop kept giving her huge chunks of money every year, but, as always, she stashed it away in her trust fund and went about her modest everyday life without questioning it.

My father learned about it, however. After Grandma Hale's death two years later, when he found it all but impossible to convince

Grandpop to part with additional monies to keep Sunrise Farm afloat, he remembered his father's firm belief about always making equal distributions of money to one's children regardless of disproportionate needs. He not only remembered it, he slyly took advantage of it.

But that was a little later, when things were getting desperate.

Chapter 7

---❖---

Practicality

M Y FIRST three hours at High Mowing School were not as traumatic as my initial introduction to Edgewood had been the year before. That was to prove misleading.

Located atop a high ridge with a breathtaking view of Mount Monadnock and the lesser mountains to the west, High Mowing was the creation of a strong-willed, energetic follower of the Rudolf Steiner philosophy of education. Her name was Beulah Emmett. Mrs. Emmett had taught at Edgewood, although I didn't know her there. When she, the Baravallis, and several other teachers found that Edgewood took less of a Waldorf approach to education than they wanted, she decided to convert her large country estate into a genuine Waldorf boarding school. She named it High Mowing. I arrived with my mother in September 1942 for the very first year of its existence.

The school was divided between the High School, which was on Mrs. Emmett's estate, and the Lower School for the younger children like me, which was situated at the edge of a forest with several open stone-wall-edged fields across the road and a large barn in back. To my surprise and relief, it didn't have that boarding school look. Rather, it resembled a small New England farm. (There is no Lower School today, and Mrs. Emmett died in 1978. But High Mowing, now one of more than three hundred Waldorf schools worldwide, and exclusively for grades nine through twelve, continues to flourish.)

Teaching at the Lower School was Erica Von Baravalli (we

115

called her Mrs. Belly Belly when she wasn't around). The housemother was a kindly, wise lady named Ann Friedl, who also spoke with a German accent. Both Mrs. Von Baravalli and Mrs. Friedl were at the door, all smiles, the afternoon my mother and I arrived.

I'd been teary-eyed throughout much of the two-day drive from Vanceboro. A mixture of sorrow, foreboding, anxiety, suspense, and gloom lay like a dead weight everywhere within my being and I was certain it would last for the next twenty-two days. But then Mrs. Von Baravalli and Mrs. Friedl kissed me at the door and spoke in their familiar German accents. I was shown around the farmhouse and noticed it had no long, dark corridors, no common bathroom lined with urinals and stalls, and no electric bells to announce things. And, perhaps best of all, my tiny corner room on the second floor was without a Michel! Maybe, just maybe, this was going to be all right.

"Just like home," I said brightly to my mother as we walked to the dining room later that afternoon. "Just like home," my mother said as she passed me a platter of home-fried potatoes, just like Bessie's, as we were eating supper with about a dozen children. "Just like home, isn't it, Juddie?" Mrs. Von Baravalli called over to me several times from her place at another table. Everyone, including me, was really trying.

Later that evening, both my mother and Mrs. Friedl tucked me into my bed for the night, saying how much I was going to love High Mowing. Mrs. Friedl left with a cheery "See you in the morning" while my mother lingered for a minute and then kissed me good-bye. "I'll call you from New York in a few days," she said, and then she was gone until Thanksgiving.

The weight inside me returned in full force as if out of nowhere, the lump slipped back into my throat, and tears again filled my eyes. It was, as I both observed and experienced it, an amazing phenomenon occurring right there in my cozy little farmhouse bedroom that was "just like home."

The next morning I was introduced to six big, frisky, scary riding horses who so dominated my life at High Mowing that I barely had sufficient time to indulge myself in my new case of homesickness. In charge of them was a strikingly beautiful twenty-five-year-old girl we knew as Miss Griffin. Miss Griffin was also an art teacher, a health nut who drank milk and grapefruit juice mixed together, and a sculptress who worked in front of a long mirror in the nude while pretty much the entire male population of the Lower School watched through an open floor register in the attic over her studio.

My mistake with Miss Griffin was not being honest with her that first day when she asked me to be her assistant in the barn. She'd heard I lived on a farm in Maine and just assumed I loved horses. I should have told her that I *did* love to feed them carrots, if I was on the other side of the fence, and that I *did* love to watch them try to roll over in the paddock. Period.

As it was, I spent a good deal of time every afternoon waving my arms, clucking, and mostly just waiting until the rear end of the horse was pointed away from me and the entire horse was located in the farthest corner of its stall. Then I would slip quickly inside the half-door, fork in some hay, pour a little water, cover the existing manure by flinging new straw over it, and get the hell out of there. Chores in the stall of a fidgety horse could take as much as an hour.

About midway through my year at High Mowing there occurred an incident that I would probably think was merely a bad dream if I hadn't recently discussed it with a witness. It happened on one of the many afternoons when Miss Griffin wasn't around (turns out she was naked in her studio) and I had been placed in charge of the horses and the barn chores. At the moment the crisis began, however, I was on the seesaw in front of the Lower School house with a sixth-grade girl, Geraldine Mathews. (Today Geraldine has five children and five grandchildren and helps run her family's custom shoemaking business called Cordwainers in Deerfield, New Hampshire.)

Suddenly one of the first-grade boys was running toward us from the direction of the barn, yelling, "The horses are loose! The horses are loose!" I later learned that it was the same boy who had unlatched all the half-doors to the horses' stalls and then fled, after closing the outside barn door. ("Just something I wanted to do," he later shamefacedly confessed to Mrs. Friedl.)

Geraldine and I ran to the barn and peeked in. The sight was a nightmare. Not only were all the horses "loose," as the first-grader had yelled, but, unbelievably, they were all fighting! One was biting another in the throat, two were kicking and lunging at each other, the gentlest of them, a large pony named Tasha, was standing still, shivering violently, with a stream of blood running down her neck, and all except Tasha were screaming out all sorts of hysterical whinnies and piercing horse cries. "It was absolute chaos, an unbelievable sight," Geraldine remembers today. Worse still, it was my responsibility to deal with it!

The nearest stall to the barn door was Tasha's, and without thinking what I could or would do, I dashed into it, closing the half-door firmly behind me. There I stood, safe, but in the midst of screaming bedlam. White-faced Geraldine closed the outside barn door and ran for help. I was alone.

I don't know how long I remained there, shivering every bit as violently as poor bloody Tasha. Maybe a minute or two. Then some little miracles began to occur. One of the horses abruptly stopped fighting and trotted directly into its own stall. Shortly thereafter, another did. Finally, all the horses but Tasha were standing in their open stalls, heaving, blowing, and bleeding. I could hardly believe it. Perhaps my guardian angel (my mother always told me I had a guardian angel and I suspected it was the Madonna-like woman who had drifted through the wall of my bedroom years before) was providing me with a rare and golden chance to be a hero.

I couldn't turn her down. With adrenaline surging, heart pounding, I dashed from the safety of Tasha's stall and in a matter of seconds had closed the half-doors to every stall.

It was over. A moment later, Geraldine, Miss Griffin—pulling a bathrobe around herself—and others came running. We all coaxed Tasha back into her stall and then Miss Griffin began administering to the various wounds the horses had inflicted upon each other. I continued to shake for the remainder of the afternoon.

I had, however, learned a couple of things. First, I began to suspect I was inherently lucky—to the point where I could probably even count on it. The second was in the area of practicality: namely, that the best solution to a bewildering crisis is often to stand by on the outskirts of it, appearing knowledgeable and concerned, while the crisis solves itself!

An unfortunate by-product of my newly acquired—and surely unfamiliar—hero status was that Miss Griffin now thought I was even more of an expert at handling horses than she had imagined. I'd been able to separate six fighting horses and return all of them to their stalls. Surely I would love to exercise the horses in the paddock and even accompany her and some of the girls (not one boy in the school, including myself, was the least bit interested in horses) on afternoon rides. However, by means of one excuse or another, I managed to avoid anything more frightening than occasionally sitting on a walking horse inside the paddock.

Then came the late spring afternoon when I simply ran out of excuses (but not, as it would turn out in the long run, of luck). Unbelievably, I found myself outside the paddock atop one of the biggest, scariest horses in the whole bunch, the one that had done most of the biting in the barn fight. "We'll just take it real slow, Juddie," said Miss Griffin as four of us slowly walked our horses out onto the road in front of the school. She must have noticed I seemed worried. (It's not easy to mask terror.)

I don't know whether my greatest fear was exposing my true equestrian inadequacies to Miss Griffin and the girls or whether it had merely to do with survival. In either case, I knew my only hope was to be sure my horse walked. Just walked.

My horse had other ideas. As soon as we reached the main road, it decided to canter. Not break into a little trot. No, it wanted to all-out run, and there was no way I could prevent it from doing what it wanted to do.

Later, everyone told me the horse bucked me off and I was knocked unconscious when my head hit the pavement. I never bothered to correct their impression.

What actually happened is that I fainted. My last memory is going higher and higher off the saddle with each of the horse's running strides, and farther and farther toward its neck. Then I lost consciousness. My next memory is lying in Mrs. Friedl's arms in a car racing down the long, winding hill to a hospital somewhere near Wilton.

Thus ended my brief association with the High Mowing horses and, for that matter, with Miss Griffin and the entire world of the Lower School. After several days in the hospital where my cracked head was sewn up (feeling the scar today is like reminiscing about old times), I was put in bed for the last month of the spring term in a room in the main building of the High School, with Mrs. Emmett in charge. I was to remain quiet until my head and face cuts healed and it was determined that the inside of my head was all right. The

specter of poor Drakie-boy's massive birth injuries arose once more
in my mother's and father's minds and so worried my mother that
she canceled the remaining engagements of a concert tour and stayed
for two weeks at the school, in a room adjoining mine.

Upon returning to Sunrise Farm that June, I made my first
specific conscious effort to control the future course of my life. One
evening at supper (Patsy and I were eating supper with the grown-
ups now), I asked my mother and father to let me remain at Sunrise
Farm the following fall and attend the Vanceboro public school, like
Patsy. I told them I didn't want to go back to High Mowing or to
any boarding school.

My father liked the idea, but my mother seemed apprehensive.
She couldn't express her real concerns to us at the time, but the fact
was she felt that Patsy, now a tall, pretty girl with long blond hair,
was already in danger of becoming too entrenched in the backwoods
farm life of Vanceboro. She'd noticed that some of the "scruffy-
looking town boys," as she described them, were beginning to hang
around Patsy while she was milking, and one of Patsy's girlfriends,
who'd been at the Mainewoods School, was rumored to be pregnant.
A couple more years at Sunrise Farm full-time, in my mother's
opinion, and Patsy would be a backwoods farmer's wife hanging
laundry on a clothesline. Consequently my mother already had plans
to transform her back into a sophisticated little lady. Patsy would
attend (and hate) my mother's alma mater, Westover School, in
Middlebury, Connecticut. But because Patsy would be entering the
eighth grade in the fall of '43, Westover was still a year away. My
mother hoped it wouldn't be too late.

As for me, she realized I didn't seem inclined toward milking
cows, riding horses, and shoveling manure, so there was less danger
of my "going native" as a permanent way of life. Still, she worried
that the Vanceboro public school would retard my education and
thus slow my progress toward achieving, as she always put it, "great
things." I never had the foggiest notion what constituted "great
things," but I always accepted easily and without question the fact
she had high-falutin' dreams for me. If one's mother didn't, who
would? (She still, at age eighty-four, hopes it will happen, and I still,
at age fifty-three, haven't the slightest idea what she has in mind.)
Perhaps I'd have had second thoughts about achieving "great

things" if I'd read one of the entries in her diary, dated June 1943. "Character is built in the storm and stress of the world," she wrote. "A man reaches full height only through compulsions, responsibilities, and sufferings. Life is not for happiness but for achievement."

As far as I was concerned, life was still for happiness, and happiness would be having my mother agree that I didn't have to go to boarding school anymore.

I'm sure the bandages on my head helped her make a decision in my favor. (As far as I was concerned, falling off the horse was a stroke of good fortune!) About a week later, after she had interviewed the woman in charge of grades four through six at the Vanceboro public school, she decided I would go there for one year, two at most. I was ecstatic—and not uninterested to note that I'd precipitated the decision myself.

Tall, square, muscular, severe Mrs. Hunter was my teacher. Her hair was cut short, her glasses were the small wire-rimmed variety that Nazis wore in the movies, and she ran her class of some fifty children more or less as Hitler might have. There was to be no talking, no laughing, no looking out the window, no fidgeting around—no *nothing*. On my very first morning, I was shocked to see her suddenly thunder down one of the aisles, yank a little boy's hand out flat, and whack it really hard with her ruler. She'd spotted him whispering to his neighbor.

Oh, how hardworking, obedient, and polite I instinctively knew how to be! After a week at the Vanceboro public school, I was the only boy in Mrs. Hunter's entire class who hadn't been whacked by her ruler.

Some of the children began suggesting I might be her "favorite," which was fairly well confirmed one late September morning during one of our study hours. I'd finished my written lessons and begun gazing out the window. Mrs. Hunter was writing material for the next lesson on the blackboard, her back to the classroom. Without being at all conscious of it, I began softly to whistle the little tune we used to play on our flutes for eurythmy class at the Waldorf schools. Mrs. Hunter whirled around violently, her large face contorted in rage, and bellowed, "Who's whistling!?"

You could have heard the proverbial pin drop. No one moved, but many eyes flickered in my direction.

"It was me, Mrs. Hunter," I finally said in a tremulous, quavering voice as I prepared myself for being whacked for the first time in my life.

Mrs. Hunter miraculously changed from a towering hulk of enraged authority to a kindly, indulgent mother about to gently admonish her own beloved child. "Oh Juddie, it was you," she said quietly, actually smiling. "We don't whistle here in class, Juddie."

"Yes, Mrs. Hunter," I said. Strangely, I haven't been overly fond of whistling or the sound of whistling in all the years since then.

As to being whacked during my two years in Vanceboro public school, I never was. And instead of being teased about being "teacher's pet," I was admired for it! I was the son of the man who was boss to almost every father in town. Mrs. Hunter, they felt, wouldn't *dare* whack Roger Hale's boy, and just maybe they were right. Or had she succumbed to my wily little ways of ingratiating myself? Either way, I was aware of a subtle power inherent in my favored status, strengthened even more by my not appearing to use it. Such "innocent" childhood guile!

Several weeks later, my guardian angel—or somebody in control —must have decided I needed humbling, that I should be aware my privileged position wouldn't always protect me and that one cannot control everything in one's life. The lesson, which lasted for slightly less than five minutes, was a staggering shock to me. And that, I suspect, was precisely what I needed.

At the urging of my mother, Mrs. Hunter had agreed to put on a school play, and I was called upon to sing a humorous song containing two dozen six-line verses. As a veteran of three Waldorf schools, I'd already been in dozens of skits and plays and had always felt at ease on stage. During all the rehearsals for Mrs. Hunter's production that fall of 1943, I sang my long song with gusto, enthusiasm, and absolute confidence.

Then came the performance. My song was first, introducing the play. The curtain went up, and I was alone on stage. The gymnasium was packed but I immediately spotted my mother in the middle of the third row, clapping an enthusiastic welcome along with everyone else. She gave me a wave and was smiling broadly as I began to sing.

I knew instantly something was wrong. Inexplicably, my throat began to tighten, my heart started to pound so hard I could hear it, all moisture left my mouth, and I began to shake. The worst of it was that these ominous symptoms were growing more intense with each passing second. When and how would it end? One part of me was engulfed in a struggle to continue singing—if the weak, quivering rendition of my song could be called singing. Another part of me, totally detached, was observing my predicament, curious whether I would indeed be able to remain standing.

By the middle of the third verse, I had come to the conclusion I probably would not be able to finish. I'd either faint, die, or go into some sort of ghastly fit. My mother's smile—I'd fixed my eyes on her —became frozen as she detected my trouble. Then, as I barely squeaked out the fourth verse, she began to sing it with me, right there from her seat in the third row. I don't know how she knew the words, but she did. And rather than utilizing her grand operatic voice, she sang at just about the loudness I'd ordinarily use were I not being strangled by a monster.

Together we got through the fifth, sixth, and seventh verses. Then I began to feel the surges of whatever had taken control of my mind and body begin to lessen. My voice grew a little stronger. By the twelfth verse, I could swallow and shortly thereafter I found myself singing alone again. I finished with all the gusto and enthusiasm I'd shown in the rehearsals.

The audience gave me a thunderous, standing ovation of the sort given an aerial acrobat who slips, almost falls several times, and finally accomplishes an extremely hazardous maneuver. I was drained of all strength but felt grateful I'd finished. Perhaps, I thought naively, no one but my mother had noticed the trouble I'd been in. Finally, I felt a sense of awe at the trouble itself. Where did this monster come from? Must I avoid similar circumstances for the rest of my life? Or might I learn how to be stronger, to summon more inner power? After all, one couldn't go through life with one's mother in the third row center!

The answers would come twenty-five years later at a speech I'd give to the Every Other Saturday Club in Rindge, New Hampshire. But that's getting ahead of my story . . .

On the day I turned eleven, March 16, 1944, my father presented me with one of his own .22-caliber rifles with a lever rather than a bolt action. "Practice with this," he said, "and when you switch to a lever-action .30-.30 deer rifle like mine, you'll be used to it." Three months later, after my first year at the Vanceboro public school was completed, we sat on the stone wall in front of the house on warm, calm evenings and shot at stumps jutting out of the water down in the duck pond while all the time he was teaching me gun safety rules.

It was the first time we had an activity we could do together. I'd never sailed with him (as even poor Drakie-boy had done before he became sick), I was scared to death of his confounded horses, photography was something he and Patsy did together along with their horseback riding, and I couldn't really partake in his interest in machinery and carpentry. So finally, with guns, we had something to share.

I was ready to use my new gun on real live things, too. Killing animals, whether on the farm or anywhere else around, was a routine part of a man's life in the north woods and I just assumed, now that I was properly armed, I'd soon be participating in that sort of thing. Sure, there were some nagging misgivings when I allowed myself to really think about the actual act of killing. I'd developed a certain sympathy even for bullfrogs. And it didn't help that my favorite book in the whole world was *Bambi*! However, I decided that with my father there to provide the strength, know-how, and approval, I could shoot whatever needed shooting just as well as anyone. All I needed was the opportunity.

It came along very soon. One morning in that same month of June, as I was having breakfast in our private wing of the main house, one of the farmhands ran in and said my father wanted me to hurry down to the chicken house and to bring my rifle along with some ammunition. When I got there, all out of breath, I saw a group of men, including my father, standing around a raccoon caught in a trap.

"Go ahead, Jud," said my father. (Only women called me Juddie.) "Go ahead and shoot it. We've saved it for you." I put a few shells into my gun and, while everyone stepped back, aimed at the raccoon standing on its hind legs, one of which was gripped in the jaw of the trap. When I fired, it was staring at me from a distance of less than two feet from the end of the barrel. The bullet grazed its face, ripping off the lower portion of its ear. It jerked and struggled against the trap for a few seconds, trickling blood, and then stood while I fired a second shot. This time I hit it in the side and the fleshy part of its hind leg. I was mangling it. As I was about to pull the trigger the third time, the desperate animal reached over with its paws and pushed the gun barrel to one side. So help me God. I fired into the ground.

At that point, my father gently took the gun from me and instantly, with one quick shot, accomplished what I'd been attempting. "Don't worry about it, Jud," he said as he heaved the animal's bloody body into the nearby undergrowth. "We'll just stick with stumps in the duck pond for a while."

We all dispersed in silence, my mind a whirl of shame, shock, and a little anger directed at myself. Finally, I consoled myself with the certainty I'd do better the next time. I didn't know then that my father would never again put me in similar circumstances.

The raccoon incident was an introduction into my father's rather brutal world at Sunrise Farm. To thrive in it one needed to be tough and resourceful, to have steady nerves, and to consider all but human life easily expendable. Admirable skills were woodsmanship, axemanship, marksmanship, canoemanship, and an intimate knowledge of every forest animal's habits and inclinations. My father, once a pampered Boston Brahmin, had become an expert in all these skills. By the summer of 1944 he could do anything in the woods that a licensed guide could do, and I believe he was prouder of that than he was of anything else he accomplished throughout the course of his life.

He didn't refer to the raccoon incident again until August. We were shooting at tin cans set up on rocks on the mainland shore opposite the northeast corner of Star Island. I was using my .22. My father was experimenting with several rifles and a number of pistols from his vast collection.

"I know you felt awful sorry for that raccoon," he said as we prepared to pack everything up and return for supper. I admitted I had.

"Well," he said seriously, looking me straight in the eye, "so did I."

Chapter 8

Expediency

He came into the world in the middle of the thicket, in one of those little, hidden forest glades which seem to be entirely open, but are really screened in on all sides.
—Opening sentence of *Bambi*, by Felix Salten (not to be confused with the Walt Disney version)

A T FIRST it sounded like a bark. It was a sharp, abrupt, guttural noise. My father, walking some ten yards ahead of me, his .30-caliber rifle crooked over the elbow of his right arm, stopped. After I walked quietly up to him, we both listened, standing as still as statues. An afternoon breeze was rustling the leaves overhead and there was a barely perceptible sound of running water somewhere in the cedar swamp off to the right of the faint trail we were following, but otherwise we heard nothing for perhaps another minute. Then, from somewhere deep in the swamp, the sound again—a little closer than it had been before. It was almost as if we were hearing Sid, our head guide, chopping wood back at camp up on the ridge a mile farther along our trail. But Sid wouldn't be making one chop every two or three minutes.

"I think it's a bull moose!" my father whispered. I had never imagined a moose could bark. My father began walking again, more slowly than before, and now he held his rifle in both hands in front of his chest. I followed close behind, as I had been doing since dawn, with the red plaid coat in which I'd begun the frigid morning now tied around my waist. Besides the new hunting knife on my belt—

126

the short-bladed variety suitable for "slicing a deer open without rupturing his stomach," as my father always said in arguing against long hunting knives—I was unarmed on this, my first day of deer hunting with my father. It was fall, 1944. Since the raccoon incident the previous June, nothing had been said about my carrying any sort of gun on hunting trips and I didn't bring the matter up. I much preferred the idea of being a sort of detached witness rather than a participant, and during all the Vanceboro years I hunted with my father, that's the way it would be.

Up to the time of the odd bark-like sounds, the day had been uneventful—but I was to learn in a matter of minutes that hunting with my father was hardly ever uneventful.

We had followed a deer trail near camp during the morning, my father stopping every few minutes to share something from his storehouse of forest information, all taught to him by old Sid. Over the years, Sid had become like a father to him, a father in the forest world he loved, as opposed to Grandpop, who represented the Boston society he'd left behind. Ironically old Sid, with his white mustache and bald head, looked much like Grandpop except for being slightly shorter and more solidly built. I never saw Sid wearing a coat and tie, however, and I never saw Grandpop without them.

Just as it was getting light, my father had pointed out to me the difference between doe and buck tracks, based on size and the fact that bucks were often too lazy to pick up their feet, leaving scuff marks in front of each hoof imprint. He showed me, too, how to tell which direction the deer was traveling, how fast, and how long ago it had passed by.

I was familiar with much of that sort of thing but from rather another point of view. By 1944 my mother and various nurses had read *Bambi* to me more than two dozen times—the original, somewhat gruesome *Bambi*, that is, written by Felix Salten and translated from the German by Whittaker Chambers. It bore little resemblance to the later Walt Disney version, which I considered not only sappy but a downright sacrilege! For my summertime evening readings on the huge pillowed sofa in the main cabin on Star Island, by the light of two Aladdin lamps, I particularly enjoyed *Winnie-the-Pooh* and *Grimm's Fairy Tales*, but it was *Bambi* I wanted read over and over again. I'd even memorized passages.

Suddenly he asked, "Who made this trail?"
"We," his mother answered.
Bambi was astonished. "We? You and I?"
The mother said, "We, we . . . we deer."
. . . They walked on. Bambi was in high spirits and felt like leaping off the path, but he stayed close to his mother.

By midmorning my father had told me how to seek mossy rocks on which to step and how to avoid cracking sticks underfoot and snapping back branches as we walked. He had shown me old deer droppings and fresh deer droppings and the difference between them. He'd demonstrated the manner in which to pick my way through dry leaves so as to make as little rustling sound as possible.

When a foot stirs them they rustle. Then someone is coming. O, how kind last year's dead leaves are! They do their duty so well and are so alert and watchful.

At noon we had built a fire next to a beaver pond, toasted our bacon and peanut butter sandwiches, and boiled tea in a small pot my father carried in his knapsack. The tea was as black as the pot, bitter, and would be judged unfit to drink anywhere but in the woods. There, it was delicious. On our fishing trips in Canada ten years later, long after Sunrise Farm was gone, my father began pouring brandy into his cups of lunchtime tea. "Tea royale," he called it. It followed many cups of "coffee royale" earlier in the morning. In 1944, however, he was still living the life he'd reminisce about someday, and his tea was pure.

After lunch, while we had sipped our tea and relaxed, my father had removed his boot and inspected the ugly red scar that ran down along the top of his left foot. Two months earlier on Star Island, he'd driven an axe through it. Patsy, Gertrude (our nurse that summer), and I were having lunch in the kitchen of the main cabin when Sid had come in for bandages and a bottle of whiskey while my father sat outside on the kitchen steps, holding his foot together.

"Is he hurt?" Gertrude had asked in alarm. Sid had said nothing. He was apt to be uncommunicative or, at best, brusque with Gertrude. While my mother and women guests were acceptable to him on Star Island, he was of the opinion women employees had no place there. They were simply in the way and infringed upon the guides' territory.

"Is Roger hurt?" Gertrude had repeated, somewhat frantically, as Sid went out the door with the bandages and whiskey. "Well," Sid finally had answered as he knelt down and began pouring all the whiskey into the open wound, "it ain't done him much good."

After he'd emptied the whiskey bottle, he bound the foot tightly with the bandages and told my father to leave it alone for the next two weeks.

There had been some debate between my mother and father as to the wisdom of Sid's medical advice. In the past, some of his "cures" had seemed all right although none had been for anything as serious as a foot practically split in two. We'd put mud on bee stings, for instance, salt pork on small cuts, a mashed-up potato and/or butter on burns, black tea on sore eyes, and wet chewing tobacco straight from Sid's mouth on banged fingers and stubbed toes. But my mother drew the line when he wanted to swab my sore throat with a feather soaked in kerosene. Also, none of us, not even my father, shared his enthusiasm for bear grease (boiled-down fat from the black bears he and the other guides trapped over on the mainland) as a cure for arthritic pains, a fly dope, a hair conditioner, and, when applied to the soles of the feet, a head cold preventative.

In spite of my mother's misgivings, however, my father had left his foot alone for the two weeks Sid prescribed. When he'd finally removed the bandages, the wound was closed and healing nicely. Now, two months later, as we slowly walked along the trail that skirted the cedar swamp on the afternoon of my first deer hunt, I noticed he hardly favored it.

The short barking sound stopped us once again. It was definitely closer. My father peered through the thick branches of the cedar trees, moving his head up and down to gain different vistas. "I can't see anything, but I think it's a bull moose all right," he whispered again. "He must be following along in there parallel with us. Thinks we're a cow." My heart was pounding at full speed.

"Are we gonna shoot him?" I asked, also whispering. I wanted him to say yes, and yet I also hoped he'd say he wouldn't.

"Moose aren't legal this year," he hissed back, and part of me deflated. "But maybe I won't be able to stop myself," he said, turning to me with a mischievous grin, and my heart went back into overdrive. "This gun hasn't the wallop we'll need, though," he muttered, peering back into the swamp. "Wish I had my thirty-ought-six."

Although he seemed to be debating whether or not to shoot if given the opportunity, I noticed he was breathing rapidly, even shaking slightly. Somewhere deep within himself, the decision had been made.

Along with the grunt-like barking, we now began to hear sticks cracking. Though still invisible behind the thick growth, something big was moving in close to us, maybe only fifty yards away.

Suddenly all noise stopped. "He's caught our scent," my father breathed, moving in slow motion a few yards up the trail to gain another vantage point. He was holding his gun in a half-ready position, pointing it toward the place we'd last heard sounds.

Then they stood still, snuffing the air.
It was He.
A heavy wave of scent blew past. There was nothing they could do. The scent filled their nostrils, it numbed their senses and made their hearts stop beating.

I remained rooted where I'd been standing, not following my father, who finally stopped twenty yards away. He seemed to be looking into the wrong area. I remembered the last sounds coming from much farther to the right. I stared through the green foliage and dead branches into what I considered to be the correct direction. Then, slowly but surely, I came to the astounding realization that two of the dead branches were, in fact, two huge antlers and a certain black area on a tree trunk was the giant head of a bull moose.

It took several seconds, maybe half a minute, before my mind digested what my eyes were seeing. Then I silently waved my arms to attract my father's attention. When I caught his eye, I eagerly pointed with greatly exaggerated motions. The moose, not moving, stared back at me.

"Let me go," said the fox, beginning to speak. "Let me go." He spoke softly and beseechingly. He was quite weak and despondent.
"No! No! No!" the dog howled.
"... Traitor!" hissed the fox. "Nobody is a traitor but you, only you."
The dog called in a deep loud voice, "Here! Here! He's here!"

My father looked to the right where I was pointing, instantly raised his rifle a few inches higher, and squinted along its open sights. I heard the distinct click of the safety going off, activated by his right thumb. It was always, in my father's way of shooting, the last sound before the roar.

The explosion of a high-caliber rifle in the forest, after many hours of silence and soft natural sounds, is shocking and nerve-shattering. I jumped, felt a momentary pressure in my ears, and as the echoes of the explosion bounced across the surrounding ridges, looked once again through the trees to where the moose had been standing. He was no longer there.

Bambi's mother said, "He throws His hand at you. . . ." "Is that so?" asked old Nettla. "What is it that bangs so terribly then?"

"That's when He tears His hand off," Bambi's mother explained. "Then the fire flashes and the thunder cracks. He's all fire inside."

My father, now calm, walked back to where I was and, in a normal, out-loud voice, said, "We'll wait a few minutes before we go in there." We both sat down on an old log. After ejecting the empty shell, which automatically inserted another into the chamber, he clicked on the safety, leaned the gun up against a tree within reach, and lit up a Lucky Strike with a wooden match he fired with his thumbnail. I can see him so clearly in my mind today as he was at that moment. With his well-worn ten-gallon western hat, stained with a dark area of sweat above the band, tipped back on his head, he could have been the perfect Marlboro Man of thirty years later. "He had that quiet, rugged look," John MacDuffie, his Harvard classmate, recalled when I visited him in the spring of 1985. "He was a little stooped but a big man—and somehow didn't quite seem like the sophisticated city fellow, like the rest of us."

To me he seemed more like a sophisticated combination of cowboy and Maine woodsman with a dash of a romantic John Wayne movie character thrown in merely to keep cold, hard, everyday reality at bay. As I reflect today on what John MacDuffie and others of his surviving Boston friends refer to as his "tragic life," I'm convinced my father, like many others, was truly happy only when he was able to live the storybook image he had of himself. At that moment, deep in the forest next to a cedar swamp, suspended between the thunderous rifle shot and the discovery of its results, casually smoking a cigarette, his little blond-headed son tensely watching his every move with worshipful eyes, the storybook image was strong and clear. Ultimately, his tragedy was that the story would end long before he was through acting it out.

"Do you think you hit him?" I asked.

"Yes, I think so," he replied. I was to learn during the many hunts we'd have in the years ahead that if my father decided to fire his rifle, he rarely missed.

I wanted desperately to run into the swamp and discover what there was to discover, but my father continued to puff slowly on his cigarette. It was a hunting ritual to which I eventually became accustomed—even thankful for—although ironically the only time it didn't work was on this, my very first hunt. During subsequent hunts, I never saw a dying deer. Every one was invariably a lifeless hunk of venison. Death throes most often require about the same amount of time it takes to smoke a Lucky Strike.

Gobo lay with his bloody entrails oozing from his torn flank. He lifted his head with a feeble twisting motion. "Marena," he said, with an effort. "Marena . . ."

"He's coming," she whispered frantically. "Gobo, He's coming!"

. . . Gobo lifted his head again feebly with a writhing motion, beat convulsively with his hoofs and then lay still.

. . . Then they heard Gobo's wailing death shriek.

His cigarette smoked and stamped out, my father finally rose and started working his way through the dense undergrowth of the swamp, motioning me to stay well behind. Neither of us attempted to walk quietly anymore.

The sight we saw upon reaching a grassy mound in an open area surrounded by mud and water is an eternal photograph in my mind. The bull moose, a gigantic animal that appeared larger to me than even a workhorse, was lying down with its head up. As we approached, it began swinging its heavy antlers back and forth in an attempt to gain sufficient momentum to propel itself back onto its feet. From its neck gushed an inch-thick torrent of blood as if from a bathtub faucet.

"Stay there, Jud," my father called over his shoulder, and he immediately walked up behind the moose's head, placed the barrel of his rifle within a few inches of the area behind its ear, clicked off the safety, and fired.

The next half minute was chaotic. Upon receiving the bullet, the moose lunged to its feet so fast my father was forced to jump back. Quickly he raised the gun, pumped the lever, and fired again. The moose turned and began to shuffle away, heading toward the spot where I was standing. A fourth explosion rumbled through the forest.

Now only a dozen yards from me, blood from the initial wound gushing onto the surrounding bushes, the moose stopped and looked back at my father, who blasted away once more, hitting it with a .30-caliber slug for the fifth and final time. (We later found bullet remains flattened out against the skull.) Even then, it took two or three more steps in my direction before almost throwing itself sideways onto the ground. There, finally, it lay still. I stared down at it. I was certain it would jump up again. My father walked over and put his arm on my shoulder. "It's OK, he's gone," he said, but I wasn't at all sure. So he grabbed one of the antlers and pulled the head toward me. Then I could see that the eyes were not the eyes that had stared into mine through the cedar branches. They were a dull, milky white, with the empty look of death.

The poacher's shirt, open at the neck, was pierced where a wound gaped like a small red mouth. Blood was oozing out slowly. Blood was drying on His hair and around His nose.

"We can stand right beside Him," the old stag began softly, "and it isn't dangerous."

Bambi looked down at the prostrate form whose limbs and skin seemed so mysterious and terrible to him. He gazed at the dead eyes that stared up sightlessly at him. Bambi couldn't understand it all.

My father's log hunting cabin, built for him in 1930 by Sid and his four sons, all of whom now worked for Sunrise Farm, was situated atop open rocky ledges sprinkled with blueberry bushes and small pines growing between the cracks. From the front porch, the ledges sloped down for several hundred yards to Eastbrook Lake, a spring-fed body of crystal-clear water three miles round, located a mile walk in from the west mainland shore opposite Star Island.

Eastbrook was truly an isolated lake (and still is today). With one exception, during the entire span of twenty autumns he and his Boston friends hunted there, my father never encountered anyone he didn't know in the woods around Eastbrook. The exception was a New York man who'd been staying at the nearest sporting camp, more than fifteen miles away on Spednic Lake. He'd been lost for three days and nights. My father spotted him staggering through the blow-down area near the outlet at the southern end of Eastbrook, and instead of immediately calling to him, he leaned against a tree until the man had walked up to within a few feet of him. Then, in a soft but distinct voice, my father said "Hi!" The man collapsed.

As we came up the trail to the cabin overlooking Eastbrook, after leaving the dead moose lying in the swamp, we saw old Sid standing out on the porch along with one of my father's best hunting buddies from Boston, "Uncle" (to Patsy and me) Charley, a textile company executive. Obviously they'd both heard all the shooting, the swamp being only a mile down from the cabin. There were additional Boston men in our hunting party that year, but they hadn't returned to camp.

"Sounded like you ran into the German army down there," Uncle Charley said as we approached. Though a city man, Uncle Charley was a fine woodsman and enthusiastic hunter. However, he had never managed to shoot a deer. The year before, my father had learned the reason. He'd been with him up north of Eastbrook Lake when they sighted one of the largest bucks either had seen. My father had whispered to Uncle Charley to go ahead and shoot—he wanted to be generous to his friend, but also it would give him a chance to observe why Uncle Charley had never brought a deer back to camp. Perhaps he was jerking the trigger too hard or not cradling his rifle solidly against his shoulder and jaw.

"Take it easy; take your time, Charley," my father had said. Uncle Charley, his face chalk-white and his teeth chattering so loudly my father later told me he could hear them, had sighted unsteadily down his rifle barrel toward the buck who, after maybe thirty seconds of looking in their direction, began to casually amble back into a thick stand of poplars. "Shoot!" my father had said. "Shoot now!" Uncle Charley, to my father's amazement, had transferred his hand from the trigger to the rifle bolt, pulled it back, and silently ejected the unfired shell from the chamber. Within a few seconds, with a rapid-fire motion of his hand and arm, he'd ejected all of the shells in the rifle, one after another. His rifle barrel remained pointing in the general direction of the disappearing buck. When every unfired shell was lying on the ground at their feet, Uncle Charley had lowered his rifle, turned to my father, and in a strained whisper said, "Do you think I hit him?"

The mystery was solved. Buck fever. My father never had the heart to tell him about it. It wouldn't have helped.

As we stepped onto the porch and greeted Sid and Uncle Charley, my father must have winked because Sid was grinning widely. "Hedgehog?" he asked, his eyes almost bursting with laughter.

"Biggest ol' hedgehog you ever saw," my father answered, confirming Sid's suspicions. "Hedgehog" was the code word used to indicate any hunting activity in conflict with existing game laws. Over the next days and even months, our moose was never referred to as anything but a "hedgehog."

There was an unwritten and rarely discussed code of ethics strictly adhered to at my father's hunting camp, but it had nothing to do with the law. Poaching animals out of season, like the moose, for instance, was fine. Better than fine. The illegality of it seemed to add an extra element of fun and excitement. And yet, while both the United States and Canadian governments encouraged the shooting of *real* hedgehogs (i.e., porcupines) by paying a bounty on them, the hedgehog was the only animal in the forest that my father and his friends would *not* shoot. Sid maintained it could be a source of food that a lost hunter could easily catch and kill with a stick.

Hunting on Sundays was illegal in both the United States and Canada, but under the special "private" code, one could track and kill a deer on Sunday if it had been wounded on Saturday. (Somehow this personal interpretation of the law evolved into the fact that *every* deer killed on Sunday was said to have been wounded the day before! Sunday hunting was always referred to as "tracking.")

It was legal in both countries to carry semiautomatic rifles, but the code didn't allow it. Single-shot only, no shotguns, and no loaded guns within one hundred yards of camp.

Jacking deer at night (hypnotizing them with the beams from flashlights strapped to the head of the hunter, who then aimed his gun for a spot between their blazing, hot-coal-like eyes) was a serious, if incredibly exciting, crime under the law but not at Eastbrook.

There it was as serious as, say, drinking a little too much whiskey in the evening. On the other hand, leaving good meat to rot in the woods under any circumstances whatever was unthinkable under the code. Hunters who did so—and we only *heard* about them— were considered on about the same level as, say, child-molesters.

Both the law and the code agreed about salt licks: you couldn't shoot deer at them. My father set out a number of salt licks during the summers as bait to attract deer for his nighttime photography. In the old photo albums I now have in my possession, there are a few dramatic photos of live deer at the salt licks (and to be sure, other photos of many *dead* deer hanging up by their hoofs). Most of these salt-lick shots, it seems, were of my father only, with no deer, or of Sid only. There are several of just my father and Sid. In each photo they have startled expressions on their faces. The black of night is behind them and they seem to be forever frozen by the flash in the act of stepping over the strings stretching from trees to the camera.

Our moose was gutted out by Sid and my father that very evening, with me holding two flashlights. Over the next week the meat was cut up and carried in burlap bags to the icehouse on Star Island, where it hung until the following winter, when it went to the lumber camps under the guise of "beef."

My father saved the antlers. Somehow they survived the breakup of Sunrise Farm and all the subsequent moves, and today they hang high under the eaves of my A-frame on an island on Lake Winnipesaukee, New Hampshire. I look at them often. They represent a tangible link to my father and our closeness in the woods around Eastbrook Lake almost forty-five years ago.

We shot many deer together (but never another moose) after the first hunt in '44—two or three every year. I remained his "eyes and ears," as he told everyone. There was never any more blood and gore, though. As we approached each deer, after he'd fired at it and smoked his cigarette, it was invariably dead.

I was so sure of "our" hunting prowess and my father's workmanship that I developed a little private ritual that I'd perform every morning before we'd leave the cabin for a day's hunting. In the dim light of early dawn, I'd stand on the porch and look out over the dark hills surrounding Eastbrook Lake and concentrate on the specific deer, out there somewhere, that was going to die that day. Was it sleeping at that moment? Or perhaps taking an early morning drink from a forest stream from which my father and I might also drink in several hours? During this private time, my thoughts were more reflective than sad, more philosophical than troubled. But I felt I owed that deer those few moments of sympathy and respect. Then, when the time to do so arrived later in the day, as it inevitably did, I'd be free to function as my father's "eyes and ears." In my mind, the deer had been dead since early morning.

I wish my father could see that I have those moose antlers hanging up in my own lakeside cabin today. He'd be pleased to know I wanted them there. It would tell him that I'm glad he and I shot that "ol' hedgehog" back in the fall of '44. He would know it hadn't turned out to be a "painful memory" for me, as he'd confided to my mother he thought it might.

It would also tell him that if he hadn't decided to up and leave so suddenly, we could have continued to hunt together after I'd grown up.

Perhaps I'd even have carried a gun . . .

"Don't follow me any further, Bambi," he began with a calm voice, "my time is up. Now I have to look for a resting place."

Bambi tried to speak.

"Don't," said the old stag cutting him short, "don't. In the hour which I am approaching we are all alone. Good-bye, my son. I loved you dearly."

Chapter 9

Prudence

WE ALL figured your father's money was a bottomless well," Paul Susee, my father's former Sunrise Farm office manager, told me during a telephone conversation we had in January 1986. After the demise of the operation in 1947, Paul and his wife, Viola, moved to Sherman Mills, but today they're retired and living back in Vanceboro. Yes, he and others in the office, including my father, were aware of the massive losses every year, but, he said, "there always seemed to be enough to carry on," adding that since my father wasn't concerned, "we didn't feel *we* needed to be."

"Next year," my father always told Paul, "next year things will turn around." Undoubtedly he was saying the same to Grandpop. But while production increased dramatically year after year, particularly in the lumbering operation, so did the red ink.

It was almost eerie for me to hear Paul's voice, a voice I hadn't heard in forty years, saying what I thought only those of us in the family knew. For instance: "Your father could sense when any of us had a problem, and he always advised doing nothing about it until tomorrow. He'd say the problem would still be there tomorrow, but that it would be much smaller and easier to deal with."

How familiar that sounded! In my early years I thought it to be good advice, too. However, when I began working for my mother's brother, Robb Sagendorph, at *Yankee* magazine in 1958, I discovered that Uncle Robb lived by exactly the opposite philosophy.

"Take care of tomorrow," Uncle Robb often said, quoting Robert B. Thomas in the 1937 *Old Farmer's Almanac*, "because it is here today." Ironically, these two men, each so influential in my life, each so different from the other, each eventually making his own decision to die, might well have tempered their own outlooks with a little of the other's philosophy.

There's no question, however, that with tomorrow of no concern, my father's philosophy was working for him during the Vanceboro years. He was sublimely happy—a state of mind Uncle Robb, for instance, never approached.

According to Paul, Viola, and others, my father's working day began with no more than one hour in the office, after which time he was inevitably on Ranger, riding up to the laboratory to consult with Dickie or to the lumber mills in town or perhaps out to one of the back pastures where the beef cattle grazed. There he'd combine his Harvard background with his cowboy dreams. After hitting a polo ball around for a while, he'd practice roping the steers.

My father enjoyed honing his cowboy skills, although there was precious little opportunity to apply them in conducting his business. An exception occurred when a pig escaped from its pen one day and was running around the barnyard, easily evading the gang of farmhands chasing it. Wearing his sweaty ten-gallon hat, chaps, and spurs, my father cantered in on Ranger and roped it. It was one of his finer moments.

Often he carried a pistol. He'd use it to blast away at woodchucks, raccoons, or any other bothersome varmints he might encounter on his daily rounds. Occasionally everyone would jump out of their shoes at the roar of a pistol or even a rifle inside the barn! "One less rat," he'd say, grinning as he came out from one of the supply rooms behind the milking area, and Patsy and I would hope it wasn't one less *cat*.

His haphazard shooting of animals around the farm came to an abrupt and permanent halt the evening he shot Timmie. Timmie was his own dog, an expensive English setter. Fully trained for bird hunting, though my father rarely used him that way, he was as devoted to my father as my father was to him. His favorite place was beside Ranger, loyally loping along, his long tongue hanging out.

On the evening Timmie breathed his last, he was in a chicken-wire pen behind the barn. He'd been confined there for several days so he wouldn't "bother" my dog, Sunny, who was in heat. (One didn't spay female dogs in those days.) Naturally, lots of dogs had been hanging around the house hoping for a moment with Sunny. One in particular, a scroungy, white, husky-like town dog who'd carried away chickens on occasion, particularly irritated my father. So after supper, muttering that he was going to "eliminate that goddamned nuisance once and for all," he walked down to the barn, saddled up Ranger, and with a rifle across his saddle, took off after the skittish little white guy, who began hightailing it toward town.

Perhaps Timmie's mission in life was to make my father realize he ought to be less casual about shooting off firearms around the farm. Perhaps Timmie saved someone's life. At any rate, fate dictated that Timmie dig himself free from his pen, chase after Ranger, and place himself exactly between my father and the fleeing town dog at the instant my father, having dismounted and aimed his rifle from a kneeling position, pulled the trigger. Timmie rubbed in the lesson, too. Instead of dropping dead right away, he ran toward my father, mortally wounded, yelping so loudly we all could hear him from the house. Then he died at my father's feet.

My father mourned Timmie for weeks, as did Patsy and I. It was our first family "death."

"If you gotta shoot a dog, guess the best thing is to shoot your own," I heard old Frankie remark several days later, but otherwise the incident was never discussed by anyone within earshot of the family. As to the scroungy town dog, well, after Timmie's demise he hung around the farm more than ever and stole chickens when he felt like it.

Like many of the men in Vanceboro, my father was both cruel and kind to his animals. The cruelty would emerge when, for instance, Harry, the frisky English riding horse, would put the bit between his teeth and run off with a guest, most often with one of the visiting anthroposophists. This would infuriate my father. "Best way to slow down a runaway horse is to bet on him," old Frankie would say interminably, always pleased with himself. There was no humor in it for my father. His remedy was to "beat on him." When Harry was recovered, usually with the shaken anthroposophist still hanging on for dear life, my father would whip the horse with a leather strap for several minutes. I hated to see it. So did Patsy, although she usually assured me it was "for Harry's own good."

After the beating, my father would hop into the saddle himself, not bothering even to adjust the stirrups to his own long legs, and run Harry at full speed around the rough pastures behind the barn until the poor animal was within an inch of collapsing. Presumably Harry would then make a mental note not to run off with an anthroposophist ever again. (If so, a horse's "mental note," I observed, lasts for a few hours at best.)

On the other hand, my father wouldn't allow Frankie to buckle a painful martingale on Harry. A martingale, a leather strap fastened to a horse's girth, passed between his forelegs, and fastened to the bit, is intended to hold down his head, preventing him from rearing. "I'd never use a martingale on a hoss," my father would say (pronouncing "horse" in a way that rhymed with "boss"). "It's a cruel piece of equipment."

The slaughtering of farm animals was something in which my father took a personal, "hands-on" interest. He'd studied the varying techniques during his years of deer hunting with Sid, and he approached the subject with both a scholarly, serious attitude and a certain dramatic flair. His pet criticism of the standard slaughtering techniques of the day was that the actual killing of the animal was "cruel beyond necessity," a seemingly kindhearted opinion that, in truth, reflected less his love of animals than it did his love of tasty, juicy, tender beefsteak! This I learned recently from reading an article he wrote in 1945 for an anthroposophical publication called *Bio-Dynamics,* published quarterly by the Threefold Foundation in Spring Valley, New York.

He called his article "Slaughtering Home-Raised Beef," and in it he strongly advised against the common killing technique of whacking a cow in the head with a sledgehammer. "Nine times out of ten this sledgehammer procedure does not go well," he wrote. (From the cow's point of view, the odds are undoubtedly not as good.) "Either the farmer did not hit her hard enough or she turned her head at the last moment and he made a near miss. Nellie is not knocked out but is hit hard somewhere around the head; it hurts and she resents it. She breaks away and, not wanting another blow, does not intend to be caught. So the whole family joins in the chase and finally she is cornered, caught and the whole process repeated. The result is a badly heated and excited animal. If Nellie's meat was good at the start it isn't by now." He goes on to explain how an "excited" animal's meat will be stringy and tough.

My father much preferred the Jewish method of killing an animal. Cut the throat, he advised, while it's still alive. "I don't know the religious significance," he wrote, "but I do know it produces the best meat. And, if done expertly and surely, it is instantaneous and humane. Also, it is easy."

I watched him perform a slaughter just once. The night before, he'd told us all at the supper table that Ferdinand, our docile old bull —thus named because he was so gentle we could reach through the bars of his pen and scratch him behind the ears—was scheduled for the ceremony the following morning. Patsy and I pleaded for Ferdinand's life, but to no avail, of course. The next morning, I'll have to confess that our sadness at the prospect of Ferdinand's passing on was fully replaced by our excitement at the prospect of seeing him go.

Ferdinand was led into the slaughterhouse next to the barn by the ring in his nose, augmented, as a precaution, by ropes extending from every part of him held by more than a half dozen farmhands. He seemed unconcerned. He probably could have been called in. I was certain he knew and responded to his name.

My father, standing in a corner at the far end of the shed-like room, was sharpening a very long knife. His article in *Bio-Dynamics* describes exactly what happened next:

"Place a short length of rope in a slip knot around both hind legs above the gambrels. Slip the other end over the hook on the block and tackle and motion the tractor driver to hoist away, smoothly but quickly—no jerks. If all this is done quietly and smoothly, the animal is perfectly calm and cool and does not sense anything unusual until the slip knot tightens. Then it is only a matter of a second before the hind feet are off the ground and she [in this case, he] is helpless."

It was a shock to see huge old Ferdinand's hind legs suddenly lift into the air. It shocked old Ferdinand, too. He bellowed. It was his last bellow, but for sure it was one of his very best and loudest. The tractor continued to move forward out the open double doors, hoisting him ever upward until just his head and neck were lying flat on the dirt and sawdust floor. Then my father, knife in hand, was on him like lightning.

"Brace your knee behind the animal's neck, grasp him under the jaw and pull his head back and around so that the under curve of the neck makes a long, taut arc. Then draw the knife towards you over the top of this arc; just one long, sure stroke with plenty of pressure. In a fraction of a second the throat is cut completely through the jugular, and because of your position behind the neck, the blood spurts away from you. I have done it many times without getting a drop of blood on my hands or clothing."

I couldn't see everything perfectly from my position outside the doors because so many people were in front of me, but in the next instant my father was standing up, backing away. He was covered with blood. Ferdinand must have violated the procedural rules by somehow moving his head and neck at the critical instant. Didn't do *him* any good, but it did mess up my father's riding britches. The tractor hoisted him higher so that his head was finally swinging free and we watched his nerves make his body twitch and thrash while the blood flowed from his open jugular onto the sawdust.

An hour later, Patsy and I rode on the stone boat (a wooden platform with rough runners but no wheels, dragged by a team of horses) that carried Ferdinand's guts a mile up the dirt road leading to Alice May Point. Jim Hansen went along with us to help bury the stuff somewhere in the woods. "Ain't a very deep grave, Frankie," Jim said pointedly, smiling, as the two of them, along with a little tentative assistance from Patsy and me, heaved the massive mound of guts, already swarming with flies, into the shallow pit they'd hastily scraped out. Frankie occasionally moonlighted as a grave digger in Vanceboro and it was well known he never dug down any deeper than what he considered to be the minimum depth necessary.

"I doubt you'll see him climbin' out of there," said Frankie. It was his standard retort to any criticism on the subject of his grave digging.

I returned alone to the slaughter shed after supper that evening and looked at Ferdinand, *sans* his innards, hanging there in the darkness. I couldn't erase his last bellow from my mind. It was, I thought, as if he suddenly realized, too late, that a docile bull was no better off than an ordinary mean one. But I felt pride in my father. He'd stepped in like a daring matador for the most crucial, dangerous seconds and then he'd ridden off somewhere on Ranger while the others did the messy work. To be sure, his performance hadn't been so perfect that he emerged without getting a drop of blood on his hands or clothing. Yet even that slight failure had a certain amount of theater about it.

A subsequent follow-up article in *Bio-Dynamics* indicated he had changed his opinion about the Jewish method in the case of "very large steers and bulls." For them, he advised after Ferdinand, "just before you slip the rope around his hind legs and while he is still comparatively quiet, shoot him, using a high-powered rifle from ten inches behind the ear, and then immediately string him up and cut his throat as described previously."

My father had always thought a lot of his riding britches.

As time went on, my father began to begrudge having to spend the first hour of the working day in his office without Ranger. So, up on the hill above the main house, overlooking the lake, he had his men build a brand-new office with a stall so close to his desk that he could pat Ranger without getting up from his chair.

He and Ranger used it for only a week. Then, just before dawn one night, it burned to the ground. Awakened by all the commotion, I looked out my bedroom window to see a bright orange glow in the sky over the hill above our house as flames consumed the structure within an hour.

There was little question it had been deliberately set. Eventually it was determined, though never proved legally, that the arsonist was a former Sunrise Farm employee who'd been caught stealing an outboard motor from my father's boathouse, had been sent to jail in Bangor for a few months, and, obviously, had returned with a grudge. According to Russell, the foreman, he was even heard to boast about setting the fire, saying he did it because Sunrise Farm was "full of German spies," and that my father himself was a German spy. Burning down the office, he implied, was his patriotic duty.

Irrational, exasperating "German spy" suspicions were always floating around the outer fringes of my mother and father's life in Vanceboro throughout the war years. (And, I'm sorry to say, even beyond.) The presence of the German-speaking anthroposophists and the fact of my mother's maiden name, Sagendorph, provided just enough "proof" as far as members of a tiny minority were concerned. It was no coincidence that these few people who supported the rumors were, like the arsonist, invariably people who'd been fired from Sunrise Farm or had some petty reason to resent my father and/or the organization.

There was nothing my father could do. One didn't exactly go around telling people one was *not* a German spy! I'm thankful he didn't read a book published in the late 1960s by the University of Maine featuring "oral histories" of early Maine lumbering years. While reading it as a candidate for our book review section in *Yankee*, I noted a mention of the Sunrise Farm lumbering operations, and then there was a passing reference to "the rumor, never proved" about my father being a German spy! I was (and am) outraged and, unlike my father, even tried to do something about it. I wrote the professor whose byline was on the cover of the book and explained how these spy suspicions originated. I even succumbed to my emotions and harangued about how my father was "as patriotic an American as any man who ever lived." Probably I protested too much. I never received a reply. It's not easy to accept the lessons therein: (1) denying a rumor strengthens it; and (2) once a rumor, *always* a rumor.

I did see plenty of German soldiers in Vanceboro and, on one scary occasion, actually came face to face with a *real* German spy! The soldiers were on the prisoner-of-war trains that rumbled through town. My three best school buddies, Aubrey, Ralphie, and Tadpole, and I would wave to them, and if they didn't wave back, we'd throw rocks at them.

Sometimes, usually at Tadpole's urging, we'd pile debris on the tracks in a wooded area across the St. Croix River when we knew a prisoner-of-war train was at the depot in town. Then we'd crouch in the bushes, waiting for the train to come along, hoping our junk would derail it and it would crash down the steep bank on the other side of the tracks, killing lots of Germans. (Thank goodness none of them ever did derail.) The worst that happened was Tadpole putting his tongue on the tracks, where it became firmly stuck. When we heard the train coming, we pulled a screaming Tadpole to safety, but a thick layer of his tongue was run over by a German prisoner-of-war train—something he perhaps tells his grandchildren about today.

My first and only view of a real German spy was outside the kitchen door of the main house one hot September afternoon in 1944. He was sitting in the front passenger seat of my father's

Plymouth sedan. Russell Nichols was in the back seat behind him, holding an axe over his head.

A serious forest fire had been raging on my father's land west of Vanceboro for the previous three days. The sky was dark with smoke, and when we climbed up onto the highest part of the roof of our house that particular day, we could see flames here and there on the horizon. Although none of them was ever as destructive as the fire that wiped out nine Maine towns in 1947, forest fires were a frightening part of almost every fall in Vanceboro. This one, because of its position and the wind direction, was threatening the entire town, including the lumber mills and the farm.

It had been set by the German spy sitting in my father's car. A couple hours before, firefighters, including Russell, had found him walking alone along a dirt road deep in the woods only a mile from where the forest was burning. Because there was, as they said later, something about him that didn't seem "right," they stopped their car and searched him. On his person they found a rough map of my father's timberland with several crosses penciled in, one of which marked the precise location where the fire had, in fact, begun. With the wind coming from the southwest, it was the perfect spot to do the most damage.

Holding an axe over his head, they drove back to the farm, picking up my father at another location along the way, and now my father was in the house telephoning the Vanceboro sheriff and the Bangor police. The sheriff, as usual, couldn't be reached, but the police in Bangor informed my father that the F.B.I. had solicited their help in attempting to locate a German agent they'd followed all the way from Florida to Bangor and as far as Lincoln, where they'd lost him two weeks before. This, everyone was certain, was the man.

"We got us a damn Nazi!" Russell yelled out the car window as he tightly held the axe. He was exuberant. Tadpole, Aubrey, Ralphie, and I came down from the roof, joined the crowd gathering around the car, and stared at the man sitting there in the front seat. He looked to be in his thirties, had a week's growth of beard, wore ordinary farm clothes but no hat, and was surprisingly dark-complected, with jet black hair cut short. (I'd thought all Nazis were blond.) He stared back at us all with a steady, rather unnerving gaze, calm as could be. He seemed oblivious of Russell's quivering axe.

Then, as my father and others came out of the kitchen and began piling into the car to take him down to the one-room jail in the Vanceboro railroad station to await the arrival of Federal agents, he winked. Looking directly at us four little boys and with a barely discernible smile, he actually winked!

I turned away for a moment. I didn't know how to react. Tadpole knew. He came to attention and gave a snappy "Heil Hitler" salute! Tadpole was always the daring one.

That evening, the wind shifted over to the northeast, bringing showers, and the hundreds of firefighters, including many from Canada, were able to save the town, the farm, and the mills. Nonetheless, about a third of my father's timberland was destroyed, along with one of the two lumber camps scheduled to be operating that winter.

Several months later, my father received a letter from the F.B.I. confirming the man's identity as a German agent and thanking him and the Sunrise Farm organization for "splendid and patriotic cooperation."

"Guess it takes a German spy to catch a German spy," my father remarked sarcastically as he read the letter to everyone at dinner one night. But I could tell he was pleased, too. He liked the idea that the Germans felt the Sunrise Farm lumbering operation was worth destroying. Therein lay no small amount of vindication.

The lumber camps were temporary affairs, operating during late fall, winter, and until ice-out in the spring. They moved to new cutting areas about every other season. Some years the hardwood logs were brought out of the woods to the mills via plowed roads on frozen Spednic Lake. News of trucks and horses going through the ice was as normal a sign of spring as sighting the first robin. "We never stopped hauling until something or somebody went through two or three times," my father loved to say.

Just before the spring breakup, logs were spread out on the ice in "bag booms," sometimes several acres in size, encircled by chained logs. After ice-out, these booms would be afloat, ready for the long, excruciatingly slow trip to the mills. When we'd see the *Milky Way* coming down the lake with a boom in tow, a great froth of white water kicking up behind her from her extra-large "working" propeller, the only way we could tell she was moving forward was to line her up for several minutes against an object on the far shore.

The lumber camps consisted of a bunkhouse, a cookhouse (or one large building housing both), several equipment sheds (one of which housed a tractor, the only machine at the camps then), and a long low-slung hovel (never called a barn) for the workhorses. Everything was built with the roughest of lumber and covered with black tar paper. When a camp was abandoned after one or two seasons, its few windows, doors, stoves, and metal chimneys were taken to the next site while the rest of the buildings became rotting homes for porcupines.

Although chain saws had been invented, they were still too slow and heavy to compete with two good men on a crosscut saw. Horse teams "twitched" the logs out of the woods on "two-sled rigs," which in effect were two bobsleds, one behind the other, connected by an adjustable piece of lumber called a "reach." An undated Sunrise Farm Christmas card in my possession today features one of the hundreds of photographs my father took of this picturesque hauling process.

Once out of the woods, the horses were also used to pull the logs up onto the trucks or open railroad cars. (The railroad was used to take some of the logs to mills other than my father's.) A pulley would be fastened to a telephone-pole-size tree or pole called a gin pole, located on the far side of the truck or railroad car. Then, by ropes running through it, the horses would haul the logs, one at a time, up a two-log ramp. Once a log was at the proper height, men with peaveys maneuvered it into position. (A peavey is a short wooden pole with a steel spike at the end along with an adjustable steel hook. It was named after Joseph Peavey, a Maine blacksmith who invented it long before my father's time.) The age of mechanization was just around the corner during the 1940s in Vanceboro, Maine—but it sure hadn't arrived!

When a lumber camp was comparatively close by, my mother and father often organized day expeditions to them, including whatever guests were on hand at the time. It was all very jolly and fun to sort of rough it for a day. Overnights, on the other hand, were rare. Lumber camps just didn't have guest accommodations, particularly for females. Aside from the teamsters—"hair pounders"—who bunked in an area attached to the hovel or stable, the men all slept together in their long underwear on wooden bunks, built sometimes three beds high and reached by crawling in through the rear. "Muzzle-loaders," they were called. There were no bathing facilities, and the bathroom consisted of a long, skinny bench (sometimes a seven- or eight-holer) over a lime-filled trench, covered by a lean-to roof but often open to the air in front. The majority of the men were a rough, tough lot, some of them having been "hired" by being thrown into the back of one of my father's trucks, stone drunk, after one of the Saturday night dances at the Vanceboro town hall.

In other words, the typical Maine lumber camp of those years was a long way from my mother and father's Boston upbringing and, to say the least, not a place where it was likely you'd ever hear much discussion about Rudolf Steiner or anthroposophy!

With one exception. It occurred on the only overnight visit to a lumber camp on which not only my mother and Patsy were along, but also, of all unlikely people, Dr. Ehrenfried Pfeiffer. He brought a regular traveling suitcase with him for his extra clothes, and a black leather bag containing tools with which he intended to obtain borings from various trees for crystallization testing in Dickie's laboratory.

My father, Dr. Pfeiffer, and I slept in the bunkhouse with the men, perhaps fifty of them, all snoring, wheezing, and snorting from eight o'clock, when the stove brought the temperature in the upper bunks to about ninety degrees, until dawn, at which time it was around zero throughout the bunkhouse. My straw mattress and half-dozen blankets (like the men, I used my jacket for a pillow) smelled like a dead horse, but I didn't mind. For me, being at a lumber camp overnight was a grand adventure.

My mother and Patsy were put in the office, a small room attached to the rear of the tractor shed. Two bunks were hastily built for them the afternoon we arrived. Every hour throughout the night, as the outside temperature dropped to well below zero, they could hear men coming into the shed, running the tractor for a few minutes, and throwing logs into the wood stove there. Of course no one came in during the night to throw logs onto the dead fire in *their* stove.

The next morning, my mother asked my father why a pile of metal in the tractor shed was kept toasty-warm all night while she and Patsy were allowed to freeze in the next room. My father laughed heartily. He enjoyed the tough priorities of backwoods living. "That tractor," he explained, "builds the roads around here. It's the one and only thing in this entire camp which *has* to be kept warm." My mother was less amused.

Like the good sport she was, however, she tried to made the best of things when we all gathered around the huge cookhouse stove in the morning. The cook, a bald, one-legged, elderly little man called Irving, had been making bread, biscuits, and doughnuts since three o'clock in the morning. Temperamental and, like many chefs, rather a prima donna, Irving was irritated a good deal of the time and our presence did nothing to lighten his mood. No one but his cookees were allowed in Irving's kitchen. His cookees were two scruffy men, too old to be either in the war or in the woods, who would be the sort to be sleeping on subway gratings if they were alive today. Patsy remembers one of them kneading dough that morning and saying, "There's no better way to get your hands nice and clean."

Together, but under Irving's firm command, these grimy old men produced immense quantities of high-quality food—at least high-quality to my way of thinking. (For perspective, perhaps I should mention that today I am also fond of greasy, burnt food, anything from a can, cold food from coin machines, and airplane food; when I was in the army, I loved C rations.)

At every meal, on the long tables in the area adjacent to Irving's cookroom ("kitchen" was a woman's area; lumber camps had "cook-rooms"), were bowls of baked beans with chunks of pork fat, mounds of fresh biscuits, and bread (made with just milk, flour, salt, yeast, and two tablespoons of chicken fat per loaf) with crusts as hard as boards, plain doughnuts, dozens of fresh pies, and, the pièce de résistance as far as Patsy and I were concerned, an inexhaustible supply of molasses cookies, some with sugar on them, each over six inches in diameter.

Also on the tables—besides porcelain pitchers of canned milk, water, and coffee ("strong enough to float an axe"), and bottles of ketchup—were large jars of molasses. Molasses was put on or in almost everything. The food, in bowls and platters, was set at one end of each table and quickly passed down the line, every man shoveling off large amounts onto his metal plate. Besides the afore-mentioned, always on hand, Irving served pancakes, hot cereal, fried potatoes, eggs, pork chops, and ham as the sun was rising, while the

ABOVE: A Mainewoods School picnic, probably in the spring of 1939. I'm in the middle, wearing a tam. The next winter our Swiss teachers were so harassed by a few townspeople (who were convinced our school was a front for German espionage) that they all returned to Switzerland and my mother had to come back from New York and take over as headmistress. BELOW: Patsy in the *Milky Way,* next to its Star Island flag, heading to Vanceboro.

Dr. Ehrenfried Pfeiffer, ABOVE, and his wife, Adelheide, BELOW LEFT, were often among the visiting anthroposophists. It was Dr. Pfeiffer who introduced my parents to "Dickie" (Mathilda von Fragstein) in Berlin a few minutes after my mother was almost arrested by the Gestapo. That's Dickie, BELOW RIGHT. She was in charge of the laboratory and the gardens.

RIGHT: When I look at this photo of Sunny and me on Star Island, I think of heaven. Because it was. It was taken during the summer of 1942, right after my second year (fourth grade) in boarding school. In late August of that same year, Grandpop paid what turned out to be his last visit to Vanceboro and the island. The photo BELOW, showing my father and Grandpop in the stern of the *Milky Way*, with Star Island visible over my father's right shoulder, reflects their conflicting moods at that time. Grandpop is worried about the appalling magnitude of the Sunrise Farm operation and the amount of money my father is already having to borrow from him—and is losing! My father, on the other hand, is having the time of his life. He's carrying out a bona fide *mission* and couldn't care less about such details as money and red ink.

My mother lived in two quite different worlds during our Vanceboro
years. The early photo ABOVE was
one of those used on programs for
her radio and concert tours throughout the Northeast during the winter
months. The late Edwin McArthur,
accompanist for the great Wagnerian opera singer Kirsten Flagstad
during the 1930s, told me years later
that my mother "could have been as
great as Flagstad if she'd done things
differently. It was a great tragedy."
Her other world was Sunrise Farm.
At RIGHT, just after the war, she sits
astride her favorite horse, Mañana,
trailered all the way to Vanceboro
from Sante Fe, New Mexico, by a
cowboy friend she and my father
had met out there in 1936.

ABOVE: Bedtime for Patsy and me on Star Island. I'm probably pleading with my mother or nurse to read "just one more chapter" of *Bambi*. It was my favorite book (the *original* version, that is). BELOW: My father poses with a moose he shot (illegally) about 1946. It's a smaller version of the one involved in the somewhat brutal experience described in Chapter 8.

There were almost always deer hanging upside down outside my father's hunting cabin on Eastbrook Lake. He and his friends hunted here for more than twenty years and only once encountered another man in the woods —and he'd been lost for over three days! It was on this porch I'd stand alone each hunting morning before dawn, communicating silently with the specific deer I was always certain I'd be pointing out for my father to shoot.

The age of mechanization never reached my father's lumbering operation. Horses still "twitched" logs out of the woods, as ABOVE, and although chain saws had been invented by the 1940s, they were still too slow and heavy to compete with good men with crosscut saws. BELOW: As seen from the hill above the farm, the *Milky Way* drags a log boom to our two lumber mills in Vanceboro village. (The opposite shore is Canada.)

Sid Robinson, ABOVE, our head guide, not only took care of everything on Star Island, including the cooking, but also became a sort of second father to my father, teaching him everything from how to use an axe or skin a bear to how to paddle a canoe without *ever* switching sides. Sid died in 1947, the year Sunrise Farm went on the auction block and the year my father and I, BELOW, took a canoe trip on the St. Croix River and Big Lake. It was the first time I noticed him pouring brandy into his many coffees.

evening meal consisted of gray beef (which in the winter of '44 was sometimes referred to as "hedgehog" by a few of the men who knew Sid), rivers of brown gravy, and canned peas. Always canned peas. For lunch, each two-man or three-man team carried a wooden pail called a "firkin" into the woods, filled with sandwiches, doughnuts, and whatever else as long as it was a *lot*. Sometimes the cookees brought hot beans and biscuits out into the woods on a sled for the noon meal.

Each meal in camp consisted of two sittings, and the long rows of men ate in absolute silence except for occasional requests to pass something. To save time, talking during lumber-camp meals was strictly forbidden.

I can't quite imagine what Irving and his two assistants thought of us all as we crowded into his cookroom that morning. My father, with his western hat, western riding boots, and heavy sheepskin coat, looked like a cowboy. My mother appeared to be a movie star in costume for, perhaps, an inexpensive detective picture involving a skiing scene. Her face was, as usual, meticulously made up and she had on an elegant white Norwegian coat with green and red stripes on the collar along with a tall, rather Russian-looking hat to match. In contrast, Dr. Pfeiffer was dressed like a buffoon. A huge man anyway, he was enlarged even more by the many layers of sweaters he was wearing, pulled down over the pants of a dark business suit. He had earmuffs on the top of his head, ready to pull down over his ears when the need arose. A gray and bright-red knitted scarf, although wound several times around his neck, hung down almost to the floor. It struck me that oddest of all in that particular setting was his heavy German accent.

"Is it difficult to know what temperature your oven should be?" my mother cheerfully asked Irving as he was removing about twelve loaves of bread. In answering, Irving did not at any time look at her or Dr. Pfeiffer.

"Well, any fool cook would always know what temperature to have his oven," he replied, glancing up at my father, who nodded amiably, as if to smooth over the brusqueness. My father was well aware one had to treat good lumber-camp cooks with kid gloves. In the ensuing silence, Patsy and I stared at the round wooden knob-like thing Irving used as a foot. Using his own jackknife, he'd cut off his real foot at the ankle years before, so the story went, when he was pinned by a tree he'd felled a long way from camp. I pictured him grinding away at it, through the gristle and joints.

After several minutes, Dr. Pfeiffer, continuing the temperature theme, asked Irving if he heated his yeast before mixing it into the bread dough. Without looking at him, Irving said yes, it should be "blood warm."

"Same as newly milked milk," one of his old cookees chimed in.

This triggered something in Dr. Pfeiffer, and right there in Irving's cookroom, he proceeded to expound on the subject of body temperature in reference to Rudolf Steiner's theories on the practice of medicine. While I remember only the gist of what he said, I can picture today Irving's grizzled face changing from a look of bored irritation to one of stunned alarm.

"Ahhh, 'blood-warm' is the temperature of man's ego," said Dr. Pfeiffer happily, suddenly entering into familiar territory for the first time in the entire trip. My father, I noticed, began to stare at the floor.

Dr. Pfeiffer went on to explain to Irving and his cookees that Steiner believed man's ego, "that element which makes him human," takes hold of the human body through warmth. Body warmth, he said, is the manifestation of the ego. In a similar vein, he continued, the force that is the source of life itself, called "Chi" by the ancient Chinese, utilizes water—i.e., body liquids—as its medium. The plant, as the purest expression of this life force, can, for instance, unfold only in the presence of water. He continued his little dissertation by pointing out that the human mental functions work into one's body through everything that is of gaseous nature, "like oxygen."

Never had any anthroposophical lecture fallen on deafer ears. "At life's end," Dr. Pfeiffer concluded, as if lecturing to students at the Goetheanum in Switzerland, "it is the ego alone which carries the fruits of its experiences and growth into future reincarnations."

Silence again. Irving had stopped flipping pancakes for a moment and was, for once, looking directly at Dr. Pfeiffer. There is no question in my mind that he was thinking that this huge friend of the Hales', with his peculiar accent, was, in lumber-camp jargon, about two logs short of a cord. Maybe more.

As I reflect now upon that early morning scene of years ago, I can readily understand why there are so many strange rumors about my mother, father, and Sunrise Farm still floating around up there in Vanceboro today. Regardless of high aspirations and good intentions, some things just don't mix.

The third serious fire at Sunrise Farm, following closely after the office and German spy fires, was the worst. Not in terms of total devastation (though it was bad enough in that way, too) but in that it caused a certain loss of spirit. After the big white barn, home to as many as sixty animals, the center of the farm and our farm life, burned to the ground one sunny, clear, bitter-cold January morning in 1945, nothing ever seemed quite the same. As a Vermont farmer said in a 1961 *Yankee* magazine article, "Anyone who has been through that—anyone who's seen his barn burn—well, they come out different. Something changes."

After hearing someone in the kitchen shout, "The barn's afire!" my first horrifying view of it was from the living room bay window in the Hale section of the main house. The barn, rising above the other buildings connected to it, was all there, dominating the entire farmyard scene just as usual. But, like a nightmare from which I'd surely wake up, there were rolls of heavy black smoke roaring out of the open hayloft door under the peak of the roof.

Although the temperature was recorded at twenty below zero that morning, I could see that the Sunrise Farm fire truck had miraculously started and was lumbering out of one of the lower sheds attached to the barn, heading for the frozen duck pond below the house. It was actually just an ordinary truck, painted red, in the back of which were hoses, a couple of ladders, axes, and a large gasoline-driven pump attached to a steel shed-like frame. So when it became stuck in the snow halfway across the field near the pond, it didn't matter. It had no water tank or pumping capability anyway. Some of the men lifted the pump off and dragged it across the field and then out onto the snow-covered ice to where others were already chopping a hole. Every section of hose was taken from the truck, linked together, and stretched out between the pond and the barn. The distance was about five hundred yards in all, exactly the amount available! So far, everything was going well.

I could see my father down there—his cowboy hat and sheepskin coat easily identifying him—directing the evacuation of the horses and cows, as well as all the saddles, harnesses, sleighs, wagons, and other equipment. I also noticed that a few flames were beginning to chase all that black smoke billowing out from the hayloft.

Within five minutes—a long five minutes—a hole had been chopped through the ice, every foot of hose was in place, and the pump was primed, ready to be started. I was relieved to see that Jim Hansen's father, Carl, the Sunrise Farm blacksmith and chief mechanic, was out there. From that distance, I couldn't see the goiter-like growth, the size of a baseball, that hung down beneath Carl's chin like a turkey's wattle, but I recognized the long black coat and black fedora hat he always wore. If anyone could start a balky, cold engine in twenty-below-zero weather, it was old Carl Hansen.

Carl wound the starting rope, whipped it back, wound it again, whipped it back—over and over. Every few cranks he'd stop to adjust the choke or whatever he felt needed adjusting. It was an eternity of cranking and adjusting. Suddenly there was a puff of smoke and the distant roar of an engine coming to life drifted up to us children and women watching from the house windows. We cheered. Maybe it wasn't too late!

The one and only serious mistake of the day was made at that point. Instead of allowing the engine to warm up for a few minutes, Carl, understandably anxious to provide water right away, threw it in gear as soon as it seemed to be running smoothly. As water surged through, we could see the hose twitch and thrash all the way along the line to where men were holding the nozzle. A stream gushed forth and began arching up toward the smoke and flames. Then it fell back—and stopped. The pump had stalled.

Carl began winding the starting rope and cranking again—and again and again. Some of the other men relieved him. And still the cranking continued. Everyone said later that it was only a couple of minutes before the engine finally started, but whatever time it took, it took too long. When they threw it in gear and began pumping, there was no place for the water to go. The water pumped a few minutes earlier had frozen rock solid inside the entire length of the hose. The Sunrise Farm Fire Department was out of business.

My father sent men off to McAdam for more hose, but he and everyone else knew they wouldn't be back in time. The barn was doomed. The only hope now was to cut away a large section of the attached buildings in an attempt to save the offices, apartments, theater, and some of the storage sheds. As the barn roof began to smoke, ready to burst into flames, my father directed dozens of men to begin hacking apart the building where the slaughterhouse was located, while others were to begin removing office files, furniture, and machinery in the event the tactic didn't work. Hundreds of men were on hand now, all of them running somewhere.

People in the house were now on the run, too. It was obvious to me that one of the most important things to do at a fire is run. Wherever. I also learned that the worst thing one can do during any sort of emergency is faint. One of my father's female employees living in the house at the time—and I won't divulge her name in deference to her children and grandchildren still in the Vanceboro area today—fainted dead away in the narrow corridor between the Hale family section and the rest of the main house where Bessie, Dickie, and other employees lived. She lay there throughout a good part of the morning with people leaping over her inert body. Nobody knew—or cared—whether she was alive or dead. In the aftermath of the day, jumping over this unconscious woman was recalled with much amusement and scorn. "She wasn't a helluva lot of help," Bessie often said later, laughing. I gathered fainting was a surefire sign of weakness. (And I would have cause to remember this lesson one evening five years later in the Choate School dining room.)

Additional hoses and pumps eventually arrived from McAdam and the fire was stopped at the slaughterhouse cut-through, thus saving the rest of the connected buildings. All that remained of the barn, however, were rows of black cow stanchions standing upright in a sea of smoking debris.

At least there had been no foul play involved this time. The cause was generally believed to be an overheated stovepipe, which extended up through the hayloft from the harness room below.

Miraculously, the only casualty, besides the barn itself, was Andy, a bantam rooster I'd kept caged in the barn as a pet. He and his mate, Gloria, had been rescued along with all the other barn creatures and placed in a fenced-in area near the carpentry shop. Capable of flight but having always been confined, Andy and Gloria had never known what it was like to take to the air. When the fire was at its height, flames roaring up from the entire length and breadth of the structure, Andy decided to find out. Leaving the less adventuresome Gloria on the ground, he spread his little wings for the very first time and flew out of the fenced-in area. Up and ever upwards he went, circling several times far above the barnyard, and then, while many people stopped momentarily to watch him, he headed directly for the conflagration of smoke and flames roaring up into the sky above the barn.

"Look at Andy!" people in the house yelled to me, and I kept waiting for him to turn back. He never did. While everyone *ooohed* and *aaahed*, he disappeared forever into the solid wall of flames. Poor, foolish, brave, beautiful, innocent Andy, I thought. But then again, what a grand gesture!

Instead of building a new barn, my father sold all but two of the cows and a few of the horses, and had sheds built to house Ranger, Mañana, and whatever other animals were left. Sunrise Farm was different from then on. A farm without a barn is not even a farm.

The following summer we celebrated V-J Day by decorating a truck with banners and flags and riding all through Vanceboro and McAdam tooting whistles and horns. Men returning from Europe that summer told wonderfully gruesome tales of combat, and I was certain there would no longer be newspapers since there would no longer be any news.

A month later, at age twelve, I was off to a pre-preparatory boarding school for boys, called Harvey, located in Hawthorne, New York (now in Katonah, New York), while Patsy was sent to Westover School, my mother's alma mater, in Middlebury, Connecticut. Our years of country school education and backwoods Maine living were virtually over and, according to my mother, "none too soon." It was time, she said, we were exposed to "culture."

In my case, being exposed to "culture" meant being exposed to the mortification of watching an entire baseball team walk five yards toward home plate whenever I came to bat. Also to the giggling, whispering rumors of the sexual shenanigans many of the little boys indulged in regularly. Although I didn't understand at the time exactly what "cornholing" was all about (and I wouldn't think of explaining it here), I was aware early on that it was something sexual considered daringly wicked by many students and just plain wicked by the teachers. I was also aware that the three boys in the room down the dormitory hall from me were, according to their own boasts, steady practitioners and that it was an activity very much in violation of school rules. Every few months a teacher would "catch" two unfortunate little boys in the act, and I noted that it was always the boy rumored to be the cornhol*er* who was thrown out of school while the alleged cornhol*ee* was, as far as I could determine, simply given some sort of reprimand and allowed to remain. The lesson to be drawn from that was, in my mind, somewhat obscure.

During my vacation back in Vanceboro in the spring of 1946, I could sense trouble. At the dinner table, once so festive and noisy, were just my father, Patsy, and I. My mother was in New York, as she had been throughout most of the winter. There were no visiting anthroposophists, the laboratory had closed, and Dickie had left to join Dr. Ehrenfried Pfeiffer at the Threefold Farm in Spring Valley. I wouldn't see her again until the summer of 1985. Even the Nichols family was gone—farm foreman Russell, his wife, Grace, so expert at catching cow urine in her glass vials, and their daughter, the butterfly dancer, Sheila.

With the cows sold and the farm operation all but closed down, the only real activity was in lumbering, and that was still going at full capacity. Both mills were turning out more finished hardwood than ever and there were over a hundred men in the woods, operating out of two lumber camps.

The biggest and most ominous clue to real problems, however, was that, on my first night home, Bessie presented my father, Patsy, and me with a platter of grilled frankfurters for supper. I couldn't believe I was seeing straight as she placed them in front of my father for him to serve. My father hated grilled frankfurters. He hated anything other than rare beefsteak, venison, lamb chops, or chicken. He'd tolerate pork chops.

While Patsy and I held our breath in dreaded anticipation of whatever was about to happen, my father stared at the frankfurters in shock. Then he went into one of his quiet, smoldering rages.

"You expect me to eat these?" he said. His voice was quiet and steady yet in some way indicated he was a living time bomb about to explode. Poor Bessie suddenly realized she'd made a terrible mistake. "Well, I just thought . . ." she began, floundering about for an explanation, "I just thought with everything happening, that maybe I should try to save money in the kitchen and . . ." She trailed off into nowhere.

Save money? Here at Sunrise Farm? By serving my father grilled frankfurters?

Needless to say, Bessie took the platter back to the kitchen within a minute. While Patsy and I sat in embarrassed silence and my father continued to smolder, she cooked and served an entire new meal. It consisted of rare, tender, juicy beefsteak, the sort of thing my father loved and expected. No matter what.

The summer of 1946 was my last on Star Island. It was a quiet summer, with no singers from the Metropolitan and no guides on hand besides Sid, who'd suddenly become old and frail. My father often talked of his plans for leasing additional timberlands, dramatically increasing the cutting operation during the subsequent winter of '47, and how he expected to realize good profits the following spring. "If we can just hang on 'til then," he'd say, "everything will turn around and be fine. Guaranteed."

Whenever I hear someone say "guaranteed" about the expected success of some *Yankee* project today, I involuntarily shudder a little. Surely the word fails to live up to its meaning more than any other in the English language.

When Patsy and I returned after Christmas vacation to our respective boarding schools in January 1947, neither of us knew we'd never see Sunrise Farm as a going operation again. I've always regretted not being able to make the barnyard rounds and say goodbye to Ranger, Mañana, Harry, Snoozy (my white cat), Gloria, and the remaining workhorses, chickens, and pigs. I don't even know what became of them all. The only animal to remain in my life was my dog, Sunny. She was to seem as out of place in New York City, our off-and-on home base during some of the years ahead, as my father. (But at least he didn't have a tail that continually jammed in revolving doors.)

I came back to the town of Vanceboro the next June for a canoe trip down the St. Croix River with my father, Uncle Charley (his Boston hunting pal), and Frank Lounder, a young Canadian guide. (Sid had died the previous winter.) However, we didn't set foot on the farm, which, as I'd learned a few weeks before, was up for sale. My father met Uncle Charley and me coming in on the overnight train from Boston and insisted we go directly to the landing below the dam, where he had gathered all our gear, supplies, and canoes. By midmorning we were negotiating the first white-water rips.

It was a spectacular six-day camping trip, one we were to repeat each June for the next few years. (My father always paid the man in charge of the dam gates to open them wide and keep them open for the three days we'd actually be on the river.) He acted on that first trip as if everything were fine, that selling the farm, the mills, the twelve thousand acres, Star Island—everything—was simply the right business move at the right time.

However, as we sat around after supper at Rocky Falls, our first camp, I heard him admit to Uncle Charley that the expanded cutting operation the previous winter hadn't worked out very well and that he had "a bit of a cash problem at present." But he also said he and my mother had already pretty much decided to "move on and do something else with our lives."

It was during that 1947 river trip that I noticed for the first time that he poured brandy after brandy into coffee after coffee as we cooked breakfast over the campfire every morning. His so-called coffee royale.

No one alive today knows all the details of my mother and father's rather spectacular failure in Vanceboro. However, by talking with relatives and friends who'd been on hand as well as several of my father's former employees, I've pieced enough together to know the gist of it.

Obviously, my father ran out of money. Which means Grandpop finally refused to give him any more. This my mother confirms today. When the final business deal, whatever it was, with the St. Croix Paper Company, a division of Eastern Pulpwood, "didn't work out," as he described it, and when much of the timber cut over the winter of 1946–47 remained lying in the woods that spring with no funds available for removing it, Grandpop was the last hope for survival. And for the first time ever, Grandpop refused to come to the rescue.

My mother says it was not until the telephone call in which Grandpop told my father "no more" that she became aware how serious their situation really was. For the first time my father informed her that their debts more than likely exceeded the value of the entire business. In short, they were facing bankruptcy, a far more devastating situation, both socially and from the point of view of ever recovering, back then than it is today. It all came as a great shock

to her. She and my father rarely discussed money or business, because, like most well-to-do couples of their generation, they both
took it for granted that those were not subjects for women to be
concerned about.

"I never gave money a thought," she recalls now. "Whenever I
was in New York and needed some, I'd just telephone a 'Mr.
Streeter' at the Old Colony and two days later there'd be a check for
$5,000 in my mail."

Apparently my father was not reluctant to discuss finances with
his sister, Aunt Mard. She recalls him often coming to her for loans
or to ask her to request money from Grandpop, knowing there was
a good chance he would then receive an equal amount.

"When Roger was little, Father went to great pains to teach him
how to save his money," she told me during one of my recent visits
to her at Sherrill House, a fancy Boston home for the elderly where
she now lives. "Made him write all his weekly expenses down in a
little black book." She thought about what she'd said for a moment
and then added, "Guess it didn't make much of an impression."

Aunt Mard is ninety-two at this writing and devotes much of her
time to playing solitaire. "I cheat to win," she says. She also says it's
"a pretty stupid life" in a place like Sherrill House but that she
figures she's "too old to do much about it."

My father probably came to her or called her in the spring of
1947, and she probably gave him some money. Not enough to save
the day—even Aunt Mard couldn't have done that—but some.

"I always loaned him something when he wanted it," she says.
"I lived a lot more quietly than Roger and Mannie did, you know,
and so I didn't need as much as they did. Of course, I don't know
if you'd call them 'loans,'" and at this point she laughed, "because
he never gave any of it back!"

My mother is certain my father also went to the Old Colony and
perhaps to other Boston banks as well. No doubt they all painted the
same picture for him: without Grandpop's signature as a guarantee,
they could not approve a loan large enough to support another year
of operations at Sunrise Farm, particularly in light of its consistent
history of losing money. As usual, Grandpop remained the key.

So, without my father's knowledge—and I'm not sure he *ever*
knew about it—my mother traveled to West Newton by herself to
plead my father's case in person. Grandpop always liked my

mother's willingness to speak up to him while everyone else kow-towed. She felt that, if anyone could, she might be able to convince him to change his mind and come through with enough to save the day. At least, as she puts it today, she intended to pull out all the stops trying.

Grandpop lived alone with his servants then, Grandma having died three years earlier. So, on the evening she arrived, it was just the two of them at the big dining room table, the one around which we'd all sat for Sunday dinners back in the Chestnut Hill days. I'd like to have been a fly on the wall. My mother has never told me or anyone all the details of what transpired, but I assume her arguments, as usual, relied on emotion; his, on his innate sense of frugality, prudent business practices, and common sense.

She has told me on several occasions that her principal point—plain, simple, and brutal—was that unless he agreed to support Sun-rise Farm for another year, his son would probably have a "nervous breakdown." This surely placed Grandpop in a painful dilemma. As a loving and generous father, he wanted to help his son out of serious trouble if he could afford to do so (a questionable point at this stage). On the other hand, would help now simply postpone greater trouble later on? He'd already decided Sunrise Farm was a harebrained operation that, sad to say, would probably never be financially suc-cessful under my father's direction.

The upshot of their clandestine meeting was a compromise, a significant compromise of far-reaching consequences for the future of my family. There were many complex details Grandpop worked out with bankers and attorneys later on, but basically he agreed to guarantee a long-term loan sufficient for my father to avoid bank-ruptcy. The catch was that Sunrise Farm had to be sold, with the proceeds locked into the loan arrangement. Furthermore, Grandpop would set up an irrevocable trust for my father as his inheritance right away. Compared to the amount given him at the time of his Harvard graduation and in subsequent "loans," it was a small trust fund, although the interest from it, Grandpop figured, would pro-vide enough income for my mother and father to live comfortably. If, on the other hand, they wanted to continue to live lavishly, well, then my father would have to make money on his own. Grandpop made sure, or so he thought, that my father could never get his hands on the principal of the trust fund.

It was a generous plan designed to bail my father out of debt, remove the cause of continuing debt, and, because he wouldn't ever have access to any large amounts of money again, force him to live within his means. I can only imagine how all this affected my father's psyche and sense of pride.

After Grandpop's death seven years later, the plan would begin to unravel, but that wasn't Grandpop's fault. He'd done what he thought was right. In retrospect, one can see that the best plan might have been to allow my father to struggle out of his self-made problems by himself. After all, nothing could have been worse than what eventually happened. But how could Grandpop or anyone have known that a man as wasteful and careless with money as my father surely was could also be a veritable financial wizard . . . in his own way?

My father's photographs illustrate the lavish eight-page sales brochure put out by Previews, a copy of which I recently found among the few Sunrise Farm mementos I have today. "A Timber Empire —A Going Business and a Way of Life," says the dramatic headline. The flowery copy makes it sound like heaven, but, then again, it was. In the brochure, however, heaven makes money.

> From logging and mill operation only, based on alternate operation of mills (i.e. 50% of capacity) and logging by both our crew and by contractors, the owner estimates gross income, at current prices, to be $344,500 and gross expenses, at current costs, to be $271,000—a net profit of $73,500 per year. The owner is offering the property for sale only because other interests unavoidably demand his presence elsewhere.

Why mention that "other interests" were actually Boston banks demanding regular payments on loans? Or that "elsewhere" hadn't as yet been determined?

The price on the brochure is listed at $214,000, seemingly low until you consider the value of the 1947 dollar and the fact that, back then, good-size farms all over New England could be picked up for under $10,000.

There were no takers. Interested parties lost interest when they became acquainted with the realities. Not only had Sunrise Farm lost money from the start but much of the property—such as the Mainewoods School, the laboratory, the theater, the Timber Village apartments, the various camping cabins, boathouses, and so forth—was just so much excess baggage insofar as operating a profitable business was concerned. And no lumber operation of that size needed to own twelve thousand acres when timberland could be so easily and cheaply leased.

Two years later, therefore, at 11 a.m. on October 26, 1949, Sunrise Farm went on the auction block. My mother and father's dream, which was supposed to render meaningful the tragedy of "poor Drakie-boy," the lifetime mission conceived at the edge of the Grand Canyon fourteen years before, was divided into three hundred and eighty-six "piecemeal lots." These included such as the timberland, the "completely equipped turning square mill" and woodworking shop, on down to, for instance, lot 163, listed in the auction brochure as "chemical glassware, precision weights and balances, and three electric evaporating ovens." I wonder if the high bidder for lot 163 was aware he'd become fully equipped to crystallize cow urine.

"That auction was like a funeral," my father's office manager, Paul Susee, told me during our recent telephone conversation. "Everything went for practically nothing, but before it started that morning your father told Vi and me to take anything we wanted. He was telling some others of his old workers the same thing."

"I remember how hard I cried," said Viola, Paul's wife.

I asked them what had gone wrong. They both mentioned "too much, too quickly" (which everyone I've spoken with cited), but Paul provided an additional insight, one that neither I nor anyone in the family had known about.

"Your father had some people working for him, right in top management, that he shouldn't have," said Paul. I prodded. "I don't want to drag any names through the dirt at this late date," he responded, obviously wishing he hadn't brought up the subject. I prodded some more.

"Well, Jud, if you really want to know the truth," he said, sighing in resignation as I assured him I did, "I might's well tell you. Your father was stolen blind!" He went on to say that a number of private homes standing in Vanceboro today were built from stolen Sunrise Farm lumber, and that "tools and equipment could hardly be replaced before someone grabbed them for themselves."

Didn't my father realize this was happening? "I tried to tell him," he said, "but when your father put his trust in someone, he couldn't change. Of course, he was so honest himself, lots of people said he could *never* be successful!"

To many a New Englander, I thought, the cardinal sin is to be an easy mark.

And perhaps second in sin is waste. Paul went on to say that at the end of every spring, particularly those of the last three years, thousands of dollars' worth of equipment and lumber were left in the woods to rot. "There was waste in everything, even labor," he said. "When a machine in one of the mills broke down, everyone sat around for two or three days collecting their hourly wages until someone decided either to fix it or maybe even to buy a brand-new machine!"

Another New England (and Grandpop) golden rule violated: "Use it up, wear it out, make it do, or do without."

Viola chimed in on an extension at this point. "We all let him down," she said. "No one realized they were killing the goose that laid golden eggs!"

Paul asked me if my father ever talked about his problems at Sunrise Farm during the remainder of his life. I told him he only reminisced about the good times, and there were many.

Before we hung up, we all agreed that whatever my father's inward distress might have been, his oft-stated philosophy would dictate he think of it "tomorrow." Surely the pain would be less then. But as we were all to eventually learn, his sense of failure only increased with each of his tomorrows. And so silently.

The rest of us in the family were not so burdened. My mother still had her singing career to think about, Patsy and I were dealing with the horrors of boarding schools, and Drakie-boy, according to the regular reports from Switzerland, was hitting himself less and was apparently happier and more adjusted to his situation there.

After the Sunrise Farm auction, my father left Vanceboro to join my mother in an old colonial house they suddenly decided to rent in Greenwich, Connecticut. My mother saw it one day when visiting a wealthy cousin and "fell in love with it," for a brief time. It would be the first stop in their seemingly aimless wanderings from there to Lake Placid, New York, to Carmel, New York, to Westport, Connecticut, from one address in New York City to another, to San

Rafael, California, to Marblehead, Massachusetts. Surely I've forgotten a few. There were still two-month trips to Europe, summers at western ranches, and plenty of roses, champagne, and caviar!

It wasn't until 1963 that we knew for certain how my father managed it all financially. Then we also knew for certain where his heart had been.

Chapter 10

———— ◆ ————

Contrariety

THE MOST important thing I learned at Choate School was how to make my high, squeaky voice low, like a man's. It wasn't important when I arrived in the fall of 1947. With only two or three exceptions, all of my classmates were high-voiced little boys like me.

I played left end on the freshman football team, which was known as the Midgets. No one weighed over 110 pounds. Once in a while there'd be somebody on one of the outside school teams we played against who'd grown man-size and man-sounding in a hurry. "Hey, he's no Midget," we'd complain to our coach, pointing to some giant thirteen-year-old warming up before the game. The coach, a kindly, slow-spoken man with infinite patience, would simply advise us to try to "tackle him low." We'd try—and the man-size boy would run over us for a touchdown every play he didn't happen to trip.

By my sophomore year, I had become aware that my high voice and small size could become a serious problem if my body didn't hurry up and rectify things. Half my class came back bigger than me and with low voices. Most of them joined the varsity football squad while I remained on the Midgets.

Up to that point in my academic career, I'd been an "A" student at every school I attended. But during my Choate sophomore year my inner priorities shifted. I can even pinpoint the change to a specific evening. While I was studying in my room for a history test, some of my friends came in to urge me to join them in a "Peeping Tom" expedition to the school infirmary. The night before, some-

166

body had seen the teenage daughter of the head nurse undressing in the basement-level apartment there. Now a dozen or so boys were on their way to see for themselves.

"C'mon, Jud, you've studied enough," they urged. "You should have some fun. C'mon!" I wavered. My studies had always been my first priority. However, on that evening they dropped down to second, and over the next seven years, practically out of sight. Replacing my desire to excel academically was an urge to be wild, funny, daring, someone with a devil-may-care attitude—anything to counteract my high-voiced, goody-goody image. Off I went with them into the night.

The teenage daughter wasn't there so we had to be satisfied with viewing her fat, middle-aged mother, the school's head nurse, sitting on the john. When the body pressure around the single window forced one boy's head through the glass, we scattered in all directions, returning singly to the dormitory where we stayed up most of the night smoking strictly forbidden cigarettes and recounting our individual "escapes" over and over again. I received a "C" on the history test the next morning, my lowest grade ever. I didn't care. It had been an exhilarating evening. My seven years of trouble were under way.

Only two of my classmates were on the Midgets when I returned for my junior year. I was becoming alarmed, and even my mother wondered whether I'd ever reach puberty. During Thanksgiving vacation in New York she took me to a doctor to see if I had a glandular problem, or something equally weird. He said not to worry. My "body clock" was just a little slow and I'd develop normally "in time." Fine for him to say. For me it was a problem that was beginning to engulf my life.

My friends began giving me advice, based on their own experiences. One said his voice had changed when he began running for the cross-country team. So I ran myself ragged around the Choate campus every afternoon following Midget football practice. Another said he matured when he began to masturbate after every meal. I don't know how he managed to find the time, place, or energy during a typically fully programmed Choate day, because I couldn't. Anyway, sex for me pretty much consisted of looking up "dirty" words in the dictionary during study hall.

A third friend's suggestion launched me into my publishing

career. He said *his* voice had changed after working for several months on the staff of the school newspaper, the *Choate News*. His reasoning was a bit suspect, but I was ready to believe anyone with a voice like his. It had the deep, modulated tones of a professional radio announcer. He said it grew to be that way after he began existing in the permanent state of total exhaustion prevalent among *Choate News* staffers, all of whom, I noted, also had low voices. They were the only students in the school allowed to remain working after the regular bedtime bells were rung, and so they felt obligated, even privileged, to work very late every night. Their hollow-eyed, zombie-like appearance during the day was considered a mark of distinction and maturity. According to my friend, it was specifically this extreme level of exhaustion that somehow triggered the body mechanism that lowered his voice. It was all I needed to hear.

Hedrick Smith, now the *New York Times* correspondent in Washington and a best-selling author, was the editor of the *Choate News* at the time. He informed me that in order to qualify for election to the staff, I'd have to "heel" for at least sixty hours during the next month, which meant running around doing flunky work late at night. Perfect. I would surely be exhausted.

He also said it would help if I brought in some advertising. So I wrote to both my grandfathers, who came through with full pages carrying "Compliments-of-a-friend" messages. In addition I managed to sell a small ad to a funeral parlor in Wallingford. The ad appeared on the first page of our memorial issue to a classmate who'd just died of leukemia, precipitating a sermon by the headmaster on the subject of "good taste."

By the winter of my junior year I'd arrived at the desired level of total exhaustion and was elected to the staff of the *Choate News*. My voice, however, continued to sound like a girl's.

I spent the summer prior to my senior year at a ranch for teenagers, called the E Bar L, outside Missoula, Montana. The day I arrived I was greeted by a boy who, in the course of general conversation, asked how old I was.

"Seventeen," I said.

"No!" was the flabbergasted reply. "You can't be." I assured him I was. He yelled to a group of his friends to come over, whereupon he asked them each to estimate my age. Most of the guesses were under twelve. One boy, sensing a trick, said, "Oh, he's probably a lot older than he looks. I'll guess fourteen."

Finally, with great glee, the first boy announced I was "seventeen!" and exclamations of disbelief poured forth from everyone. I stood there, smilingly agreeing with them, and felt like a freak.

The following September I discovered I was the only senior on the Midgets, possibly in the history of the school. It precipitated two moves, each of them born of desperation. First of all, every evening at the mandatory chapel service I inwardly implored my guardian angel to pull whatever strings she could with God so He'd change my voice, promising it would be the only request of Him I'd make for the rest of my life. Second, on the chance that playing on the Midgets was actually *keeping* me a midget, I screwed up all my courage to the sticking point and went to the varsity football coach, a man named J. J. Maher, to ask if I could be listed on and practice with his varsity team. I assured him, in my gentle, squeaky voice, that I was tougher than I appeared.

J. J. Maher was *very* tough. He'd been a Ranger or a paratrooper or perhaps a Storm Trooper in the war, and rumor had it he'd once strangled the Yale bulldog with his bare hands prior to a college game in which he'd played.

The night I went to see him, J. J. Maher seemed as tough as his reputation. In his fifties, he was powerfully built, with a face like chiseled granite and a voice like a hoarse John Wayne. He told me I'd get hurt playing with bigger, tougher varsity players and to make the best of the Midgets. I must have appeared crestfallen, because as I was leaving his office, he called after me that he'd "think about it."

A week later, I came within three steps of what I believed would surely prove to J. J. Maher and the entire school that I was as weak and frail as I appeared to be. I almost fainted in the dining room. Probably from exhaustion. As I felt myself blacking out and the room revolving, I rose from my table and headed for the swinging doors leading to the outside, perhaps twenty yards away. Never have I been so determined to walk a certain distance.

I awoke on my back at the head of the stairs outside the dining room. I'd made it. But my relief turned to dismay when I realized who was kneeling over me, loosening my tie (everyone wore coats and ties in boys' boarding schools back then) and gently telling me in his John Wayne voice that I'd be all right. It was J. J. Maher. He'd been the only one to notice me reeling toward those swinging doors and he'd followed me out.

After I sat up for a few minutes recovering my equilibrium, J. J. Maher led me *by the hand* to his car and drove me to the school infirmary. We were met there by the head nurse, whom I could never look in the eye after having observed her sitting on the john two years before. "Take care of this little guy," I heard J. J. Maher tell her. "He's too tough to admit he's under the weather." *Tough!* It was my second-best moment at Choate School. The best was soon to come.

When I returned to school after three days of solid sleep in the infirmary, J. J. Maher called me into his office. In a gentle, concerned manner, he advised me to take advantage of my small size by becoming a coxswain on the crew. That had never occurred to me.

My first crew race was against Taft, or maybe Kent, and naturally I considered it very important. So at evening chapel the night before, I threw in another request besides my standard, everyday "voice" one. I asked my guardian angel to tell God I only wanted "to do my best." I figured both she and He would like that. They'd think well of me for not asking "to win."

As we pushed off the dock to go to the starting line, the coach's last instructions to me were "don't oversteer." Too much rudder would be a drag on the boat. So, as the race began with me shrieking commands at the top of my voice, I hardly steered at all. As a result, we rowed off to the left of the course into a swamp area near the shore. The other boat stroked straight down the course while we attempted to slog through lily pads. When I finally began to steer us out of the quagmire, we were at least ten lengths behind, and yet we almost caught them at the finish line. The coach cruised over in his motorboat and announced through his bullhorn that we'd lost by one foot. Well, well, I thought. So much for my guardian angel and praying. I wouldn't bother with *that* again.

On thinking back to the incident a few months later, I realized I'd missed the simple and obvious lesson. Praying before the race hadn't been my mistake. We'd lost because I failed to *steer!* I recalled, as I should have at the time, old Sid's advice when confronted with an angry bear. "Don't kneel and pray," he'd say. "*Run* and pray!"

As we rowed slowly back to the dock, everyone in the boat told me not to worry about it, that we'd proved we could do well, et cetera, but I felt terrible. I felt terrible, that is, until I said something. I think it was "Sorry guys, my fault" or some such, but suddenly I was ecstatic beyond measure. Unbelievably, my voice came out sounding low, exactly like a man's voice! *That* was my best moment at Choate.

Unfortunately, it didn't turn out to be a permanent miracle. My voice didn't change, nor did I begin to grow to my present six-foot-three-inch height, until the middle of my freshman year at Dartmouth. My voice sounded low after the crew race because it had become hoarse from shouting the cadence and racing commands. Fine with me. At least I now had a procedure that would allow me to *sound* normal, if only for short spurts.

So for the remainder of my senior year at Choate, I'd hang back in my room every morning while everyone else headed for breakfast. Then I'd shout rowing commands into my pillow for approximately ten minutes or until I was hoarse. After lunch, if time allowed, I'd race back to my room for a short "touch-up" pillow-shouting session, sufficient to last me for the rest of the day.

As Norman Holmes Pearson recently wrote in his introduction to the works of Hawthorne, "Human experience is so diverse that a man can be estimated only by the depth with which he understands what chance has thrown his way." I already knew in my heart who controlled chance. How could I have ever doubted my guardian angel for even an instant?

Reaching puberty during my freshman year at Dartmouth launched me toward a series of typical adolescent milestones that most other boys my age had already experienced years before. At one moment I was a little boy, shouting desperately into my pillow each morning and particularly dreading my freshman Navy R.O.T.C. class on Wednesdays because that was my day to call the roll. And then, in a flash, I was, in sound and appearance, a young man. At long last.

Unfortunately, my sudden physical maturity didn't eliminate my little-boy insecurities. I still wanted to be thought of as wild, funny, daring, someone with a devil-may-care attitude. Only now, with the appearance and sound of normalcy, my capability for doing so was increased a hundred times over.

The first two milestones were innocuous and routine, though each had a large potential for trouble. They were, in order, my first drink (followed on the same occasion by my second, third, fourth, and fifth) and my first kiss. Both occurred on the same evening, with the latter being sort of forced upon me. As a Green Mountain College girl I'd known for ten minutes and I sat side by side on a couch in my dormitory room, my roommate playfully snapped off the lights and left. We were both too immature not to feel compelled to attempt a tentative kiss. It was awkward, closed-mouthed, dry— even embarrassing—but it *was* the first!

The drinks were exclusively my own doing. Shortly after the kiss, they caused me to abandon the Green Mountain girl in order to throw up on the door of the bathroom down the hall, the first of many college episodes in which, sad to say, alcohol played a major role.

Even my memories of first love and, shortly thereafter, first sex, if indeed that's what it was, are dimmed by the alcoholic haze surrounding them. The "love" entailed drinking premixed whiskey sours with her in the black 1946 coupe I called the Crow ("just caws," I delighted in saying when someone asked me about the name) somewhere on the Middlebury College campus. Then there'd be the long drive back to Dartmouth as the sun was rising and waking up in my Economics I class with my professor's angry, somewhat contorted mouth yelling at me from one foot away. There was something about my sleeping in his class that grated on his nerves.

Sometimes she'd come to Dartmouth, and it was during one such visit that *the* first occurred, or if not, a reasonable facsimile. We were parked in the Crow on the Dartmouth golf course, there were the usual whiskey sours and hours of silent fumbling around, but as dawn was breaking and hundreds of birds began singing like crazy, we crossed over that mysterious line between pretend and real for perhaps two minutes. Or maybe I just *thought* we did.

At the bourbon-and-milk-punch party at my Phi Kappa Psi fraternity house the following noon, after I'd put her on the bus going back to Middlebury, I stood apart from my friends and attempted to strike a pose that would appear as mature, wise, and worldly as I felt. Later that same afternoon, I joined a few others in sailing 78-r.p.m. records across the living room at the stuffed moosehead hanging over the fireplace. Parts of records remained imbedded in the plaster there for many years.

I know today that my Dartmouth years, overflowing as they were in a sea of beer, milk punch, and, yes, those whiskey sours, were a waste of precious time. In fact, the pace of my education slowed to a crawl just as I was exposed to everything one of the finest educational institutions in the country had to offer.

According to our professor-chaperone, I even wasted my first trip to Europe during the summer prior to my senior year. It was a two-month "political and economic" tour of thirteen countries, arranged by half a dozen eastern colleges. Students would be able to interview government leaders, attend legislative sessions, and analyze economic conditions. Three other boys and I, however, devoted our waking time exclusively to local bars and late-night clubs. By day, while everyone else was being bused around to the various appointments, we slept.

"Why did you come on this tour, Jud?" the professor asked me when we were halfway through the summer. "You could have accomplished everything you've accomplished so far with us right at home." Not really, I thought. For instance, I couldn't have kissed a beautiful, tall Texas girl under the Arc de Triomphe while the sun was rising on Bastille Day following a night that began with dinner at a posh place called Monsignor, where we were surrounded by no fewer than twelve violinists at our table, followed by a bottle of champagne during the second show at the Lido and dancing through the wee hours at a place on the Seine called the Crazy Horse Saloon.

A few weeks later, we were in Belgrade, Yugoslavia, and the nightlife was dismal. I decided to leave the tour for ten days in order to visit my brother, Drake, in Switzerland. I was twenty-one, he was twenty-seven. It would be our first meeting.

On the day I'd left New York on the *Rotterdam*—crammed to the gunwales with college students—my mother had coached me on what to expect if I found the opportunity to see Drake. Bring him food as a gift, she said, but too much candy wouldn't help his already somewhat rotten teeth. Give him nothing heavy or solid because he'd only heave it out his fifth-floor window to see it *fliegen* (fly). She warned me that his mouth hung open, he had a tendency to rock back and forth, he liked to keep his hands clasped together inside his sleeves, his voice had a guttural sound as though there was always a frog in his throat, and he spoke only German. I'd taken two years of German at Dartmouth specifically for the purpose of being able to communicate with him someday. Now I was going to have my chance. It would, I thought, be a momentous occasion.

Upon checking into the Three Kings Hotel, built on the edge of the Rhine in Basel, after precisely thirty-seven hours on trains, mostly the stop-and-go one through Yugoslavia, I was bone-tired and suffering from an intestinal disorder. But I was determined to take the trolley out to the *Sonnenhof* (the "Sunshine House"), where Drake still lived, that very afternoon. With no toilet facilities on the trolley, it was a painful trip. As I finally ascended the steps of the *Sonnenhof,* the very ones my mother, father, and Drake had first walked up twenty-three years before, I was armed with a box of sponge cake—I figured he could heave that out the window without damaging results—a family photo album, and an English-German dictionary. But instead of experiencing the sort of emotional feelings one would expect when about to come face to face with an older brother one had never seen, finding a bathroom was the only thought on my mind. The body, I dimly noted, can be callous and downright rude even during the most important of life's dramatic occasions.

I was met at the door by a nurse who immediately cried out happily, *"Da ist Drakies Bruder!* (Drakie's brother!)," hugged me warmly, and then, in halting, broken English, introduced herself as Frau Benitzer, one of Drake's nurses. She explained that she recognized me from the photo my mother had sent her in anticipation of my visit. To my embarrassment, which exists now in even the recollection, my greeting to her was in the form of a one-word question. "Toilet?" I asked.

A few minutes later, feeling slightly relieved, I was climbing the four flights of stairs with Frau Benitzer to the fifth and topmost floor where Drake, by now twice as old as the next-oldest "child" in the *Sonnenhof,* had lived since the fall of 1930. As we reached the top landing, I felt waves of nervousness in my stomach, accompanying the other problems, and my mind was racing through the possibilities of what I might say and he might say. Would we hug or kiss or shake hands? Would I *feel* that he was my brother?

We stopped at the entrance to the bedroom at the end of the short, dark hall and there he was, sitting on his bed, dressed in pajamas and a loose-fitting pale blue bathrobe. He was rocking gently back and forth and his hands were clasped together inside the bathrobe sleeves.

"*Schau, Drakie! Dein Bruder ist von Amerika gekommen, um Dich zu besuchen!* (Look, Drakie! Your brother has come to see you from America!)" said Frau Benitzer, and I stuck out my hand. Frau Benitzer gently pulled his right hand from his sleeve and placed it in mine. It was very soft and limp. He stopped rocking for a few seconds and glanced furtively up at me before quickly turning away. At first, his general appearance seemed just as my mother had described, but then I became conscious of a familiar Sagendorph look around his eyes, rusty-red hair like my mother's, and a strong Hale nose and long fingers. To see him there, a stranger so familiar, was like a dream.

"Hello, Drake," I said, pulling a nearby chair up to his bed and sitting down. "*Wie geht es Ihnen?* (How are you?)" It was the only German phrase I could think of and it immediately sounded inadequate.

Drake turned to Frau Benitzer and began speaking very rapidly to her, his voice little more than a loud whisper. I could not distinguish one word from another. I waited for her to translate, but instead she replied directly to Drake in German, speaking equally rapidly. He responded with another long stream of German, and back and forth they went for several minutes. I felt certain he was somehow indicating to Frau Benitzer how he felt about my presence there. He must, I thought, have a million questions.

Finally, she turned to me and capsuled their entire exchange into eight English words. "He wants to know what's in the package," she said, pointing to the box of sponge cake I held in my lap.

I placed it on his lap. He removed his hands from his sleeves and carefully opened it, folding the paper neatly and placing it to one side. When he got down to the actual contents, he began to eat without hesitation, pulling the cake apart and slowly stuffing large chunks of it into his mouth.

"*Ist gute?* (Is it good?)" I managed to ask but Drake didn't reply. So I watched him in silence while he consumed more than half the cake. "*Genug, Drakie* (Enough, Drakie)," Frau Benitzer told him at long last, and she placed the box on a nearby shelf out of his reach.

For the remainder of that first meeting, I couldn't think of a single additional thing to say. My intestines were hurting again, and emotionally I felt deflated. What I'd expected would be meaningful was turning out to be meaningless. Despite my mother's warnings, Drake was a more pathetic creature than I'd imagined and I felt incapable of any sort of normal interaction with him. We'd get along fine, I thought, if only I could turn into a sponge cake.

Frau Benitzer began paging through the photo album I'd brought with me, punctuating each page with *"Hier ist Deine Schwester, Patsy"* or *"Hier ist Deine Mutter und Dein Vater in Amerika."* Drake looked at each picture intently but didn't say a word. Occasionally Frau Benitzer would turn to me and laugh and I'd join in, just as if I'd understood whatever little joke she'd said.

By the time I rose to leave an hour later, I'd thought of a parting phrase. *"Ich komme morgen wieder* (I'll come again tomorrow)," I said haltingly, and Drake stood up. I was surprised to see how tall he was. Tall and thin, just like me. Then he pulled his limp, long-fingered hand out of his sleeve and held it out for me to take. Suddenly touched, I grasped it in both of mine.

"Wo ist Mommie? (Where is Mommie?)" he said in a soft, almost conspiratorial tone, looking directly into my eyes for the first time.

"In America, Drake," I answered softly. "She sends you her love," I added in English which Frau Benitzer, in a loud voice, immediately translated for him. I had the impression he'd understood without the translation. We remained holding hands, gazing directly into each other's eyes, and I felt comfortable—mentally, emotionally, and even physically—for the first time all day. You are my brother, I thought. You are my brother.

For the next week, I spent several hours every day with Drake and Frau Benitzer. After that first day, Drake was always dressed for my visit in a blue pinstriped suit, a white shirt, and a loosely tied necktie. When I wasn't with them, I'd walk the various paths around the *Sonnenhof,* paths my mother and father had walked so many times over the years. One meandered up to an ancient castle on a hill; another to the Goetheanum, the huge, molded-cement headquarters of the international Anthroposophical Society, occupying a commanding position overlooking the villages of Dornach and Arlesheim. At Frau Benitzer's urging, Drake would recite, in a mindless, breathy monotone, long passages he'd memorized from Goethe.

And we'd attend afternoon art shows and concerts on the *Sonnenhof* premises.

During the second day I was there, while sitting in the audience of children and nurses waiting for a concert to begin, I may have appeared somewhat alarmed at the myriad of screams, violent hiccups, and other loud sounds that filled the hall and would, I supposed, pretty much drown out whatever music was about to be played. Suddenly a tiny hand reached across Drake's lap to pat my knee. It belonged to a little English mongoloid boy who loved to be near Drake though Drake ignored him. Like most of the other children in the hall, he'd been staring at me. "Don't worry about all the noises," he said in a husky, low voice with a pronounced British accent. "That's just what we *do*, you know." I smiled and nodded while everyone around us laughed merrily, relieved to know this tall, blond stranger from the outside world had finally been put at ease.

As the first few notes of the orchestra began, the noises ceased as if by the wave of a wand. I understood then why music is such an important element in the Rudolf Steiner treatment of retarded children.

Drake's favorite activity with me was walking the quarter mile down to the picturesque village of Arlesheim for the purpose of eating ice cream. As we spooned in our heaping dishes of vanilla, always vanilla, he'd communicate his pleasure to me by throwing tiny smiles in my direction. Sometimes, as I tried to say something in German to Frau Benitzer, I'd notice he'd be almost laughing. My efforts with the language obviously amused him. I'd laugh in return, and he'd turn away to gaze off into the distance with a pleased expression on his face, looking all but normal and as if he knew much more about everything than anyone could imagine.

On my last day, he took my arm as we slowly walked back to the *Sonnenhof* from town. When we reached his room, he seemed more talkative than usual, bombarding Frau Benitzer with rapid-fire questions I couldn't understand. Her replies, spoken warmly as she touched his arm and hugged him several times, I could understand without difficulty. "*Oh, Nein, Drakie,*" she said many times, "*Nein, Nein.*"

"What's he saying?" I asked her. "Oh, he's just being silly," she said, reluctant to explain further. Drake and I persisted, he with his questions and I with wanting to know what he was asking. Finally she turned to me and said simply, "He asks if he can go with you to America."

It took me aback. My response, spoken directly to him in the best German I could muster, was, "*Drake, Ich werde Dich ein andermal nach Amerika mitnehmen, aber fur dieses Mal muss ich Auf Wiedersehen sagen* (Drake, I will take you to America someday, but for now I must say good-bye)." He became silent. I put my arm around his shoulders for an instant and then left him there. As I started down the stairs, I turned back and waved to him. He was standing outside the door to his room, slightly stooped at the shoulders, dressed as usual in his blue pinstriped business suit. He didn't wave in return. His hands were tucked up inside his sleeves.

Before taking the trolley back to Basel and boarding a train for Zurich, I decided to walk over to the Goetheanum for one last visit. The afternoon before, I'd noticed some stairs to the right of the two-storey entrance hall. They were roped off with a sign saying "*Kein Eintritt!* (Do Not Enter!)," which is probably what aroused my curiosity. There was no one about in the Goetheanum that afternoon, so I stepped over the rope and began to climb. Arousing my curiosity even more was the faint sound of piano music emanating from somewhere far above me. At each stairwell landing, dimly lit by a single trapezoid-shaped window, another rope with another "*Kein Eintritt!*" sign blocked the next set of stairs, but I continued to climb, stepping over each of the ropes as I came to it. The sound of the piano grew ever louder, and at about the fourth landing, I realized someone was playing the music from the final scene in the third act of Wagner's *Die Walküre*, the same famous aria that Edwin McArthur and Friedrich Schorr had performed together on the old lumber scow tied to the wharf at Star Island many summers before. The music soared. Whoever was playing was obviously a superb professional.

Eventually I ran out of stairs. I was on the top level, in front of a massive wooden door perhaps ten feet high, the upper third of which was shaped like an off-center triangle, so typical of Rudolf Steiner architecture. At this point, the music coming from the other side was thunderous.

I quietly, carefully, pulled back the iron latch on the door and ever so slowly opened it. Inside was a room about the size of a gymnasium with a raised stage at the far end. Folding chairs were piled high in one corner. Without doubt it served both as a theater and as an area for eurythmy classes. Just below the stage was a grand piano, its top raised, and a woman playing it. Her back was to me and her long, straight blond hair hung down below the piano stool to within a few inches of the floor. She wore a dress of layered orange and green chiffon, almost exactly as I remembered the dress Sheila wore for her butterfly dance at my mother's production of *Cinderella* in Vanceboro. I felt almost dizzy with emotions I couldn't even identify.

With the stirring Wagnerian "fire music" still reverberating about the room, she placed her hands in her lap and there was silence. I wanted to clap, but then I wanted more to disappear, to fade quietly from the scene. As I pulled the door toward me, preparing to slip back down the stairs unnoticed, it creaked. The woman whirled around on the piano stool and faced me from across the room. She was hideous. She had been burned, or something very horrible had happened to her. There was only a hole where her nose should have been and her skin was solid scar tissue.

"*Es tut mir leid* (I'm sorry)," I called across to her softly. She stared back at me, seemingly stunned at my presence. With a tentative wave in the way of an additional apology, I closed the door tightly and walked back down the stairs to the outside, where I stood on the terrace looking across to the gardens and fields leading to the village of Dornach and on to the lush green hills beyond. It was a beautiful, pastoral scene, like those on so many Swiss postcards. Birds were singing, a car honked down in the village, and two shepherd dogs were romping on the lawn in front of me. I drank it all in—almost desperately.

The following day, I flew from Zurich to Berlin to rejoin the tour, which ended a week later in Holland, where we boarded the *Rotterdam* once again. The voyage back to New York took around thirteen days, although I wasn't sure of the exact number even at the time. I do know that three or four of them were spent drinking ten-cent bottles of beer while on the floor of the lounge, sitting in pairs, back to back for stability, as the ship barely maintained headway into the mountainous waves of Hurricane Carol.

During the winter of my senior year at Dartmouth, my sister, by this time a Bennington graduate, married a prep-school teacher in

Lake Placid, while I had several dates with a pretty brown-haired Skidmore sophomore with a reputation for being unwilling even to hold hands. Her strict adherence to her Catholic religion did not, however, preclude her willingness to heartily join my friends and me in the steady intake of alcohol that seemed to be the basic prerequisite to any sort of "fun" during my Dartmouth days. Her name was Sally Huberlie, she was from Rochester, and when we kissed in front of her dormitory in Saratoga Springs one cold evening after we'd attempted to have a drink in as many of the town's ninety-nine bars as possible, I felt complimented. She didn't just hand out kisses as a matter of routine. Also, my recently acquired "Peck's Bad Boy" reputation seemed somehow to balance easily with her reputed "straitlacedness," and we had felt mysteriously comfortable with each other from the moment we were introduced by our respective college roommates.

There were a few more dates, a few more kisses, an exchange of letters; but then the series of silly events leading to my expulsion from Dartmouth, two months prior to graduation, swept me off in a different direction. I wouldn't see Sally Huberlie for another four years, but by then the timing would be as right as the relationship.

"Is it true you were thrown out of Dartmouth for vomiting on the dean of the college?" is a question I'm often asked these days. I used to refer to the incident humorously in speeches to various organizations around New England. I stopped doing so after a 1975 live television talk show in New Haven, in which the host up and asked me whether or not I had had an alcohol problem at Dartmouth. That somehow didn't seem so funny.

Yes, it's true I was expelled for throwing up on Dean Joseph MacDonald. But that was only part of the problem. I threw up on Mrs. MacDonald, too. And over fifty other people, I'm told. All in about thirty seconds.

The real blame lies in exactly ten "if only I hadn'ts" . . .

1. If only I hadn't driven the Crow over the lawn in front of the dean's office after a heavy spring rain and become stuck there (the Crow had no reverse gear, so I couldn't back out of my parking place), Dean MacDonald would not have demanded I turn over the Crow's keys to him for a period of two weeks.

2. If only I hadn't given Dean MacDonald the keys to the secret

meeting room in my fraternity basement and kept the keys to the Crow, I would not have been arrested for speeding on the road to White River Junction two days later and so been listed in the local newspaper that Dean MacDonald read every day.

3. If only I hadn't consumed a countless number of whiskey sours at the fraternity cocktail party prior to the annual variety show put on in Webster Hall every spring, and

4. if only I hadn't decided to go to the variety show anyway, despite my general condition, in a friend's black hearse (Dean Mac-Donald having by then appropriated the Crow).

5. If only I hadn't parked the hearse on the front steps of Webster Hall, having failed to have found a convenient, more acceptable parking place, and

6. if only I hadn't been a friend of the two ushers who thought it would be funny to allow me inside.

7. If only they hadn't given me a seat down front, and

8. if only I hadn't almost immediately gone to sleep and awakened a half hour later knowing I was about to be sick.

9. If only I hadn't decided to try for the men's room in the back of the hall, running up the full length of the aisle, my hand over my mouth, spraying secondhand whiskey sours in both directions.

10. If only Mr. and Mrs. MacDonald hadn't been sitting in aisle seats that evening.

When I called my mother in New York to inform her and my father that I'd been expelled from Dartmouth and would be home the next day, she was furious—at Dartmouth.

"I knew you should have gone to Harvard," she said. She had never understood why I'd chosen Dartmouth over my father's alma mater. At the time I had explained to her that I wanted a country college where everyone hiked in the mountains, went on canoe trips, fished, and that sort of thing. She said no one did those things in college, and as it turned out for me, she was right.

She was also angry at Dartmouth for allowing me to be "drummed out of the United States Navy for cowardice" during my sophomore year. It's true I'd been dropped from the Navy R.O.T.C. program for flunking the written gunnery exam that year—but then, to give my friends a laugh, I'd ripped the buttons off my uniform and painted a yellow stripe down the back of my navy overcoat. She came across the coat in my closet during Christmas vacation and so I laughingly told her I'd been literally drummed out of the navy in an elaborate ceremony performed in front of the entire student body. When it was obvious she believed me, there was no undoing it. She was convinced it had happened.

"How could you allow one of your sensitive young boys to be subjected to such a mortifying experience?" I heard her demand on the telephone the evening I returned home. It turned out she was speaking with the president of Dartmouth College, John Sloan Dickey. President Dickey had accompanied my father on fishing trips to the St. Bernard Fish & Game Club in Quebec on several occasions, along with former Dartmouth president Ernest Hopkins, but her tone on the telephone that evening was anything but friendly. She wanted him to reinstate me at the college "immediately," saying Dartmouth and not her "Butch"—somewhere along the line she'd acquired that private name for me (which she still uses today)—was solely responsible for "everything." Whatever minor transgressions I may have committed, she told him, were simply a reaction to being drummed out of the navy in front of the entire college!

Evidently President Dickey investigated "the incident," because a friend of mine told me later that a Navy R.O.T.C. professor announced to his senior class during the last week of their final term that "contrary to a silly rumor instigated two years ago by some joker," the United States Navy had *not* "drummed" anyone out or painted a yellow stripe down anyone's back since the days of John Paul Jones! President Dickey's investigation must also have convinced him that Dartmouth College was, indeed, better off without Judson Hale. My expulsion stood.

In order for me to recover from the trauma of my Dartmouth "experience," my mother decided on the spur of the moment to take me on a vacation in Europe. I needed a "change of scenery," she said. So within a week after my involuntary departure from college, she and I flew to Paris on Pan American's posh "Ambassador" flight, in which, after dinner, sleeping berths were made up just like the ones on a train, and for the next two months we toured the French and Italian Rivieras and spent a week with Drake, and I walked for perhaps a hundred miles along the streets of Paris. I happily reveled in my troubled life and uncertain future. I would sit moodily for hours on the banks of the Seine as if contemplating the great questions of life and death. In truth, my mind was often blank or perhaps weighing whether or not to purchase another small bottle of wine. For a rather spoiled, immature, twenty-two-year-old New England preppy, life's problems are a game. There's a seemingly infinite expanse of time out ahead in which to maneuver and recover.

On the other hand, I sensed it was my mother who was having to face real-world problems. Her time was running out, at least as far as her singing career was concerned. During the eight years since Sunrise Farm had failed, she'd greatly expanded her operatic repertoire beyond Wagner to include such Italian roles as Tosca, Aida, Desdemona in *Otello,* both Mimi and Musetta in *La Bohème,* and both Sustazza and Lola in *Cavalleria Rusticana.* She also learned Marguérite in *Faust* and could sing Rosalinda in the English version of *Die Fledermaus.*

We spent an evening discussing her career at a small outdoor restaurant, with candles on every table, up on Montmartre overlooking the city of Paris. At that time, she said, she could sing any one of twenty-two major operatic roles, plus seven small roles, on four hours' notice. But she also told me that evening that although she intended to continue her voice lessons and maintain her roles, her operatic career had probably ended the year before in Dusseldorf. She'd been auditioning at various European opera houses that winter, including at La Scala, with the idea that she'd join one of them and eventually become successful enough in Europe to attract the attention of the Metropolitan Opera Company in New York. (That was the typical route to "the Met" in those days.)

She'd turned down several small companies, but when she was given an offer to join the well-known, prestigious company in Dusseldorf, she was ready to accept. It would mean, of course, living abroad for at least a year.

"The morning I was preparing to go over to sign the contract, I received a letter at the hotel from Rog saying how much he missed me and that he had a cold," she said. "It made me wonder where my responsibility lay, and I ended up coming home." I told her there'd be plenty more opportunities, but she disagreed. "When I had the *perfect* opportunity, I'd shown the color of my flag," she said. And

as we drank a little more champagne, with the lights of Paris twin-
kling below us, she talked to me about "seizing life's moments" as
they pass on by. I only half listened.

We sailed to New York on the *United States,* sitting at the
captain's table every night, naturally. My father met us at the dock,
and a week later he and I sat all by ourselves in the third row of an
old theater somewhere off Broadway while my mother, accompanied by Edwin McArthur on the piano, sang the Sieglinde role
from the second act of *Die Walküre.* "Musically, this is an extremely
difficult part," she warned us before beginning, as if she wasn't sure
how well she'd get through it.

When she finished, she looked across the empty orchestra pit to
us. My father had tears streaming down his face. It was the only time
I saw him cry, and it's one of my mother's most cherished memories
of him today. "Until then, I don't think he thought I could *really*
sing," she recalls, and then she sadly adds, "but it was too late."

A month later, despite holding down a regular salaried job for
the first time in his life, my father joined my mother for yet another European trip. He had enrolled in the conservation program
at Yale in 1950, a year after Sunrise Farm was auctioned off, received his Master of Science degree there two years later, and had
then joined the New York Conservation Foundation (now in
Washington), becoming one of the vice-presidents shortly thereafter. Over the next seven years, he was to become a respected
early voice in the national conservation movement, speaking at colleges and universities and participating in seminars of, for instance,
the Natural Resources Council of America and the North American Wildlife Association.

I have recently read through a four-foot-high stack of folders
containing his letters, articles, and speeches from those years. His
expertise was obviously on the subject of conservation education at
the college and graduate school levels, but his letters also indicate a
lively interest in the problems of how to control the deer and other
game populations in the national parks. "As an old poacher, myself . . ." several of them begin. In a long letter to the Commissioner
of the Department of Conservation in Albany, he urges that the
phrase "public hunting" be avoided even when, in fact, public hunting was being utilized. "I suggest the term 'herd control' or some-

thing similar," he writes. Clearly he had learned that the euphemisms of politics are useful in the successful practice of conservation!

Included are a number of "Dear Rog" letters from Laurence Rockefeller, referring to forthcoming or past conservation seminars in which both participated. There are indications they often saw each other at the Cosmos Club in Washington. The longest and, I'm sorry to say, the dreariest of the speeches in all these papers is the commencement address he delivered in June of 1960 to the Waldorf School in New York City. ("We do not always know the consequences of our actions. We develop plans; we put them into execution, and the results very often turn out differently from what we expected. . . .")

It is also clear from the material in his files that his commitment to his new career was less than total. Liberally sprinkled throughout the correspondence are such phrases as "I'm sorry I won't be able to attend because Marian and I will be in Florida for the next two months" and "Expect to be on Martha's Vineyard during August" and "I'll be away at the seashore with Marian at that time" and "Can't make it as we'll be sailing for Europe next week if the maritime strike is over." But sometimes he attempted to keep his hand in even while vacationing all winter. From their rented house in Palm Beach he wrote a member of the Soil Conservation Service in Washington, "If you're interested in real pollution, you ought to see the oil on the beaches down here."

When Fairfield Osborne, then president of the New York Conservation Foundation and, therefore, my father's boss, hinted in a letter that he wished his "associates" would be more "associate," my father wrote back to say that he wanted his salary cut in half so he could continue to travel and vacation with my mother without, as he told me at the time, "feeling guilty about it." Fairfield Osborne accepted the suggestion, and there is evidence in the files to indicate that not long after that most of the other vice-presidents at the Foundation did exactly the same. A year later, my father gave a speech at Windham College in Vermont entitled "Conservation Is Not a Dilettante Affair."

My mother and father sailed for Europe in late June 1955, leaving me to mow the lawns at their current country home in Weston, Connecticut, until I received my army draft notice, expected momentarily. Of course, I was also free to visit their penthouse apartment on New York's Central Park South on occasion. They were barely past the Statue of Liberty before I'd made up my mind to make a *permanent* visit to the penthouse apartment. When they returned in September, they found a note pinned onto the apartment door. It said simply, "I'm in the Army now. Love, Jud." They had to call the Pentagon to learn my whereabouts. Out at their eighteenth-century farmhouse in Weston, purchased from singer Jimmy Melton the year before, the lawns had turned into pasture.

Waiting for almost two months to be drafted into the U.S. Army while living in a penthouse apartment in New York turned out to be a delightful experience—I think. It consisted mostly of drinking martinis out on the balcony and watching the glittering lights of Central Park while discussing the problems of love and the world (90 percent love, 10 percent the world) with my Dartmouth friends who stopped by. The same general routine was followed when my frequent guest was a certain Syracuse freshman who insisted on playing Frank Sinatra's "My Funny Valentine" over and over while she lamented losing the love of her life, a forty-year-old married English professor. There were also evenings listening to Conrad Janis blast forth on his trombone at a downtown beer joint called the Central Plaza, and early mornings dozing on the bar at the uptown Hickory House while Marian McPartland performed her moody piano magic. And everywhere I walked within "my" penthouse apartment, I was confronted with images of myself disappearing into infinity on the myriad of wall mirrors in almost every room. Sometimes, far down the line, one of the more distant ones would slowly raise his hand and wave at me before I could turn away. I'd wonder which was real, him or me.

My draft notice came none too soon.

Chapter 11

The Work Ethic

While standing stark naked in a line of more than a hundred equally naked men, I called out someone's name and inadvertently changed the course of my life. We were waiting for a physical examination. It was the day, in August of 1955, that I had been inducted into the U.S. Army at Fort Dix, New Jersey. Looking down the long line, I spotted a Dartmouth friend, one of those who'd shared the martinis and the view of Central Park many times during the previous two months. I didn't even know he'd been drafted.

"Jim!" I yelled, "Jim Wallace!" He turned, smiled, and waved, but we didn't have a chance to speak to each other until two years later when he and his bride were courageous enough to visit me in the army hospital in Frankfurt, Germany.

Saying something, anything, in that line of naked men was against the rules. The second I did, a tough-looking sergeant yelled, "Button up, soldier!" Then he took down my name and instructed me to tie a towel on the end of my bed before I went to sleep that night. At 2 a.m. I, with three others who'd committed similar minor infractions, was awakened and ordered to report to the kitchen for dreaded K.P. (Kitchen Police) duty.

After twenty-seven straight hours of washing pots and pans, we returned to our barracks to find them empty, awaiting the next group of inductees. All the men I'd been with, including Jim Wallace, had been transferred to the regular training facilities at Fort Dix while we four bad-boy K.P.'s were arbitrarily picked to fill four vacancies in the 33rd Battalion of the 3rd Armored Division, then already in training at Fort Knox, Kentucky.

For me, the transfer to Fort Knox meant sailing to Germany with the 3rd Armored Division the following spring and contracting tuberculosis a year later while on tank maneuvers along the Czecho- slovakian border. Tuberculosis, in turn, was responsible for my rein- statement at Dartmouth and, shortly thereafter, thanks to disability payments, for enabling me to accept a position on my Uncle Robb's struggling little magazine called *Yankee*.

In short, if I had not yelled "Jim Wallace!" while standing naked that first day at Fort Dix, I would very likely be living today where many of my best Dartmouth friends have their homes—in the state from which, mysteriously, all New England innkeepers originate: New Jersey. Such is the capricious nature of Lady Chance.

My seven-year period of misconduct, misdeeds, and mindless- ness, originating with the Peeping Tom night at Choate, virtually ended one warm October afternoon in the tank motor pool at Fort Knox. The five of us who made up the crew of an M-47 tank were supposed to be cleaning the 90mm gun and performing other equally redundant maintenance chores in preparation for the first week-long maneuvers of the division, scheduled to begin the next morning. Instead, we were lying beneath our tank, out of the hot sun and out of sight of wandering sergeants and officers, drinking beer.

My official tank position at that time was "loader." The loader was the least responsible position in the crew. Besides helping with the interminable cleaning and maintenance chores, his only official function was to heave three-foot-long shells into the chamber of the 90mm gun during combat, or, as in our case, while on the firing range. Next above me, in order of rank and prestige, was the bow machine gunner, who sat down low to the right of the driver. He was in charge of a .30-caliber machine gun positioned there. Driver was the middle position. In fact, in order to become one you had to undergo considerable training and pass a road test, after which you were issued a tank-driving license. Ranked over the driver was the gunner, in effect the tank's trigger man. Finally there was the tank commander, whose job it was to stand tall in the turret, look confident, and sound good saying things like "Baker 1, this is Baker 5. Over" into his radio mouthpiece.

"All of you under there! Fall in!" I heard my bone-skinny platoon sergeant yell. He was squatting next to the tank, looking beneath it. I crawled out sheepishly, as did the others. We were all slightly inebriated, having been under there for almost two hours.

"Besides you," he said, pointing to our driver, "do any of you drive?" and I instantly said I did. I'd put nearly a hundred thousand miles on the Crow in the last three years alone.

"You got your license?" he asked. I said yes, but that it was in my wallet back in the barracks.

"Good," he said. "We're short one driver for the maneuvers tomorrow. You'll drive Baker 3."

It was then I realized he and I had been discussing two sorts of driving and two sorts of licenses. I meant cars. He meant tanks. I started to point out the misunderstanding and then stopped myself. What an opportunity for a promotion. Though my heart was suddenly pounding, I said nothing. All at once, for reasons I'm unable to explain even to myself, I wanted to do *well* once again. This would give me the chance. And somewhere floating around in the back eddies of my mind was a statement my mother had made while we were discussing her singing career at the restaurant on Montmartre, something about seizing life's "moments."

At dawn the next morning, I was sitting in the driver's seat of Baker 3. The engine was roaring—yes, I'd managed to start the thing, thanks to last-minute instructions from a tank-driver friend the night before. I'd even remembered to press the two starting levers *before* activating the tank's internal radio system. "Start the engine with the radio on," my friend had warned, "and you'll blow up a hundred-thousand-dollar radio." Surely that was the sort of little blunder that might alert my tank crew to the fact their new driver was not exactly "experienced."

"Move out!" came the order over my headphones from the tank commander standing tall in the turret far above me. It was just becoming light. I pushed the single lever located on my right into the forward position, pressed gently on the accelerator, and fifty tons of steel began to rumble forward.

"Stay fifty yards behind Baker 4," the voice on my radio instructed. Thank goodness the pace of our long line of tanks, each with its guns pointing backward, was slow through the base area, perhaps 5 m.p.h., with many stops. It gave me a chance to calm down, but only a little.

Once on a tarred road outside the base, the tanks in front of me accelerated. Baker 4 was already several hundreds of yards ahead and gaining more speed when my tank commander's voice cracked through my headphones: "Get going, driver!" I slowly increased my foot pressure, passed the point in speed where I still felt reasonably comfortable, went on beyond to where I was frightened, and thence, after another bark through the headphones, to being out of control.

Unlike the later-model M-48 tanks, which had a small steering wheel, the M-47 was steered by moving the shift lever. But at the top speed we were traveling, somewhere around 40 m.p.h., I learned one did *not* steer by moving the shift lever right or left. One controlled a speeding tank by merely *thinking* about moving the shift lever right or left. More pressure than that meant trouble.

I was in trouble. When I oversteered to the right, I overcorrected to the left. Then I'd overcorrect to the right. We were weaving at breakneck speed (believe me, 40 m.p.h. in a fifty-ton tank is like going 80 m.p.h. in anything else!) in ever-widening curves, which, if continued, could only end in catastrophe. In fact, I figured catastrophe was two, perhaps three, overcorrections away.

"Jesus Christ! What-the-hell-are-ya-doin!?" The voice on my headphones almost pierced my eardrums. A gas station was looming up in front of us. As we flashed by, barely missing the two pumps, I was conscious of a brief crunching sound, which I later learned was the attendant's motorcycle. Seconds later, we'd swooped over to the other side of the road and were beginning what appeared to me to be our last overcorrected turn. If continued, it would be adequate to take us over the bank leading down to the dry riverbed running parallel with the road. The voice now coming over my headphones was so loud and shrieky I couldn't decipher the words.

Finally, I exercised my only remaining option. I slammed on the brakes. My tank commander was not catapulted out, only because his foot caught on the .50-caliber machine-gun mounting next to the hatch cover. The gunner later showed me his front teeth, loosened considerably when his radio mouthpiece passed by them on its way to the back of his throat. The bow gunner and loader had bruises.

But I'd avoided driving over the bank and, at the suddenly reduced speed, was able to break the overcorrecting cycle. At long last we proceeded down the road in a straight line, my foot shaking so badly I could barely keep it on the accelerator. As we began to catch up with the tanks ahead, I repeated the words "Don't steer!" over and over to myself out loud, between tightly clenched teeth. "We're gonna ease to the left—but *don't steer!*"

I'd learned how to drive an M-47 tank—and, more important, I'd learned that the best steering is done with one's *mind.*

It took many hours of driving without further mishap that day to convince my new tank crew they weren't going to die. But they eventually calmed down and even laughed about it. I remained a tank driver on Baker 3, *sans* official tank-driver license, for the remainder of the year. In January 1956 I was very proud to be among the fifty "good hard workers," as my battalion commander described us, chosen from the entire division to spend six weeks in the Mojave Desert learning how to operate and shoot America's newest big tank, the M-48. We'd return as instructors.

We shot real .30-caliber machine-gun bullets at each other's buttoned-down tanks out there, and sometimes, when there weren't any officers around, we'd let fly a 90mm projectile at the top of a nearby mountain. I'd been promoted (legitimately!) to the position of gunner when we arrived in California, so I was usually the one who activated our "flying geese" ranging device at some snowcapped peak and pulled the trigger. Then, while the projectile was flying on its way, I'd crawl out the top hatch to join the rest of the crew on the tank's back deck to wait for a puff of white smoke far above us, indicating the projectile had arrived.

We stopped shooting at mountains the day I missed one completely. The projectile, containing explosives, soared past it to the left and on in the general direction of the town of Barstow. Lord knows where it actually landed. Gunnery just didn't seem to be my forte.

Our voyage to Europe in the spring of 1956 was not particularly reminiscent of drinking champagne at the captain's table on the *United States.* On the troop ship, all our waking hours were spent standing in long winding lines for meals while seasick soldiers threw up in barrels placed about for that purpose. Throwing up over the side was forbidden, in deference, I suppose, to those on lower decks.

Our new home in Germany was in the quaint little town of Gelnhausen, just outside Frankfurt, where my five-tank platoon moved into the fifth floor of a barracks formerly used by a Nazi S.S. unit. Once every week, sometimes more often, all sixty-odd tanks in our battalion would charge out of our motor pool in response to an "alert." Alerts meant racing pell-mell through several towns in order to join other tank battalions in a certain wooded area where, if it was ever for real, we would begin shooting at Russian tanks. Because every World War III alert invariably occurred at precisely 3 a.m., many of the drivers were in approximately the same shape they'd been in upon returning to the barracks two hours earlier from an evening in Frankfurt. As a result, the Army Corps of Engineers necessarily followed in our wake as a matter of routine. Their job was to repair the sheared-off corners of buildings, replace fencing, curbstones, shrubs, and trees, restore partially destroyed bridges, and no doubt spend considerable time apologizing to the irritated residents of the villages we thundered through.

The most tragic "alert" was one that never happened. On the night Russian tanks were rolling into Hungary to quell the uprising there, I was on temporary duty as the colonel's orderly at battalion headquarters. When I returned to the barracks, I decided to tell everyone I'd just heard that President Eisenhower was ordering the Seventh Army, of which we were a part, to Budapest that very night. We were going to war! I thought it would be funny to see how people reacted.

Some took it seriously and grimly began packing their gear in preparation for combat. A few of my close friends spotted the twinkle in my eye and proceeded to hang me out a fifth-floor window by my feet until I'd admitted the hoax. While that was going on, two men deserted.

One returned an hour later, having learned we were not, in fact, being sent to Hungary. The other was apprehended in Frankfurt two days later, charged with being absent without leave, and brought back to Gelnhausen under guard to await shipment to the United States, where he'd receive a dishonorable discharge. It was an extreme punishment under the circumstances. Similar cases were ordinarily taken care of by a few days in the stockade. But none of us was surprised. The man happened to be a tall, gentle, loose-jointed, slow-talking black named Harry who was persona non grata to our southern cadre. For some time they'd been blatantly searching for an excuse to remove him from our company entirely. I'd inadvertently helped to provide the excuse.

Harry's basic problem seemed to be that he was either unable or, more likely, unwilling ever to come fully to attention. As he'd stand somewhat slouched over at the shoulders or with his weight more on one leg than on the other, our sergeants would yell "Attention!" over and over at him until their faces were every bit as red as their necks. At each yell, delivered at a distance of perhaps six inches, Harry would straighten up another half inch and no more, always maintaining a calm, somewhat amused expression. It was a daily war.

"Harry, I apologize," I said to him, extending my hand as he was climbing into a truck a week later to be taken to the airport. He was being guarded by a man with an unholstered, fully loaded .45-caliber pistol. He turned, took my hand in both of his, and said with what I thought was a sad smile, "It don't matter, Jud. They can't get me. Like the old song says, 'I'm goin' home tomorrow; I'm goin' home tomorrow; I'm gonna see my baby!' " As the truck drove away, he was humming that old song softly to himself.

I decided that from then on I needn't add any more practical jokes to those already provided by ordinary, day-to-day living.

Tuberculosis came my way during bitterly cold winter tank maneuvers on the Czechoslovakian border. The donor was my skinny platoon sergeant, who was so sick with what he thought was the flu that he could barely smoke down his daily three packs of cigarettes. Perhaps I shouldn't have borrowed his water canteen or used his radio headset during days he remained bundled up in his tent.

Upon our return to home base in Gelnhausen, he was whisked off to sick bay, his real problem as yet undiagnosed, while I was given command of his tank even though, as a corporal (specialist third class), I was a grade below the usual rank for a tank commander. By this time I was already coughing all day and suffering from what seemed like excessive fatigue, but nonetheless I was thrilled to be the one chosen. To be sure, I couldn't at first fathom *why*. God knows —as did everyone else—it wasn't due to any skills in "tank stuff" like mechanics, communications, driving, or gunnery. However, as the one soldier in our company willing, even eager, to do my absolute best at any job handed me, even unto cleaning out the bathroom urinals with a razor blade, I had recently acquired a reputation as "a worker." For the rest of my life, I decided, I would remain "a worker" and surely everything else would naturally fall into place around me.

So for three predawn alerts I had the opportunity to stand tall in the turret of my old platoon sergeant's M-48 tank, its engine roaring beneath me, and say marvelous military things like "Baker 3, this is Baker 5. Over" into my radio and then, as the long line of tanks on my right would begin to peel out in semidarkness toward the motor pool exits, to bark "Move out, driver!" The almost euphoric sense of raw power generated by this sort of thing surprised me. Finally I fully understood what Dartmouth philosophy professor Rosenstock Heusy meant when he once told us that the most dangerous side of war is its seductiveness.

Euphoria ended quickly, as it always must. Several weeks after becoming a tank commander and a week after every soldier in the 33rd Tank Battalion had, for reasons not explained to us, been given a blood test, I was standing in the usual morning formation prior to marching to the motor pool when two orderlies pulled up in an ambulance truck. One of them handed my company commander a slip of paper. "Hale!" he yelled. "Sir!" I answered from severals rows back.

"In the truck, Hale," he said, and then, as I stepped out of the formation and was about to climb in through the rear door, he scared me. For the first time since I'd been listening to his daily yells and barks, he spoke in a soft, gentle voice. "Good luck to you, son," he said. Jesus, I thought to myself, what does he mean by that?

As it turned out, I never saw him or any of my friends again. In fact, I never even saw the stuff in my locker again! One minute I was about to begin a routine army day and the next I was bouncing along in an ambulance truck on my way to the army hospital in Frankfurt. As I entered a doctor's office at the hospital, he was placing a white gauze mask on his face. Another scary signal!

"According to the blood test you received last week, Hale," he said, "you have tuberculosis. You were the only one besides your platoon sergeant to test positive." He went on to tell me I'd be kept in Frankfurt for a few weeks and then flown to the army hospital in Valley Forge, Pennsylvania.

"How long will I be there, sir?" I asked, and his answer was somewhat numbing. "It could be as long as seven years," he said.

Visitors were not allowed on the fourth floor of the hospital, and I was the only one up there. My platoon sergeant was in a more-intensive-care area on the third floor, being prepared for an operation that would remove much of both lungs. When the nurse came into my room with a meal tray, she'd hold her breath until she was safely back out the door.

For the first week, my only activity was being taken downstairs for x-rays, over and over again. I guess someone just wasn't doing them right. Otherwise, I was pretty much left alone to write "brave letters," which I very much enjoyed doing. "Don't bother trying to get me reinstated at Dartmouth," I wrote Dean Joseph MacDonald. Several months before I'd written to ask if I could return for my final term following my discharge from the army, and he'd replied that, although he'd look into it, he thought my chances were "slim."

"Just forget it," I wrote him from the Frankfurt hospital, absolutely reveling in the self-pity of it all. "I have tuberculosis and probably won't recover for seven years, if I ever do." It was deliciously dramatic. He wrote back a sympathetic, friendly note saying he'd personally see to it I was reinstated "no matter how many years from now that must necessarily be." At long last Dartmouth was on my side again, though, to be sure, the method utilized was not the sort to be widely recommended to others.

My letter breaking the news to my mother and father, I decided, ought to be more upbeat. I felt the kindest approach would be an attempt at humor, so I described the hilarious way some of the nurses held their breath whenever they came near me, how my "luxurious private suite" was the deserted fourth floor of the hospital, that my only treatment was to be "zapped by x-rays all day long," and that at least it appeared I would "get a good rest" over the next seven years. Needless to say, my mother and father were not even slightly amused by the letter. The very morning they received it, my father telephoned Robert Cutler at the White House. An old friend of my father's from the Boston days, "Bobby" Cutler had been openly ambitious over the years, even considered somewhat "pushy" by some of his more staid friends, and was then an aide to President Eisenhower.

"I hear Bobby Cutler has become pretty successful," one of his classmates reportedly remarked one noon hour while rolling dice for drinks at the Harvard Club. "Oh yes, he has," someone replied, "but of course only on a *national* level." The exchange has since become one of the classic "Boston snob" stories.

Well, Bobby Cutler *was* influential enough, if "only on a national level," to impress the appropriate general at the Pentagon that a certain Corporal Judson Hale, sick with tuberculosis up in the empty, dark fourth floor of an army hospital in Frankfurt, Germany, was important—even if no one along the line could fathom why!

Everything changed overnight. I was moved down to a large corner room on the third floor, I was provided with snacks as well as almost-gourmet meals, several doctors came to see me twice a day, and I was started on a brand-new antitubercular medication, taken in pill form, that would miraculously eliminate tuberculosis sanitariums all over the world within a few years and cure a mild case such as mine within months.

A week later, I was lying, masked, on one of dozens of stretchers, mostly occupied by men with broken limbs or accidental wounds, in an army plane droning its way across the Atlantic toward home. Although it was the middle of the night, no one was asleep. We were all silently watching the copilot, who was shining a flashlight out a passenger window onto one of the starboard engines, which had stopped running. "Guess we'll make it," he muttered under his breath as he turned to walk back toward the cockpit. The plane suddenly erupted in a chorus of voices shouting "You *guess!* You better *know*, buddy!" It occurred to me that up there we were a long way out of Bobby Cutler's sphere of influence. But, as it turned out, the copilot guessed right.

My eleven months in the tuberculosis ward of the Valley Forge Army Hospital consisted of becoming proficient at bumper pool and shooting rubber bands at the ceiling in such a way as to have them land within a painted circle on my chest, an activity resurrected from childhood "rest periods" in Chestnut Hill and Vanceboro. We also watched Sugar Ray Robinson's career fade away on the Friday and Wednesday night fights, flirted with the masked high school girls who came every afternoon to teach us how to hook rugs and make leather wallets, and after lights out, consumed the Dewars White Label my Dartmouth friends from New York and New Jersey smuggled in to me every weekend.

I also wrote Dean MacDonald that, thanks to the brand-new tuberculosis medication, I'd be ready to return to Dartmouth the following winter. He confided to me later that several college officials were reluctant to go along. My recovery following so quickly after my "I'll-probably-die" letter seemed to indicate a continuation of my erstwhile college shenanigans, but Dean MacDonald, true to his word, helped me *in* every bit as much as he'd helped me *out* three years before. (We corresponded as friends off and on until his death in 1983.)

When I was released from the hospital in December 1957 and retired on 50 percent disability pay, I returned to my mother and father's home in Weston and, of course, to the penthouse in New York. (How my father managed financially to support all of this plus the trips to Europe would not become apparent for another five years.) It was at Central Park South, while cleaning out the desk I'd occasionally used during vacations from college, that my hand felt the edges of a crumpled piece of paper that had become partially wedged behind one of the drawers. I pulled it out in several pieces. It was a four-year-old handwritten letter from Sally Huberlie, that cute-but-strict Catholic girl from Rochester I'd dated a few times at Dartmouth. The one my friends predicted would never kiss me— but who did. The one I never thought could match me drink for drink throughout a bar-hopping evening in Saratoga Springs—but who did. While I sat there placing the pieces of the letter together, I wondered what in the world had ever happened to that girl. Probably married, I thought, with two or three children already.

The desk drawer still didn't operate smoothly. Reaching even farther back, I pulled forth a crumpled envelope with her address on it, and it was then, on a sudden, perhaps mysterious, impulse, I picked up pen and paper and wrote her a note. I don't have to remember what I said, because the note is before me now, one of many "Jud Letters" Sally has saved over the years in a white cardboard box, so labeled, tied with a sickeningly pink ribbon.

Dear Sally,

    Are you still on this globe? Do you remember a ne'er-do-well from Dartmouth (Bob Hayes' roommate) who helped you discover all ninety-nine bars in Saratoga Springs one rainy evening long, long ago? Are you married? Engaged to be? Can you still be reading this note—if you've ever received it, that is? Would you be even slightly interested to know I'm fatter now, a little wiser (I hope) and that I no longer harbor "the poet's disease" you may have heard about from your old roommate, Joan, who, as you surely know, married my old roommate, Bob!? Incidentally, I'll be back at Dartmouth next month for another go at graduation! The Indians forgave me! Want to come up some time?

Sincerely,
Jud Hale

P.S. The Crow passed away, God rest his soul.

A week later I received a letter with a Rochester, New York, address in the left-hand corner. I was rather surprised to note that my heart was pounding as I opened it. "Yes, yes, no, no, yes, yes . . ." it began, and our lives began to intertwine.

Three months and several dates-with-Sally-at-Dartmouth later, I found myself driving to Rochester for a three-day weekend in order to conduct a serious, even profound, conversation with her—perhaps with her parents too—on the subject of the possibility of our undertaking a mixed-religion marriage. Once one was finally a mature, responsible individual, I thought, one didn't leap impulsively into anything. One analyzed all the pros, cons, pitfalls, and advantages of, for instance, joining her supposedly strict Catholicism to my odd, convoluted mixture of skepticism, New England Puritanism, mysticism, anthroposophy, and guardian angels. How would it all affect our children? After three days of thoughtful discussion, perhaps then we could intelligently sort out our individual priorities and make whatever plans seemed appropriate according to the conclusions we'd arrived at through the orderly analytical process.

Our discussion lasted less than a minute. "The fact our religions are different doesn't really matter to me," I said. "Does it to you?" "No," she answered. We were sitting next to each other on the couch in her parents' summer cottage on Lake Canandaigua, a few miles west of Rochester. Her mother and father had just gone to bed, and we were prepared for a long night and the most important conversation of our young lives.

"It doesn't?" I said, surprised at her simple answer. "No, it doesn't," she said firmly. "Oh," I said. We looked at each other for perhaps a full minute. Finally I broke the silence by saying, "Well,

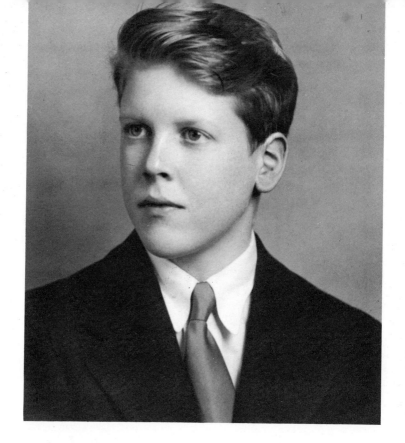

Because it made me look so much older than I *really* looked, I secretly loved the formal photograph of myself, ABOVE, taken for my graduation from Harvey, a pre-prep boarding school then in Hawthorne, N.Y. I was fourteen. Everyone at Choate the following fall thought I might be eight, perhaps nine. For the next five years, my desperate attempts to look and sound older were downright bizarre (Chapter 10). Patsy, on the other hand, looked lovely for her formal graduation photo, LEFT, from Westover School, my mother's alma mater. Westover was a school for "finishing" young ladies, but Patsy's heart was still with her beloved cows and horses at Sunrise Farm, which, by this time, was no more.

ABOVE: Grandpop's eighty-ninth birthday, August 1951. From left: Cousin Robert (Aunt Mard's son), who died of polio in 1953; my mother; Aunt Mard; Patsy; and I, about to be a Dartmouth freshman. Seated: Robert's brother, Cousin Frank, who survived polio a month later; Grandpop; Frank's wife, Eloise; and their children. (My father snapped the picture.)
BELOW: My mother and I at Dartmouth, the year before I was thrown out.

When my platoon sergeant in Germany went into the hospital with tuberculosis, at first undiagnosed, I was given command of his tank. That's me, RIGHT, cleaning my .45-caliber revolver the day before my first scheduled practice alert as a tank commander. The euphoria wouldn't last long, however. When this photo was taken, I had tuberculosis, too—but didn't know it. BELOW: Almost two years later, in June 1958, somewhat heavy from my medication and still smoking cigarettes (as my army doctor encouraged me to do!), I was in a happy mood the day following the evening Sally (that's her, of course!) and I became engaged. We're on her father's boat, *Hub's Tub,* on Lake Canadaigua, N.Y.

Arthur Rickerby, *Life* magazine © 1966 Time Incorporated

Robb Sagendorph, my mother's brother and founder of *Yankee,* at his desk, studying a copy of *The Old Farmer's Almanac,* in our Dublin, N.H., office. The time is early 1960s, when Robb still successfully promoted the magazine by telling potential subscribers that "there's nothing much in it."

Arthur Rickerby, *Life* magazine © 1966 Time Incorporated

ABOVE: Robb driving his old wooden outboard motorboat to his island on Highland Lake, Stoddard, N.H. BELOW: The last photograph of my father. He, my mother, Sally, and I are celebrating my thirtieth birthday at the Copacabana in New York—March 16, 1963. Patsy, in particular, had recently been worried about our father's drinking, so I called her the following week to say, "Dad seemed fine." But he ended his life a month later.

Arthur Rickerby, *Life* magazine © 1966 Time Incorporated

ABOVE: Aunt Trix confers with Robb about a controversial stone sculpture she wanted placed next to the Yankee headquarters across the street. For the most part, however, Trix devoted her days to painting *Yankee* covers in her studio, leaving Robb to his domain here in Dublin village. BELOW: Rob Trowbridge (Robb's son-in-law) and I with Robb in Robb's new office.

ABOVE: The *Yankee* lunch table at the Dublin Inn. As usual, I'm threatening to snag some food off Robb's plate. It was one of our ongoing jokes, but because Robb was so seriously ill at this time (1969), my attempts at humor were rather desperate. BELOW: Sally and I with our boys in 1968. She was in trouble then, though I wasn't fully aware of how serious it was.

Epilogue: Thanksgiving 1986, when Judson Drake, Jr. (behind Sally), 27, was an ad salesman in Boston for Yankee Publishing; Daniel, 26, was helping to restore the historic William Pitt Tavern in Portsmouth, N.H.; and Christopher (the one out on a limb), 22, was a junior at Bates College.

let's get married." "Yes," she said, without hesitation, and we kissed. It was done. A few minutes later she ran into her parents' room to tell her mother. My excitement matched hers exactly, and for the next three hours we chatted happily about pure love, emotion, instincts springing from the subconscious, and how the quickest method of smothering all three was through intellectual analysis!

The next morning, her father, a genial, loving, self-made man who'd just turned his fuel-oil business over to Sally's brother, put his arm around my shoulder with the casual, midwestern ease I so admired but could never duplicate, and said, "Welcome aboard!" It all felt very, very right.

Following my Dartmouth graduation in June 1958—seven years after first arriving there as a squeaky-voiced little boy who spent much of his time shouting into his pillow—I began looking for work in New York City. The wedding day was set for September 6, and surely it would be awkward not to have found a job by then.

"What can you do?" was the age-old question put to me by the people who interviewed me at advertising agencies and publishing houses. I would laughingly reply that, well, I could drive a tank and had majored in English at Dartmouth. Few laughed in return. I said I had worked on my high school newspaper. At that piece of news, their eyes would glaze over.

"My brother is putting out a little magazine he calls *Yankee,*" my mother remarked to me as I was seeing her off on the *Ile de France* one evening in July. She was sailing to Europe to see Drake again, scheduled to return just before the wedding. "He may know people in publishing. Why don't you write him? But don't say I suggested it."

I'd met my Uncle Robb Sagendorph only twice before. The Sagendorph family was not the sort to favor get-togethers. What few had occurred over the years had ended, far more often than not, in some sort of unpleasantness. Besides, my mother never forgave Robb, her older brother, for the way he once introduced her to a certain Harvard classmate she admired when she was a giddy but beautiful teenager. "I'd like you to meet 'the shrimp,' " Uncle Robb had said as my mother came down the stairs in her debutante gown. Today, at age eighty-four, she still refers to it occasionally, saying it was "a rude way to introduce a girl—and, besides, I was already five feet six inches tall!" Some things live forever.

Uncle Robb's four-page, handwritten reply to mine began, "It is interesting to hear you want to go into the 'publishing' business" and went on to describe no less than "eighteen subdivisions" within the industry. "I believe it is important for you to decide which of these you want," he went on. "My usual advice is on the *distribution* end, as basically all eighteen subdivisions depend largely on this mysterious (nobody really knows the answers) relationship between author-editor and newsstand, subscriptions and bookstores and mail-order buyers. The *highest* pay and rewards in the industry are to be found among those who understand and are experienced on this end. Authors, editors, production, design, and ad men come and go, but a good distribution man can practically name his own ticket."

As I was to learn over the next twelve years, my Uncle Robb, bless him, the man who would be a more profound influence on my life than any other, was at his very worst when giving personal advice. However, it didn't matter. I couldn't fathom what he was talking about in that first letter, anyway—until I reached the bottom of page three.

"I have an interesting little opening here at the moment," he wrote. That I understood. "The pay wouldn't be too hot—$55 a week . . . there'd be a lot of proofreading, layout and detail work . . . but you'd be in a focal spot where you could familiarize yourself with just about all the angles."

Perfect, I thought. Six months or perhaps a year with Uncle Robb's little New England magazine and I'd return to the big city able to say I could do a few things besides drive a tank! My father, on seeing the letter, said Sally and I could never get by on only $55 a week, but I pointed out to him that my monthly disability payments would keep us afloat. (Surely, as it all turned out, no one in this world has ever been so downright fortunate to have contracted tuberculosis!)

Incidentally, Uncle Robb paid me slightly less than $50 a week and denied offering $55. I did not, however, resort to showing him his letter (which I now have framed on my office wall). Like my mother and all the Sagendorphs, Uncle Robb never responded particularly well to proof.

My mother flew into Rochester from Switzerland the very day of our wedding in the Catholic church in the small town of Webster,

New York, where farmers were realizing huge profits that year by selling their land to a company called Xerox. She joined my father outside the church about fifteen minutes prior to the ceremony, dressed in white feathers, including a white feather hat. She looked pretty flamboyant for Webster, New York—but stunning.

After I greeted her in the church parking lot and introduced her to some of Sally's relatives who were filing into the church, she pulled me to one side.

"Butch, are you *sure* this is what you want?" she asked, gazing steadily into my eyes as she'd always had the rather disconcerting habit of doing. While about three hundred mostly Rochester people were gathering inside the church, I had the distinct impression that, as far as she was concerned, I could easily have responded with, "Well, come to think of it, I guess not," and the two of us would have walked out to her rented car and driven away to have a champagne brunch somewhere in town. That would have been the sophisticated, Cary Grant–style reaction. Instead, my answer was a regression to the time I was ten or eleven years old. I was the little fair-haired golden boy again, being lovingly patronized by my glamorous mother, who always seemed to approach each of life's important events as if it were a scene in an ever-so-romantic storybook or movie.

"Oh, Mom!" I said, maybe even stamping my foot, and turned to walk into the church. My mother followed, smiling, the absolute star of the show, knowing she still maintained her own mysteriously subtle brand of control.

Chapter 12

---◆---

Shrewdness

I WANTED to be early for my first day on the job at *Yankee* magazine, so I came in at 7:30 a.m. Robb Sagendorph had already been there for an hour. It was Monday, September 15, 1958, nine days after my wedding.

"Look at this, Jud," said Uncle Robb, holding up a small brownish almanac as I came into the room on the second floor of a red clapboard building in the center of tiny (population 1,000) Dublin, New Hampshire. Uncle Robb's small, battered old desk was in one corner; mine, newer and bigger, in another; and there were three other people scattered about the room as well. My presence that first morning instantly increased the editorial, advertising, and production staff of *Yankee* by 20 percent.

"It's an original 1793 edition of *The Old Farmer's Almanac,*" said Uncle Robb, carefully leafing through the tattered pages for me to see. His hands, I noticed, were extraordinarily large, like the rest of him. He wore a bright red bow tie and suspenders, the sleeves of his white Brooks Brothers shirt were rolled back to the midway point of his long forearms, and a lighted cigarette was hanging from his mouth. Most noticeable to me, however, were the deeply etched lines in his face. They were placed perfectly, as if by a sculptor.

"Robb always looked like the Old Man of the Mountain," recalled John MacDuffie, a Harvard classmate of both Uncle Robb's and my father's, at a memorial service following Uncle Robb's painful death in 1970. By then I'd become used to hearing people associate Robb Sagendorph with mountains.

"He always made me think of Mount Sugarloaf here in South Deerfield," Mrs. Eva Cane, one of the librarians at the Jones Library in Amherst, wrote to *Yankee* after the same ceremony. "A great prow of New England surging forward with good-humored irony through the homely littleness of our days." Did he, I often wondered, deliberately mold his character to conform to his craggy, mountain-like appearance? Surely it couldn't have been the other way around!

"Very valuable," said Uncle Robb, continuing to turn over the pages of the 1793 almanac. "Probably less than a dozen in existence and I have three." I noticed the ash on his cigarette was becoming long. As time went on during our twelve years together, I grew familiar enough with him to often cry out, "Robb, your cigarette!" and he'd take it from his mouth and search for an ashtray, during which time the long ash usually fell off anyway. But on that first morning, I couldn't do that.

"Life holds more meaning," he went on, "when the past ties into the present," and with that he picked up a copy of the just-printed 1958 edition of *The Old Farmer's Almanac* lying on his desk and held it up next to the old one. "When this happens, one gains the assurance the present will tie into the future," he said, suddenly looking directly up at me with a smile made somewhat crooked by the continued presence of the cigarette.

The smile dislodged not only the long ash but the lighted head as well. I watched in some alarm as it fell directly onto the 1793 almanac and began smoking its way through the first few pages.

My expression alerted him to the crisis and in the next instant we were both galvanized into action, blotting, slapping, and finally blowing away burnt pieces of almanac from his desk.

"Perhaps not *quite* as valuable now, Robb," I said laughingly, conscious I omitted the word "Uncle" for the first time. He laughed, too. My mother and others had warned me he was stern, serious, imposing, and, as they always said, "difficult." Yet in less than five minutes I felt close to this complex mountain of a man. It was the beginning of a bond between us that would outlive him by many years.

"Goddamnit!" he said, suddenly serious again, examining the almanac. Then he seemed to brighten. "Well, they say grief but aggravates the loss." He was quoting from something echoing in his

mind from years of prolific reading. "So grieve *not* for what is past!"
he said, and with that he literally flipped the blackened almanac into
an old wicker basket he had beside him on the floor.

"Come on," he said, rising briskly as he spoke, "let me show you
what I'd like you to do this morning." Though he was not quite sixty
years old, his six-foot-four-inch frame was somewhat bent at the
waist as he walked across the room. I noted later, however, that there
were times when he chose to walk ramrod straight.

One of Robb's two daughters, Jane, recently wrote in an article
about him that "he was an independent thinker, following his own
conscience rather than any orthodox creed." On a Saturday morning
during my first September at *Yankee,* I became aware that unortho-
doxy was an integral part of his day-to-day life.

I was at my new desk on the second floor, making up "reader"
questions ("What's the origin of 'Down East'?" and so on) for a
question-and-answer column called "Sayings of the Oracle," written
(the answers, that is) by a crusty old newspaper columnist for the
Vineyard Gazette, Joseph C. Allen. (A few years later, we finally
began receiving a sufficient number of *real* reader questions for Joe's
column.)

Robb was downstairs in the bathroom, which, I might add, was
not in any way so designated. At some point I became aware of an
elderly woman's quavering voice crying out from somewhere on the
first floor. "Helloo," it bleated several times. "Anybody home?" I
started down the stairs but stopped when I realized Robb was taking
care of the matter.

"Oh, you're Robb Sagendorph," I heard her exclaim. Then a
different lady's voice chimed in with, "We've seen you on *What's My
Line!*" "And," a third voice added, *"I've Got a Secret!"*

Robb was mumbling something I couldn't quite understand as
the ladies continued with "We didn't expect to meet the famous
Robb Sagendorph himself this morning!" and "Aren't we the lucky
ones!" all in an onslaught of enthusiasm, each voice overlapping the
others. I decided I'd better help him out.

When I reached the bottom of the stairs, the scene before me was
one I will never forget. There were three nicely dressed elderly
ladies standing around Robb, who was sitting down, a weak smile
on his face as he looked up at them. Odd, because Robb would not

ordinarily remain sitting while ladies in the room were standing. He was always a gentleman, in every sense of that old-fashioned word.

Unbeknownst to the three ladies, however, Robb was sitting on the toilet. I could see his pants crumpled around his feet but the newspaper he'd been reading more or less covered his bare knees.

The ladies were now wishing to purchase subscriptions to *Yankee,* so Robb began to write their names and addresses on a small pad he carried in his shirt pocket. At the point where he had to accept their money and make change from his wallet, which he took from his pants pocket lying at his feet, I turned slowly and climbed back up the stairs. There are a few times when a person in trouble ought to be left alone.

Ten minutes later, Robb trudged slowly back up to our office. I could still hear the happy chatter of the ladies, but now it was outside in the parking lot. Apparently *Yankee*'s circulation had increased by three. Without a word, Robb sat down at his desk and worked in silence for perhaps fifteen minutes. I wasn't about to tell him I'd been witness to one of the most unorthodox subscription efforts in the history of publishing.

"You know, Jud," Robb said, suddenly breaking the silence, "we've got to find something for visitors to do around here other than watching the editor and publisher of *Yankee* and *The Old Farmer's Almanac* sitting on the john!"

Then we both laughed until tears ran down my face, possibly his too. Obviously he'd spotted me at the bottom of the stairs. Later the incident sparked an editorial in which he wrote, "It is only when we can learn to laugh with and at ourselves that this whole world idea makes any sense at all."

It also sparked the idea of establishing a health food store! Something for our visitors "to do." It might have become successful, too, had certain ladies, usually from Massachusetts, been better able to negotiate the ramp leading down to the cash register. On a surprising number of occasions, one of them would find her upper body moving down the ramp at a slightly faster speed than her feet were traveling. Fortunately, none were seriously hurt in the inevitable crash landings at the lower-floor level, but we worried about lawsuits.

Robb's "solution" was to place a heavy chain across the bottom of the ramp. But when a Rhode Island lady cartwheeled over the chain, landing on her back (again, miraculously unharmed), it was the final straw. Robb decided the health food business was anything but healthy and cast his eye about for new entrepreneurial adventures. A restaurant was the next failure, followed by another restaurant and then a money-losing gift shop. Previously there'd been a town newspaper and, after Robb found himself the owner of a cement block machine at a local auction, a cement block business.

Meanwhile, *Yankee* magazine was beginning to show signs of real growth. "Why don't we just concentrate on the magazine, Robb?" I asked often, and his answer seldom varied. "The roof can fall in on a magazine anytime," he'd say. "Magazines, after all, are still just candy for the brain."

As *Yankee*'s circulation has grown to more than a million in the fifteen years since Robb has been gone, his "candy for the brain" assessment has always been my mental weapon with which to fight off whatever complacency and smugness might be meandering in quietly during the dark of night.

Within three months I had abandoned any thought of ever returning to New York for a "real job." Coming to *Yankee* and Dublin was a little like returning to Sunrise Farm and Vanceboro. I felt at home, as if I belonged. Sally and I started a child—and a house on a field overlooking Mount Monadnock. I joined the local fire department, became secretary of the Community Church, and drank a few beers with men in the local garage after work each night. And as my commitment to *Yankee* grew stronger, my working day grew longer. Within a year I was spending evenings and most weekends at the office attempting to accomplish all the tasks at hand so that Robb wouldn't hire anyone else to do them. I feared he'd bring in someone better than I, someone whose skills would show me up for what I was, an amateur. As in the army, I figured long hours and hard work would mask my professional deficiencies. And they did.

At first Robb wasn't aware that I'd subscribed to a mail-order course in magazine design. When the instructor, located in Mendota, Illinois, would send examples of two-page designs appropriate to certain subjects, I'd copy them *exactly* for the next issue, regardless of subject matter.

I learned not to disturb images in readers' minds when writing captions. "Don't describe a sunrise under a photo of one," Robb would tell me. "Just tell them where it is—Second Beach, Newport, Rhode Island. Period. Let their minds and the photograph do the rest." I became aware that hundreds of readers truly cared if I incorrectly identified a barquentine as a schooner, as I did in the July 1959 issue. When we published a fiction story the next year entitled "Silhouette of a Wedding," based on a true marriage in neighbboring Peterborough between the daughter of a Boston Brahmin family and a black man, I was witness to the dark side of our readership. " 'Silhouette of a Wedding' made me have to go into the bathroom and vomit into the toilet," was the gist of letter after letter, always expressed in surprisingly (to me) graphic terms of that sort, or worse.

I spent a day with Pearl Buck at her home in Danby, Vermont, and later told Robb I'd convinced her to write a *Yankee* article "for free." In truth, it took no convincing on my part. "If you had to pay me," she said, as her Chinese servant served us some sort of oriental tea while we sat, she in a floor-length silver satin gown, in a room furnished like an old New England country store, "if you had to pay me," she repeated, thinking about it to herself, "well, you just couldn't afford me." But she wanted to publicize her restoration work then under way in the village of Danby.

I managed the same arrangement with Erle Stanley Gardner, who also had an axe to grind. He wanted New Englanders to appreciate the work of a certain Frances G. Lee, a ladyfriend of his who constructed miniature murder scenes with dollhouse-like figures and furniture as an exercise in crime investigation for members of the New Hampshire and Massachusetts State Police. Ted Kennedy wrote an article for *Yankee* because he was eager to have his Boston Harbor Islands plan publicized, though my discussions with him were always through members of his staff. In other words, in those early years we made whatever "deals" we could—at the sacrifice, in some cases, of the "editorial integrity" all of us at *Yankee* so ardently protect and defend today.

Robb particularly enjoyed haggling with writers. It fitted into his sense of how a Yankee editor ought to be. In 1979, for example, I received a letter from writer Elliott Merrick of Asheville, North Carolina, recalling his early dealings with Robb. "The last piece I had published in *Yankee*," he wrote, "was so long ago that the magazine was just struggling to its feet. Robb Sagendorph paid me a year's subscription and the opportunity to buy a suit of clothes at a discount from some Boston tailor who advertised in the magazine." After suggesting an article theme, he ended his letter with "I trust your rates have gone up!"

Robb's favorite fee for an article, no matter what its length, was $87.50. "That sum makes them think we figured it out, maybe counted the words or something," he'd say.

Right from the beginning, one of my jobs was to investigate New England real estate opportunities for a monthly column entitled simply "House for Sale," with no byline. I enjoyed hiding my identity (and continue to!) so I'd be free to say a house was overpriced, a roof was falling in, or perhaps that the town was "dumpy" or, as I once wrote in regard to Duxbury, Massachusetts, "snooty." This sort of "honest" language naturally infuriated some readers, particularly those owning properties I criticized, and, I fervently hoped, tickled others. I usually heard only from the furious ones. In my reply letters under my own name, I'd wholeheartedly agree with their outrage and usually end by observing that "our real estate moseyer, unfortunately, seems to be without a smidgen of sensibility to the feelings of others."

While moseying around Pittsburg, New Hampshire, in search of available real estate one November day in 1959, Connecticut photographer Larry Willard and I walked into a deserted house we'd heard was haunted. We intended to create some ghostly photographic effects inside with some mosquito netting we'd brought for the purpose. As we walked in the door, we both yelled out for whatever real ghosts were in there to "go away!" The place was dark, suddenly quite cold, and very spooky. Our yelling bravado provided us both with the little extra courage we were surprised to note we needed. At the instant we yelled, however, about twenty miniature flashbulbs in Larry's pants pocket exploded, the blast from the heat actually burning his thigh. I doubt if either of us has ever exited from a house so rapidly. A silly reaction, I suppose. But there were plenty of other available properties in the area.

Everywhere I traveled around New England in those days (as well as now), people loved telling me their favorite stories about "real Yankees." "You can put this one in your magazine," they'd begin. I became aware early on of the popular Yankee image: he was male, *never* young, and lived in either Maine or Vermont. I noted, too, that he was not wealthy, not well educated, but very smart and heterosexual.

The day following my haunted-house experience in Pittsburg, I learned there exists at least one New Hampshire Yankee, and as far as the typical stories go, he may be the only one! After leaving Larry in Pittsburg, I'd swung west to the hills above Woodstock, Vermont, where Cousin Frank—by then the only surviving son of my father's sister, Poor Aunt Mard (Cousin Robert having died of polio)—and his wife, Eloise, had just purchased an old farmhouse. The night I arrived, he told me the "almost perfect" Yankee story, despite its New Hampshire locale, and in all the years since, I've never heard one with as many of the proper ingredients. Including, of course, the required conversation-stopper at the end.

One of Cousin Frank's friends was the Right Reverend Charles F. Hall, then the Episcopal Bishop of New Hampshire. Bishop Hall had been to dinner at Cousin Frank's the week before, and the story concerned one of his own recent personal experiences. He'd been visiting the northern portion of his diocese above Colebrook, on the Vermont border, and was spending the night at the home of a warden of the church, an elderly widower living alone. The man was so quiet and reticent that even the gregarious and outgoing bishop had difficulty drawing him into conversation. As they were eating a meal at the kitchen table in a rather heavy silence, Bishop Hall groped vainly for a subject that might spark the old gentleman's interest.

Finally, looking out the kitchen window at the scene of pastures with cows, rolling hills beyond, and a magnificent mountain as a backdrop to the west, he said, "Surely you must derive a great deal of pleasure, sir, from looking out at that beautiful mountain during all seasons of the year. It must be particularly spectacular in the fall and later, when covered with snow . . ." and he went on in this vein for as long as he could. There was a long silence once again, followed by the old gentleman observing, while rubbing his chin as if deep in thought, "I suppose you could say that is a beautiful mountain." Another silence. "But, of course," he concluded, "that mountain's in *Vermont.*" (Thanks, Frank.)

Besides investigating real estate, my new job also included taking the *Yankee* garbage to the dump in a trailer once a week; calling on major advertisers like B&M Baked Beans in Portland, Maine; sometimes spending most of a day unloading cartons of magazines from trucks; interviewing the New England personalities of the time, like "Bossy" Gillis, the jailed bad-boy mayor of Newburyport, Massachusetts; taking product photographs, for which we charged ten dollars apiece; and writing the monthly departments under false bylines like John Mason, Geoffrey Elan, J. H. Drake, and Damon Ripley, a few of which "live" to this very day. Robb felt that by utilizing many different bylines, *Yankee* would seem more like "a *real* magazine," the sort able to afford lots of outside writers.

Covers were painted by Robb's wife, Beatrix, a strong-willed woman who nonetheless possessed an unfathomable childlike innocence, perhaps enhanced by her ardent devotion to her Christian Science faith.

"What are you eating?" she asked me once as I was coming out of the little greasy-spoon restaurant then located next to our office building. "It's a hot dog, Aunt Trix," I replied. "A hot dog," she said, pondering the word. "I don't believe I've ever had a hot dog." There were times when I didn't know quite how to respond to Aunt Trix.

A *Yankee* illustrator who'd talked with Aunt Trix at a Boston Copley Society exhibit described her to me, not knowing I was her nephew. "The lights are on in all her windows," he said, "but nobody's home."

It was my duty to discuss with Aunt Trix each month the subject of the next cover painting. Robb allowed me that "responsibility," knowing Aunt Trix did exactly what she wanted to do anyway. Once, after several years at *Yankee* had increased my confidence, I suggested to her that the next month's cover be an Eric Sloane.

"You mean not use one of my paintings?" she asked.

"Just for variety, Aunt Trix, maybe we could use an outside artist, as so many other magazines do?" I said, already sensing trouble.

"Without me, there would be no *Yankee,*" she said in her simple, straightforward, honest manner. An independently wealthy Montgomery Ward heiress, she had financially supported a struggling *Yankee* during the thirties and forties.

I hurriedly gushed forth with praise for her work (which, in the majority of cases, I genuinely felt) and furiously back-pedaled from the silly suggestion about using an outside artist on the next cover.

"I just meant some month in the *future*," I said lamely, "to more or less fulfill your and Robb's initial dream to have *Yankee* be a medium for New England writers *and* artists." She stared pleasantly back at me, perhaps coming within a whisker, or so I feared, of saying "Without me, you wouldn't have a job."

During our next monthly cover meeting, Aunt Trix suggested we use an Edward Hopper, followed by a Maxwell Mays. And so it was I had a fleeting glimpse of a shadowy, elusive figure passing quickly by one of Aunt Trix's "lighted windows." During Robb's horrendous struggle for life a few years later, I'd see that figure again.

Within several months I could sense that the basic ingredient in Robb's intimate relationship with his readers, as evidenced in letters, phone calls, and visits, was a sort of humble self-deprecation that would certainly horrify publishing experts today. Now even the professional promotion writers *Yankee* hires feel compelled to boast. In their mailings to potential subscribers they describe *Yankee* as "beautiful," "fascinating," "exciting," "heartwarming," and, using a word I've recently grown to dislike more than any other, "folksy." (I would rather *Yankee* crawl away into the forest and die than actually be "folksy"!)

Robb promoted his beloved magazine with his hat in his hand. "Here's your *Yankee* for this month," he wrote in a subscription advertisement in the magazine about a year after I arrived. "Don't bother to read it. There's nothing in it that can compare with the amusement that you'll get out of a thousand and one other things these next few weeks."

When someone didn't renew their subscription, he'd send them what we called his "cemetery card." "Because we haven't heard from you," it said, "we're trying to accept the possibility you don't wish to renew your *Yankee* subscription. Taking your name from our subscriber files will be like taking another friend from town on his last journey to the cemetery on the hill. If *Yankee* hasn't been good enough, well, guess we'll just have to sulk. And try harder. But if you want to give us just *one more chance*, then . . ."

And *Yankee* grew and grew, with a steady 87 percent renewal rate year after year, the highest, I'm told, of all magazines nationwide —even the *real* ones!

* * *

Much of my early education at *Yankee* resulted from us all being in one room. There were no private offices. As a result there were no meetings, no interoffice memos, no speculation about what anyone was doing, no protecting of one's own "turf," no appointments —and very few misunderstandings. Communication was instant and constant throughout the working day. (One learned to concentrate amidst the hubbub.)

"Yes, they put the advertising rates up again," I overheard our advertising manager, Mrs. Annabelle Dupree, say on the telephone one morning. "No, I don't know why. They just did." Mrs. Dupree was a no-nonsense, hardworking New Hampshire native who considered her position at *Yankee* to be a good lifetime job but certainly not a "career." Careers were for city people, or maybe artists or actors. "They," not she, made important decisions like determining the advertising rates, and she was perfectly content to put it in those terms when talking on the telephone to our customers.

In this case, I felt duty-bound to call the customer back. "It's not really that our rates have gone up," I said, attempting to smooth what I felt must surely be the ruffled feathers of a heretofore steady advertiser. "What Mrs. Dupree meant is that our *circulation* has gone up and so every advertiser, like yourself, will be buying more apples in the barrel, but at the same rate per apple!"

"How's that?" said the advertiser, who ran a small furniture company in North Conway, New Hampshire. "I'm selling furniture, not apples."

"Right," I said, feeling myself sinking into some obscure morass. "I use apples as an example. You see, our rates are based on a certain cost per thousand subscribers, so . . . ."

"Wait a minute," the customer interrupted. "Will I have to pay more for my advertisement?"

"Well, yes," I admitted, "but . . ."

"Well, that's what your Mrs. Dupree told me ten minutes ago. I *understood* her!" and after he'd hung up the phone, Mrs. Dupree called across the room for me not to worry, that the man had already extended his contract six months—at the higher rate. I had a new respect for Mrs. Dupree's "no frills" sales technique: just say it straight and plain.

A few days later, a customer stopped by the office to pay an advertising bill that was three months overdue. While he stood next to her desk, Mrs. Dupree searched for several minutes through her file drawers for his records. Suddenly she brightened and reached for a large manila folder on the shelf behind her. "I remember now," she said in her matter-of-fact tone of voice, "you're here in my file of deadbeats." Across the room, I cringed. Surely she'd gone too far. But not at all. As he wrote out a check for the amount he owed, the man apologized, and on his way down the stairs he called back that he'd try to live the rest of his life in such a way as to avoid being included in "anyone's file of deadbeats." Mrs. Dupree didn't reply. She was already busy with something else.

Every day a steady stream of people came to talk with Robb, and I often benefited from eavesdropping on the conversations.

"If this isn't Oliver Ingersoll, it should be," I heard him say to editor/writer Richard Heckman, who'd come in to discuss the photographs for a book he was editing for us, entitled *Yankees Under Sail.* Oliver Ingersoll, a Massachusetts fisherman in the early part of this century, later became one of New England's most celebrated storytellers. Sea tales, of course.

Dick Heckman replied he wasn't at all sure the photograph in question actually *was* Oliver Ingersoll.

"Well, this guy looks the way Ingersoll *should* look," said Robb, examining the photograph. "I'll bet not one reader in a hundred would know whether or not it's *really* him." Just then, Miss Esther Fitts walked across the room. Esther was a tall, attractive gray-haired lady then in her mid-fifties who'd never married. She'd been Robb's father's secretary at Penn Metal Company in Boston for many years and had recently returned to her hometown of Peterborough and become Robb's secretary. (Later she would work for me, thus making her professional life a three-generation family affair.)

"Esther," Robb called out to her, "come here for a minute. Doesn't this look like Oliver Ingersoll?"

"No," said Esther. Like Mrs. Dupree, Miss Esther Fitts was not one to beat around the bush.

"Whaddaya mean 'no'?" Robb said. "How would you know Oliver Ingersoll isn't this salty-looking old sailor?"

"Because," answered Esther firmly, "I've seen the photo we have in our files of Oliver Ingersoll and not only is he not the man in that photograph, but Oliver Ingersoll doesn't look like a sailor at all."

"All right, good," said Robb. "We'll use this photograph. We wouldn't want a photo of some prissy landlubber who doesn't look salty."

So on page 43 of *Yankees Under Sail,* now many printings later in both hardcover and paperback, is a photograph of a bearded "salty-looking" old guy sitting in a fishing dory, captioned "Oliver Ingersoll." Of course it *isn't* him. But it sure looks as if it ought to be! Robb always felt an image was not only important but real. In some cases more real, perhaps, than "reality."

When China Altman, a stunning thirty-year-old brunette, walked into the office with her long-haired sculptor boyfriend one day, Robb decided to be the epitome of the crusty, shrewd, laconic old Yankee. She was a reporter for *Life* magazine, assigned to write a feature about Robb.

Yes, he admitted to her rather grudgingly, he was a Harvard graduate. Yes, he'd gone to Harvard Business School. But, he hastened to add, he didn't think even a high school education was necessary up in the country. "Around here it's best to start as young as possible on the main business of life," he said. What was that, China wanted to know, not at all aware her leg was being ever so gently pulled. "Well, pretty much just living by your wits," Robb answered, "fleecing the summer people, marrying smart women, doing about anything that comes to hand but avoiding really hard work, and of course, keeping the town taxes down." She loved it. Seven months later, the New England image, personified in the character Robb chose to play that day, went nationwide on the pages of *Life.*

An evangelist brought out a quiet, reflective Robb. As the man actually fell to his knees in front of Robb's desk, calling upon him, in an alarmingly loud voice, to prepare himself "for the life everlasting," Robb said quietly, "I would judge this *is* the life everlasting."

His oft-repeated advice to the many who came to unload their troubles (usually winding up with the marital variety): "Climb up on some hilltop at sunrise. Everybody needs perspective once in a while and you'll find it there." When someone seemed overly pessimistic: "Keep an eye out for what can *always* be beautiful in life, not just on a given day in given circumstances." And his old standby: "If you know yourself, you can be true to what you are, yet control it."

I've pondered the latter off and on over many years. Why did he always use the word "yet" instead of "and"? At any rate, the first time I overheard him so advise anyone was when a man named Allan Fox stopped by. Allan had decided to give up his sales engineering career in the city, move to Dublin with his wife and four teenage children, and operate a farm-animal zoo on land once part of a large summer estate on Dublin Lake. Because he'd heard that Robb had changed careers years before (from a Boston steel company executive with his father to the magazine business in the country), Allan was interested to know how he felt about changing life's course in midstream. Also, because "the Sage of Dublin," as many called Robb, knew so much about the area, Allan wanted to find out whether he thought a farm-animal zoo in town could generate enough income to support a family.

On the first question, Robb was on solid ground with his "know yourself" advice, suitably wise counsel to anyone under any circumstances. On the second, however, he violated what I've since decided is the golden rule of advice-giving: never *ever* get specific, because chances are, as in this case, all the specifics have already been decided upon. Thus your advice is a duplication (and therefore a waste of time), won't be taken, or, worse still, will turn out to be wrong. In this case, Robb drew the latter two!

"Don't do that," he said. "You'll go broke with a zoo in this town. Stone broke."

Within six months, buses loaded with children from all over New England were coming to visit Allan's farm-animal zoo. He called it the Friendly Farm. It was such a success he considered franchising it to other towns.

Robb, however, never wavered from his belief that Allan Fox would "go broke."

"How's it going?" he asked when Allan stopped by the office for a friendly chat a year later. "Fine, Robb. Just fine," Allan replied and then diplomatically shifted the conversation to the subject of the building of a new firehouse in town. Robb had by this time retired from sixteen years as a selectman but had recently been elected moderator, so town business remained one of his favorite subjects. They began chuckling about the debate at the preceding town meeting regarding whether or not to keep the old fire truck after purchasing a new one. "Christalmighty, maybe we *should* keep it," Robb said. He swore most when discussing town business. "What in the world for?" replied Allan, who, though he seldom swore, would become a selectman himself two years later. "Well," said Robb, "we could always send it out on false alarms!"

There was a momentary silence after they'd both laughed, and then Robb asked Allan how he felt about Vermont's Kurn Hattin School for underprivileged boys, saying he was thinking about making a "sizable" donation to it. Before Allan could reply, I heard Robb's voice suddenly lower. "By the way," he said, almost in a whisper, "do *you* need any money?" Allan's reply, too, was barely audible. "Thanks a million, Robb, but no, I'm all right. I'll be fine."

There were, of course, other facets to Robb's diamond-like personality that bore little resemblance to the generous one that, for an instant, he shined on the Allan Fox family (and, as I've discovered over the years, on many others). Arguments over money were continually drifting over to me from across the room, and his basic position in them could almost always be best described by the word "niggardly."

"It's no 137 miles to Hardwick, Vermont," I heard him say to a free-lance writer who'd come in to submit his expense account, including mileage. The writer argued that it was. Robb began rummaging through his desk drawers, finally pulling out a mileage wheel he'd sent away for. After setting the scale on it to a New England map that also emerged from the drawer, he rolled the thing along the route to Hardwick. The mileage, visible through a small window in the handle, came to 102 miles. The writer objected to the fact that Robb hadn't followed all the curves in the road. So Robb rolled along the route to Hardwick a second time, taking care to move the wheel along the curves. Eventually they compromised on 131 miles, but I had the feeling neither ever wanted to do business with the other again.

In keeping with the proverbial Yankee image, acting outrageously stubborn and sometimes downright cantankerous was a role Robb felt duty-bound to perform—although his *natural* ability was considerable! When a matronly Girl Scout leader with a rather lilting soprano voice shepherded a dozen little girls up to our office on a tour arranged with Robb the week before (but forgotten by him), Robb, hunched over writing at his desk, refused to acknowledge their presence in the room. He didn't, in fact, as much as look up. The woman carried on gamely, pointing out things on the wall such as an eighteenth-century barometer, some small figurines on a shelf, and an old weather chart Robb used for his almanac weather forecasting. "And sitting here before you, children," she finally gushed, "is the editor of *The Old Farmer's Almanac,* America's oldest continuously published periodical, old Abe Weatherwise himself!" The children stared open-mouthed at Robb while he continued writing. I was up from my desk and starting to walk over to help fill the void when Robb finally spoke. "Don't let the little buggers steal anything," he said without raising his head from his work. There was not much void-filling I could do after that.

Robb never lost arguments. In order to prevail against him, one had to do so before he became aware an argument was in the making. During an editorial conference in 1967, for instance, I failed to convince him that the word "gay" had, in modern times, taken on a meaning other than "bright and cheerful." Before I could persuade him to the contrary, he'd already dug in his feet. "For God's sake, Jud, 'gay' doesn't mean *that,*" he said. As a result, our one-page memorial to a long-time *Yankee* cartoonist, Al Banks, was entitled "God's Gay Cartoonist." When several people from Worcester, Massachusetts, Al Banks's hometown, telephoned to object to our using "that word" in a memorial, I chose to join Robb and ignore the implications. Wasn't Al, I said to each person, one of the most cheerful, happy men they'd known?

Once, just once, I did in fact overhear Robb surrender to another's argument. It was one morning a few weeks after the death of his mother, my maternal grandmother, Grandma Jane. My mother, Beatrix, and Robb had already sprinkled her earthly remains around a tree in Concord, Massachusetts, just across the bridge from the statue of the Minute Man. ("It took us forever to find the right spot," recalls my mother today. "The three of us wandered around the park there, Robb holding this urn with Mother in it, but whenever we found what we thought would be a nice place to sprinkle the ashes, we'd notice a 'No Littering' sign stuck in the ground. So we'd move on.") Robb's father, my maternal grandfather ("Da"), had divorced Grandma Jane several years before, had recently remarried at age eighty-five, and was, therefore, otherwise occupied. So Robb was in charge of the distribution of Grandma Jane's belongings, located in a house in Lincoln in which she'd spent her last years alone. Accordingly, he'd hired a moving company to transport the furniture to various relatives' homes around New England. It was to the head of the moving company that he lost the argument, possibly his only loss in a lifetime.

"This is over twice what you estimated the moving would cost me," I heard Robb complain to the man, who'd come personally to our office to deliver his bill. "I don't think I should have to pay a penny more than your estimate. This is an outrageous amount . . ."

The man was patient. He allowed Robb to rave on for a while and then, quietly, he said, "Mr. Sagendorph, allow me three minutes to explain. If, when I've finished, you still feel my bill is 'outrageous,' well, then you can pay me what I originally estimated." Robb, somewhat taken aback, agreed. The man began, in a low monotone I could hardly hear, by saying that when they arrived at Grandma Jane's house with two trucks, they were met by Aunt Joan, Robb's and my mother's younger sister. (That's "Poor Aunt Joan," the one who'd had the lobotomy in the 1930s and had spent all her adult life in institutions or under the care of nurses.)

Since Da and Grandma Jane's divorce, Robb had assumed responsibility for Poor Aunt Joan, often speaking with his father on the telephone at the office regarding details of her medical expenses or, for instance, whether or not her somewhat disconcerting habit of relieving herself on the first tee before a game of golf, one of her favorite "outings" from whatever home she was in, should preclude her access to public golf courses. Visitors to our office, I noted, were usually startled to hear craggy, gnarled, old mountain-man Robb speaking on the telephone to someone he addressed as "Papa" about how to convince his sister she oughtn't to pee in public.

Poor Aunt Joan was, the head of the moving company continued, accompanied by an older man who "didn't seem as though he was at all interested" in what she was doing. That would be Fred, I thought to myself, as I strained to hear the man's words from across the room. Fred had been Poor Aunt Joan's male nurse off and on for years, although I personally was never quite sure who really ought to be caring for whom.

The first thing Poor Aunt Joan did when the trucks arrived,

according to the moving man, was to order them to load the grand piano. "Put it in your blue truck, here," she said. Seemed logical enough. So the men went up to the second floor of Grandma Jane's house, carried a grand piano out, and loaded it into the "blue" truck.

"No, no, no," said Poor Aunt Joan, once the piano was securely tied in, "not *that* piano. *That* piano should be in your red truck."

So the men struggled and heaved and transferred it to the "red" truck.

"That's not right," said Poor Aunt Joan. She was probably beginning to have a pretty good time. "Put it back in the blue truck. I can see it won't fit with the other things I want in the red truck."

I could picture the men beginning to roll their eyes as they transferred the piano back to the "blue" truck.

"Now bring the living room sofa and put it in the red truck," said Poor Aunt Joan. They did. "Oh, *that*'s the sofa which belongs in the blue truck, sillies," she said pleasantly and they transferred the sofa to the "blue" truck.

The moving man's story, complete with verbatim quotations delivered in his steady, slow monotone, continued along this line for another few truck-switching episodes. Robb sat back in his chair, one long leg resting up on the corner of his desk, his arms folded back behind his head, and listened without commenting. The moving man eventually paused, took a deep breath, looked Robb directly in the eye, and leaning slightly forward, said, "Mr. Sagendorph, it was three hours before we realized your sister is *nuts!*"

At that, Robb laughed. It was one of very few moments of merriment Poor Aunt Joan ever provided him or any members of the family throughout her entire unfortunate life. (She died in 1985.) Then he grabbed his checkbook from a drawer and wrote the man a check for the full amount of the bill. "Guess you earned it," he said as he handed it over. The man got up and left the office, somewhat hurriedly, it seemed to me. And he hadn't as much as cracked a smile throughout, even at the very end. Well, perhaps it was no laughing matter . . .

"You've got a fine-looking son there," said the doctor, smiling, still wearing his surgical gown, as he came down the long hospital corridor toward me. It was one of life's special moments, to be remembered always with an inner glow that never diminishes. We named him Judson Drake Hale, Jr. A good choice, I thought, until he inadvertently received my paycheck and I his the week he began working for *Yankee* twenty-five years later! Daniel, a beautiful red-head, came along the following year. With the births of J.D., Dan, and, five years later, bonnie Christopher, I was surprised to feel a growing sense of vulnerability. Prior to their existence, when youthful arrogance was at its peak, I was sure I could maneuver almost any situation to my advantage. I was healthy. I received disability checks every month from the U.S. government. I was lucky. (Somewhere along the line, I began thinking of my "guardian angel" as simply very good luck. Seemed a more mature concept. I'm sure she doesn't mind.) My smile was a friendly one. I had a regular, normal man's voice with which to speak. Surely, with assets like those readily at hand, I'd always be in control! Then into my life came three basically uncontrollable entities—three human beings on whom Sally and I would depend forever for our emotional survival. Nothing would ever be nearly as important as each of them. It was downright scary!

Robb was not particularly comfortable around small children, nor were my mother and father when they came to visit. Further, my mother and father weren't particularly comfortable around Robb. They referred to him privately as "a funny duck" and couldn't fathom what "little *Yankee*" was all about. As to *The Old Farmer's Almanac*, it was just something one stuffed into stockings at Christmas. My father said I should be paid more, and my mother was already asking when I'd be getting back to New York in order to begin "a real career."

Nonetheless, one warm, sunny October Saturday in 1962, with three-year-old J.D. and two-year-old Dan wearing life preservers, my mother, father, Sally, and I all piled into Robb's old wooden outboard motorboat at his ramshackle boathouse at the edge of Highland Lake in Stoddard, New Hampshire. After an eternity of cranking, Robb managed to fire up the motor and we started up the lake to his five-acre wilderness island for a family picnic.

As usual, Aunt Trix didn't come along. Years later she confided to me that she felt Robb's properties on Highland Lake and even our office building in nearby Dublin were "his domain," not to be in any way affected by wifely influence. Whether or not this contributed to their long and successful marriage is impossible to say for certain. But surely the fact she had thoughts on the matter was a help.

The foliage was beautiful, the water glassy calm, as we put-putted along, and the Indian summer sun was warm on our backs. In retrospect, however, I have to describe that family day as "strained."

To begin with, it was obvious to me Robb didn't wish to hear my father's mechanical advice when the outboard motor conked out about midway in our trip. As we drifted quietly, Robb fussed, tinkered, and cranked while my father reminisced about the *Milky Way* and his fancy speedboat *Polaris* in which he used to commute between Star Island and Sunrise Farm. "When *Polaris* wouldn't start," he said, "I'd pour clear alcohol into the top of the carburetor."

Robb finally rummaged around in a wooden, somewhat water-logged tool chest in the bottom of the boat and brought forth a rusty, oily-looking sparkplug that he used to replace what looked to be a shiny new one. "This old one worked before," he muttered, while I began looking about the boat for oars. With one crank the engine came to life and ran smoothly the rest of the way.

Because Robb wanted us to hear the many varieties of wild birds singing as we landed at a small, wobbly pier on his island, all of us, with the exception of my mother, spoke in whispers for the first half hour there. My mother had never been much interested in birds. She spoke in a normal, out-loud voice, and eventually there was little point in the rest of us doing differently.

The meal itself turned into a minor disaster. Robb intended to cook hamburgers on a multi-tiered grill-like arrangement which, as usual, he'd purchased through the mail. It fit precariously over an outdoor stone fireplace he'd constructed near the water's edge and had various hooks on it for, I suppose, pots or God-knows-what. In the face of my father's advice that he wait until the roaring wood fire had calmed down a little, or perhaps *because* of it, Robb attempted to slap all the hamburgers on at once by thrusting and twisting a platter of them in the general direction of the grill and then, as they flew through the air, jumping back from the intense heat. His aim was excellent. But as they landed on various parts of the grill shelves, one side of the contraption gave way, instantly throwing them all into the roaring inferno below. I marveled at how quickly things can change in this world. At one moment we had plenty of hamburgers for lunch. A second later we had no hamburgers at all.

Later, while we ate toasted hamburger buns, my mother described the new house she and my father had just acquired, located on a rocky ledge next to the lighthouse out on Marblehead Neck, Massachusetts. They'd given up their New York penthouse, their home in Connecticut was for sale, and they were, after all the years, "coming home," she said, to the town in which they'd summered with Drake, then with Patsy and me, before moving to Vanceboro in the early 1930s.

"I could never figure out why you and Rog ever *left* Marblehead," said Robb as he fiddled with the grill he'd eventually retrieved from the fire. Sagendorphs just seemed to want to goad each other every so often. My father, sensing impending unpleasantness, interrupted my mother's reply with some suggestions to Robb on how he might expand his rickety dock to include a picnic and sitting deck, as we had on Star Island, and space to accommodate more boats.

Robb said he didn't want more than one boat, that the island was mostly a place for him to come to be by himself, and that, therefore, he felt inclined just to "leave everything as is." My father, sipping scotch and lake water from a tin cup he replenished every once in a while by means of a silver flask he'd brought, was silent for a few minutes, digesting Robb's statement.

"Maybe that's what I should have done," he said finally, more to himself, as he stared out across the lake to the hills beyond. It was, I thought at the time, an incongruous statement coming from my father. Out of character. He wasn't one to reflect verbally on what he should or shouldn't have done in the past. Besides, at sixty-two he was still young enough to be looking to the future. Although he'd just retired from the Conservation Foundation, his plan was to continue lecturing on conservation subjects at universities around the country. And at Marblehead he'd write articles, perhaps buy a sailboat again, and certainly he'd be seeing his old Boston friends on a regular basis. He was, indeed, "coming home."

I felt a stirring of uneasiness as I watched him during that beautiful October day out on Robb's island, an uneasiness that, unfortunately, I dismissed before the day was done.

"Rog seems unhappy," Robb said to me the following Monday morning in the office. "Oh, I think he's tickled to death to be out of New York and coming back to his old friends and the ocean at Marblehead," I said. But Robb Sagendorph, for all his eccentricities, for all his propensity to play the cantankerous, shrewd, stubborn old Yankee, was a tender, gentle man, wise in human matters—perhaps even those beyond his own understanding.

Chapter 13

Tenacity

M Y SISTER, Patsy, was the first to sound an alarm concerning my father's drinking. "Dad seems to be consuming twice as much alcohol as he ever did before," she said to me. We were walking along the road around Marblehead Neck on Christmas afternoon, 1962. It was a cold, gray day with a damp wind coming in off the ocean, but Patsy, uncharacteristically, had asked if she could speak with me alone and we'd decided a walk was the best way. Sally, my mother, and Patsy's husband, Whit, were taking care of the various children, toddlers all, at my mother and father's spectacular new house overlooking Marblehead Harbor. My father had disappeared shortly after we'd finished opening the presents around the tree a couple of hours before. It was the first (and only) time Patsy and I joined my mother and father with our spouses and children for a Christmas.

I'd never thought about my father's drinking. It was just his way of life. Coffee royale in the morning, a couple of martinis before lunch, cocktails at the end of the afternoon, and scotch highballs after supper. Seemed as if he'd been doing that for years.

"But have you noticed there's no longer any time between his last coffee royale and his first martini?" Patsy asked. I *had* noticed, chalking it up to holiday celebrating. He didn't seem drunk at any time. He didn't slur his words.

"Well, you know Dad has always been able to hold his liquor," she said. I could tell she was really worried, but because I wasn't, I didn't quite know how to react.

As we came around the northeast end of the Neck, where the grand old summer "cottages" face the open ocean, the wind increased and we walked faster. We were approaching the lighthouse on the harbor side when Patsy stopped, putting her hand on my arm for me to do the same. I looked ahead, as she was doing, and saw my father. He was sitting on a bench next to the lighthouse, his back toward us. Clouds of mist were blowing past him. He seemed to be staring at his new house on the promontory a hundred yards down the rocky shore, toward the inner harbor. The collar on his city coat was drawn up tight around his neck, and I was surprised to see he was wearing his sweat-stained old ten-gallon hat, the one he always wore when riding Ranger at Sunrise Farm. I hadn't realized he'd kept it all this time.

Patsy and I stood there for a moment, not knowing whether to walk up to him or not. Obviously he'd come to the lighthouse to be alone. Then, in unison, we turned and walked back along the route we'd taken, leaving him there undisturbed.

I've often created a different scene for that Christmas afternoon moment. In my mind, I see Patsy and me walking up to the bench and, one of us on either side, sitting down next to my father. "You seem a little depressed these days, Dad," Patsy says. "Want to talk about it a little?" I say. It's the ideal place and the ideal time and my father opens up to us. He says he's worried about his debts. He says he feels he hasn't ever been able to succeed at anything on his own throughout his life and he wishes, with all his heart, he was back in those lovely, golden days of Vanceboro. Yes, he admits, the bottle has become a crutch he can no longer control. We suggest he seek professional help and he agrees to do so. We both hug him and then the three of us walk along the shore to the house, arm in arm. We say things like "Anything can be overcome if we just all support each other with love." My father brightens noticeably and begins to talk enthusiastically about the future.

But that scene, in reality, never had a chance. Too many Yankee Hales and too many Yankee Sagendorphs in our blood precluded discussing anything that could be categorized as "personal problems." It would have to remain for all time simply an impossible "what if . . ."

When we got back to the house, going the long oceanside way, we spotted my father still out there by the lighthouse, still sitting on the bench. We both walked out onto the terrace in front of the house and waved at him. When he spotted us, he jumped, as if we'd indeed walked up behind him and startled him. Then he stood up and waved his cowboy hat, gallantly swinging it back and forth above his head.

"He's probably just feeling sad about retiring," I said to Patsy as we waved again and then went into the house. "Let's talk about it again later," I added. She agreed. But we never did. At least not while our father was alive.

Oblivious as I was to the problem of his drinking, I was equally insensitive to his money difficulties. Not that there hadn't been plenty of hints. A month before that Christmas in Marblehead, during Thanksgiving at our just-completed house in Dublin, he'd asked me to sign an agreement with the Boston bank that managed Grandpop's trusts, enabling him to withdraw up to $60,000 of principal from the trust held in his behalf. That was exactly opposite to Grandpop's intention. After the financial debacle of Sunrise Farm, Grandpop's plan had been to have the interest, *just* the interest, from the trust go to my father each month—it was enough for him and my mother to live on comfortably—with the principal distributed to Patsy, Drake, and me only after my father's death. Grandpop wasn't about to risk my father ever again "dipping into principal," one of the cardinal sins of any proper Bostonian—and, for my father, a proven path to financial ruin.

"Patsy signed one like this a few weeks ago," he said, handing me the agreement, and I noted it also indicated my approval of the trust (consisting of our inheritance money) purchasing the Marblehead house and then renting it back to my father at a nominal monthly fee. It was abundantly clear my father was in the midst of some rather desperate financial maneuverings, but I attached no special significance to it. I felt my father had more moral claim to Grandpop's money than I did. I signed without hesitating.

Even my mother was not aware of the assorted debts my father had accumulated by continually living slightly over his income since leaving Vanceboro. The $60,000 of principal, we learned later, didn't begin to bail him out. Only his death, which would automatically release *all* the principal in Grandpop's trust, could do that. And therein lay the tragic flaw in Grandpop's well-intentioned plan for his only son's future well-being.

There were other subtle warnings that Thanksgiving weekend in Dublin, too.

"If I should suddenly die, God forbid," he said to me one afternoon while he was watching me dig out a drainage ditch at the bottom of a steep bank behind my house, "I'd want you and Patsy to be sure your mother is always financially comfortable.

"Also, if that did happen, God forbid, think of my death as happening a year or so after it does."

That was a peculiar thing to say. I stopped, leaned on my shovel, and looked up at him. "Why is that, Dad?" I asked.

"Well, because then you wouldn't mind using a year's income from your inheritance to pay off all the pesky little bills I always seem to have hanging fire."

"Oh, right," I said absently, returning to my ditch digging. Christmas came, and my walk with Patsy around Marblehead Neck.

The following March, my father invited Sally and me to join him and my mother for a weekend in New York without the children. It would be my thirtieth birthday present, and he said he'd pay for everything. On Friday evening, we had champagne and caviar in their room adjoining ours at the St. Regis, followed by the theater and the late show at the Copacabana. The next morning, my father took me to Brooks Brothers, introduced me to several of the salesmen who seemed to know him well, and told them to "give my son here anything he wants and send me the bill." I bought a blue suit with a vest. That night he took us to dinner at "21" and kept us in gales of laughter with his funny stories about our old guide, Sid, Frankie the teamster, Dr. Ehrenfried Pfeiffer lecturing about anthroposophy at a lumber camp, the Metropolitan Opera singers at Star Island, and on and on. He was in rare form.

If I *had* been worried about his drinking, his finances, or even just his quiet, reflective moods of late, that birthday weekend in New York would have set those worries to rest. I wasn't conscious that he was drinking more than any of the rest us were (a test of dubious validity, perhaps). He cheerfully spent money as if he'd just won a million-dollar jackpot, and he seemed happy, even content, for the first time in years. We had a wonderful two days with him. I believe now he made *sure* we did.

"Dad really seemed fine last weekend," I told Patsy on the telephone the following week. "I don't think we need to worry about him." (Two months later, she and I sorted through the hundreds of "pesky little bills" my father left "hanging fire," amounting to nearly $100,000. Tabs for everything we did in New York during that lovely last weekend were mixed in amongst them, including one for my blue suit with vest. I felt that our paying them was an act of love.)

My father killed himself just before 11 a.m. on Monday, April 29, 1963. He was alone in his new Marblehead house. He died on the kitchen floor, beneath a large picture window overlooking the harbor and the town of Marblehead beyond, with Abbott Hall dominating the skyline. A frying pan with water in it was on the stove, as if he had been about to "drop" (poach) his regular morning eggs, though the heat was not turned on. There was a bottle with an inch of brandy in it on the kitchen table, along with an empty coffee pot and several cups. The kitchen wastebasket was full of empty bottles that had contained an assortment of prescription medications my father used for various minor aches and pains. Later, the official coroner's report cited "a combination of drugs and alcohol" as having been the cause of death. That alone could be construed as carelessness. But Robert, my father's handyman, who discovered the body at noon, knew better, and so, eventually, did a few of us in the immediate family. There was a penciled note to my mother in my father's hand which left little doubt the act was deliberate.

My mother was in New York City, at the St. Regis. Her singing career was over but she still loved to visit New York for as much as a week at a time, all by herself. She'd attend the opera, do some shopping, take a few German lessons (at this writing, she's *still* occasionally taking German lessons!), see some of her musical friends from the old days, and just generally "get away," as she put it. Not the sort of thing generally done by your standard old-line Boston Brahmin wife of her generation, but then again that's not a description that was ever applicable to my mother. "Mannie is always just, well, Mannie," one of her old-time friends said to me recently. I *think* she meant it as a compliment.

April 29, 1963, was the one day of her life my mother deeply regretted being in New York. She had, however, talked with my father on the telephone that morning. He'd called her twice. Both times they discussed trivial matters—specifications for the new refrigerator they were ordering, what tasks Robert ought to do around the house that afternoon. My father ended the second call by saying "I miss you very, very much," but he ordinarily spoke in romantic terms to her, although recently, as she now recalls, he'd been getting "a little maudlin."

At 12:25 that afternoon I was sitting alone at my desk in the *Yankee* office. It was a New Hampshire state holiday called Fast Day, and I was the only person working, although I expected to see Robb come in soon and maybe we'd have lunch together. He'd spent the morning viewing property he might buy. He loved viewing property he might buy, and he bought and sold a lot of it over the years.

When the telephone rang, I was in the midst of designing and editing an article entitled "Mr. Baker's Acres," which would appear in the June 1963 issue. It concerned the nineteenth-century amusement park, now sometimes referred to as "the Disneyland of the last century," called Ridge Hill Farms, located in Wellesley. Today I can't help but divide my almost thirty years with *Yankee* into personal little eras: the one before "Mr. Baker's Acres"—and the one after.

"Jud, I have to tell you your father died this morning." It was Charley Purdey, one of my father's Boston friends, the Uncle Charley who always suffered from buck fever up at the hunting camp on Eastbrook Lake. He'd telephoned the house ten minutes before and talked with Robert, who was waiting for the ambulance to arrive. He'd wanted to make a date with my father for lunch at the Harvard Club later that week. "I was going to gather some of the old hunting gang to welcome your father back to Boston," Uncle Charley told me at the funeral. (To Uncle Charley and others of his ilk, it seemed that anywhere within an hour's drive of Boston, including Marblehead, was considered essentially "Boston.")

"What did he die of?" was my first question when he called. Uncle Charley said he didn't know but guessed it was a heart attack. Robert wouldn't tell anyone but the doctor, my mother, Patsy, and me about the note my father had written, addressed to "Marian, dear" and ending with the two words "I love . . ." When I saw it the next day, I found myself morbidly fascinated by the fact that the "e" in "love" extended all the way down and off the bottom of the sheet of paper. If he had signed it, his signature would have been invisibly written on the linoleum of the kitchen floor.

After my brief conversation with Uncle Charley, I hung up the telephone and sat there for several minutes, knowing that I alone in the family possessed information that would change all our lives. I could feel my body vibrating with shock, hurt, anxiety, bewilderment—sorrow hadn't as yet settled in. (That would come later.) And then I began steeling myself for what I knew would be the most difficult telephone call of my life. My mother's voice was happy when she heard mine. Then, when I told her, it went an octave higher and stayed there for the next fifteen minutes, until I hung up. The last thing I said to her was that I'd be at the St. Regis to pick her up in five hours.

Patsy's voice was calm, cool, distant. I ached with the knowledge that she was furiously, desperately, throwing up her outer barricades around the devastating inner wound my news was inflicting upon her. "See you in Marblehead," she said, and we hung up.

The drive from New York to Marblehead could conceivably have been worse had we known the cause of death. We'd learn the truth of that from Robert as well as the doctor later in the evening. But it was a heartwrenching trip nonetheless, with my mother continuing to speak in a high voice and weeping. I'd never been witness to her weeping before—or since. She stopped when we entered the house at Marblehead. From then on, her voice was strong and normal again, and no one but I would see her tears.

The next day I accompanied her to the funeral home. We had to "make the arrangements" for burial, and besides, my mother wanted to see him. I didn't want to, fearing that the image of his dead face would replace forever the image I had of him alive. So as the two of us walked into the room where he was laid out on the table (my mother commanded the funeral director to remain outside), I walked at an angle, making sure my head was turned away. We stopped next to him. A sheet was covering all but his feet. I was aware that my mother was pulling it back from his face. Then she said, in a clear, matter-of-fact sort of voice, "Yes, it's him. That's Rog. But he's gone." She seemed to derive strength from the finality of viewing him there.

I recognized him, too, although I continued to keep my head turned away. I was staring at the scar, the one caused by an axe up on Star Island. It had gone right through his foot, and Sid had filled the wound with whiskey. I was picturing him bathing it during our lunch in the woods the day he and I killed the bull moose up at

Eastbrook Lake twenty years before. In a way, I've always wished I'd looked at his face, as my mother did.

While many members of the family were sitting at the kitchen table having coffee early in the morning of the funeral, Aunt Trix was dancing outside. Literally dancing. She would appear, wreathed in smiles, first at one window, then another, while Patsy and I rolled our eyes at each other. Everyone else, numb from the tragedy of it all, didn't pay much attention. Bizarre behavior was never particularly unusual when all the Hales and Sagendorphs got together.

Later, upon reflection, I realized that Aunt Trix, with an innocence that always seemed to free her spirit, was attempting to help. As a devout Christian Scientist, death as such didn't exist for her. It was rather a continuation of life but in the immediate presence of God. So from that point of view, it was a time of joy, even celebration, and she was making a generous effort to transmit that feeling to us. I later regretted that I had rolled my eyes.

I told the minister we didn't want music played during the service. Music, some of us figured, would surely make it impossible for us not to cry. It was, therefore, short, simple, and unemotional. As I stared at the mahogany casket before me, I concentrated mightily on not allowing the lump in my throat to surface into tears. Patsy said she did the same. It was a Herculean effort on both our parts, but successful.

Sally, on the other hand, the only non–New Englander among the several hundred mostly Bostonians present, wept easily and audibly throughout. She wept for all of us who were too proper, too self-contained, too, yes, too goddamn *stuffy* to weep! I was proud of her—and grateful.

And a few days later, we laid him to rest in the cemetery in Newton, Massachusetts, next to Grandpop, his eternal protector, and his mother and Cousin Robert. There is no escaping one's origins. But I wish he could have been buried by himself out on Alice May Point, where the stage for our performance of *Cinderella* had once been. He should be facing Spednic Lake where the north wind comes down from the wilderness forests around Star Island and where, to the south, you can still hear an occasional freight train whistling as it approaches the crossing west of McAdam, Canada, on its way to Vanceboro.

Chapter 14

————◆————

Common Sense

W HAT makes you think he's any good as a designer?" Robb asked
me. Three of us were sitting at a table at the Dublin Inn, a small
restaurant located a ten-minute walk down the hill from the *Yankee*
office. Ordinarily we sat at a round table large enough for ten—a few
of us from *Yankee* plus the local minister, whoever he happened to be
at the time (ministers came and went about every two years, each one
invariably experiencing marital difficulties), a local psychiatrist
friend, and "visiting firemen," as Robb referred to an assortment of
writers, artists, photographers, printers, and suppliers.

On this particular noon hour, I'd risked Robb's irritation by
insisting he and I sit apart from the others with a man I'd known
for several months. I introduced him to Robb as we sat down. He
was Austin Stevens, an illustrator and designer to whom I'd already
given several assignments. Brought up in neighboring Walpole, the
son of the local doctor, Austin liked wearing ascots and had the
appearance of a younger, more handsome, James Coburn. He spoke
(in a natural rather than affected manner) with the cultured New
England accent of someone who might have attended St. Paul's
School, which he did, and Harvard, which he didn't. He'd been
living in Boston for years, designing and editing *Boston* magazine as
well as illustrating for many of "the biggies," as we used to refer to
large-circulation magazines. Now he was toying with the idea of
returning to Walpole with his wife and two children. To do so, he
needed to find work, which was why he was having lunch with

Robb and me that day. I wanted Robb to hire him as *Yankee*'s first professional art director.

"I've never seen anything he's designed," Robb persisted, continuing to refer to Austin in the third person. Without a word, Austin produced several four-color book promotion brochures he'd designed and spread them out over our soup bowls. Robb studied them critically.

Until then, I'd never have admitted (except perhaps to myself in the dead of night) that a professional art director, trained in magazine layout, could design *Yankee*'s pages more attractively than I had been doing with the aid of my little mail-order design consultant in Mendota, Illinois. That sort of foolish admission might put me out of work! Lately, however, my confidence had begun to build. I was learning that an editor's job doesn't depend on one skill but rather on a sort of inner personal commitment to the excellence of the magazine as a whole, to be achieved through any means—or any person—possible. Another confidence builder, I'm reluctant but compelled to add, was my suddenly improved financial situation. Grandpop's trust money, after two years of paying off debts following my father's death, had finally been distributed to Patsy and me. It allowed me to feel I could survive on my own. At about the same time, Robb elevated me to the position of managing editor along with a hefty raise in pay. In keeping with one of Murphy's laws, my salary increased as my dependence upon it lessened.

So I began to urge Robb to overcome not only his reluctance to increase the payroll but also his past tendency (for which I'll always be grateful) to hire only friends and relatives—people who, as Austin Stevens loved to say to me in later years, "walked sideways." I was becoming convinced that in order for us to compete with the proliferation of new magazines "discovering" New England as a region, we needed professionals on our staff. People who walked *straight*.

"This stuff is too slick for us," said Robb as he continued to look over the promotion brochures spread out before us. "He wouldn't understand *Yankee*," he added, looking over at me as if Austin didn't exist.

I pointed out that *Yankee*'s small page size and its general subject matter could never be "slick," no matter how well designed. "Well,"

Robb finally muttered, still looking at Austin's work, "what would we have to pay him?"

"I'd need a minimum of twelve thousand dollars, Mr. Sagendorph," Austin answered quickly. "But I guarantee I'd be worth every penny of that to you."

"*Nobody*'s worth any twelve thousand dollars a year," said Robb, looking directly at me.

"Considering what he could do for us, Robb, I think that's a bargain," I answered.

"Christalmighty," said Robb, shaking his head and shifting into his "old native" language and accent, "I don't see how he could do enough to justify any twelve thousand a year. He's not that good."

"He *is* that good," I replied firmly.

Austin was looking anxiously first at Robb, then at me, as if watching a tennis match. Everyone else in the dining room, including those at our regular round table nearby, had fallen silent.

"Maybe he could design a few books for us, too, and help with our advertising brochures," I said.

At that, Robb stopped talking and began eating his soup. While we were waiting silently for the main course, Robb turned to stare at Austin for the first time. "Well," he said, "don't get too goddamn *slick.*"

A week later, during Austin's first day at *Yankee,* I learned something about sharing the creative process. It was a somewhat brutal lesson.

"Here's an article about Deerfield's retiring headmaster, Frank Boyden, we need designed for the June issue," I said to Austin, showing him the photographs and my rough sketches indicating how I thought they should be arranged on the pages. He was standing, looking over my shoulder, as I sat at my desk. "I think we should start with this photo of him, full page, next to the title, which is 'Dean of Headmasters,' maybe in red," I continued. "On the next two pages we should show him talking with the students and then at the end, use this one of him waving, as though he's saying 'good-bye.' All right?"

Austin had listened in silence to my directions and remained so now. "Can you fix it up?" I said finally, turning to look up at him. He was rigid. "I don't see that it requires 'fixing up,' " he answered icily (and Austin Stevens was as capable of being icy—or, for that matter, warm and witty—as any man). "Well, it needs the professional touch . . ." I said, growing uneasy at his reaction.

"Apparently, what you need here at *Yankee,*" replied Austin, "is not an art director but rather a lackey who can simply follow your directions," and with that he walked out of the curtained-off area of the main room I'd made into my "private" office.

I was stunned. But the lesson was crystal clear. If one hires a virtuoso violin player, one doesn't tell him how to play—much as one might like to! From that day on, Austin conceived as well as implemented all the page layouts for *Yankee* articles, and surprisingly, I found myself swelling with pride when I viewed his finished work. A new era had begun in my professional life.

As for Robb, he continued to stare suspiciously at Austin whenever the two happened to meet on the stairs outside our office. "Who *is* that guy, Jud?" he asked me one day. "Robb, you know full well," I answered with some irritation. "That's Austin Stevens, our new art director, and he's doing a fabulous job."

"Well, don't let him get too *slick,*" Robb muttered as he walked stiffly back to his desk, carrying his old wicker basket chock-full of a week's supply of submitted manuscripts.

One member of the family, hired in 1965, did not, even by Austin's high standards, "walk sideways." Quite the opposite. Rob Trowbridge, married to Robb's daughter Lorna, was a true professional in his own right. We called him "Trow" in those days to avoid confusion with Robb.

Son of well-known Episcopal minister Cornelius Trowbridge of Salem, Massachusetts, Trow had graduated from Princeton and Harvard Law School, had practiced law in Philadelphia, and had traveled the world as an assistant to international financier Charles ("Goldfinger") Englehard before deciding to move permanently to New Hampshire to help his father-in-law with the publishing side of the business and to become active in state politics.

Described by the *New Hampshire Times* a few years later, when he'd become a state senator, as having "a superficial physical resemblance to actor Telly Savalas but with more sophistication," Trow played semiprofessional hockey once a week during winters, spent summers winning the tennis and golf championships not only at the Dublin Lake Club but at clubs in surrounding communities as well, was active in town affairs, sang in several church choirs, served on multiple committees and boards around New England, played banjo in a local band, and generally felt compelled to help any group or individual who happened to cross his path. Austin described him as "one plagued by a hornet in his rear end." But while others sometimes criticized Trow for his impatience and occasional rudeness (the latter obviously fueled by the former), Austin's criticisms were tempered with real affection as well as admiration for Trow's intelligence, honesty, energy, and strong instinct to always "do the right thing."

"He may be hard to take when he's on a scent," observed Austin to me once, "but he's the man I'd want in a foxhole with me when the enemy began to charge." Of course, over the years many of us discovered that there was also a profound sense of humility following along in Trow's turbulent, frothy wake.

Coming into the business from the outside meant Trow was free of the sentiment involved in many of the "old-crony relationships," as we all referred to them, that Robb had developed with printers, distributors, circulation fulfillment companies, and paper manufacturers. To be sure, Robb recognized the need for change. However, he found it difficult, for instance, to inform his old friend Warren Osborne, president and owner of Sun Printing Company in Pittsfield, Massachusetts, that *Yankee* had outgrown the Sun facilities and would have to move elsewhere. *Yankee* was almost 80 percent of Sun Printing's business, and Robb had attended Warren Osborne's daughter's college graduation. (When we left, it did, indeed, fold.)

Likewise, the president of the New York company that distributed *The Old Farmer's Almanac* to newsstands across the country had been one of the few people on earth Robb had invited to his island on Highland Lake. So when Trow told him this man "has been stealing you blind for years," Robb didn't want to hear it. Yet he knew it was probably true. So he gave Trow the green light to make the changes he knew in his heart were necessary, and he consoled himself by complaining about Trow's subsequent actions to me at every opportunity.

"That Trowbridge moves too goddamn fast," he'd say. Or: "If our readers ever find out we're printing the magazine in Nashville, Tennessee, Jesus . . ." and "What the hell are we doing on the newsstand in New York City? Next thing you know we'll be out in California, for God's sake." (Today there are almost as many *Yankee* subscribers in California as in Maine, Rhode Island, and Vermont combined.)

When Trow decided *Yankee* ought not to wait for advertising orders to drift in by mail or telephone to sometimes-testy Mrs. Dupree, he hired a young advertising salesman who'd just moved to Dublin from Port Chester, New York, a man named Steve Avery. "I hear you're a salesman," I heard Robb say the first morning Steve came into the office.

"Yes, Mr. Sagendorph. I'm pleased to be working for you," said Steve.

"They paying you enough money?" asked Robb. I knew Robb always sort of vaguely meant Trow when he said "they," but Steve didn't. He looked momentarily confused but then, always quick on the trigger, answered with, "Well, can I have more?"

"Talk to *them*," said Robb, turning back to his writing, thus leaving Steve to ponder his first conversation with his new boss.

The staff continued to expand rapidly. A large three-floor addition was built onto the rear of our building and suddenly we were a honeycomb of private offices—just like a *real* publishing company! One Sunday morning I came in to prepare for the following week and found Robb carefully pacing off the boundaries of the area that would become Trow's new office. With arms outstretched for balance, he was meticulously pacing heel to toe as he attempted to maintain a perfectly straight line. "Goddamn!" he said upon completing the boundary. Immediately he began pacing again. "What's the matter?" I asked. "Trow's gonna have a bigger office than me," he said.

The next morning I heard him instructing the builder, Earl Proulx (who, years later, would write a monthly fix-it column for *Yankee*, entitled "Plain Talk"), to extend the length of his office by five feet. That would, he said, make it three feet longer than Trow's office. Competitive fires burned fiercely in Robb, too.

It was at about this time, during a lunch at the Dublin Inn, that the seed of a near-tragedy was sown. Trow happened to mention that he was interviewing candidates for the job of circulation director. He said he liked a certain prospect, an experienced circulation man from Boston, but couldn't seem to get a handle on what he was really like. "He's got all the credentials," he said, "but everything about him is almost *too* perfect. I wish I could find a way to get to know him better."

"If you want to discover what someone is really like," said Austin from across the *Yankee* round table, "just take him out for a few drinks. That'll soften his reserve."

Trow liked the idea. A week later, he, Austin, and I met the prospect at the Keene airport, drove with him back to the Dublin Inn, and settled ourselves at a small table in the bar off the dining room. The plan was to have "a few drinks" before lunch. Robb didn't join us, saying he'd meet the man at the main table when we eventually joined him and the other regulars.

We didn't, as it turned out, join the *Yankee* table that day. We'd run into a problem. The man, wearing a dark three-piece suit and a watch chain, was as reserved and proper after two martinis as he was when we sat down. So, exchanging meaningful glances with Austin and me, Trow was forced to order a third round. Then a fourth. Robb and the others at the round table finished their lunch and left. Still we hadn't discovered what this potential circulation director was really like.

By two o'clock, we were attempting to draw him out by launching into long, humorous (?) reminiscences about our respective childhoods. Finally we began exchanging graphic "first love" anecdotes.

"My first love was my wife," said the man when it was his turn, and that was the extent of his "story." However, he laughed politely at our stories, long and tedious as they doubtless were.

At three o'clock, Johnny the bartender announced last call until five o'clock, and suddenly we realized we had merely a half hour to get the man back to Keene for his return flight to Boston. Austin volunteered to drop him off and then continue on to his home in Walpole. Trow and I decided we'd be going directly home, too. The afternoon, we repeated happily to each other over and over, was "shot."

I don't think any of us paid much attention to the brief, formal little speech the man gave as we rose to leave. Something about how enjoyable the "lunch" had been, how he felt he'd finally gotten to know us all extremely well in just a short time, and how much he'd like the job of circulation director. It was, I thought vaguely as I struggled mightily to walk straight on the way out to the parking lot, the perfect thing to say. Just perfect.

That night I received a call from Austin's wife, Cynthia, saying Austin wouldn't be at work for perhaps a week. He was in the hospital with a broken arm, several broken ribs, and multiple bruises. On his way home from the Keene airport, she said, his car had rolled over several times, barely missing a tree that surely would have killed him. She added that a local policeman friend of theirs told her he'd been driving as if he were a champion race-car driver in the Indianapolis 500! "I've never known him to do that," she said. I laughed, feeling relief in the knowledge he'd survived and would be all right. "Guess now you know what your husband's *really* like!" I said, only half in jest.

Trow didn't hire the Boston man. Someone he liked better from nearby Peterborough came along. Besides, none of us could ever remember that stuffy guy's name.

After our third son, Christopher, was born in 1965, I noticed that Sally was drinking more at home—and less at the many cocktail and dinner parties we began attending during those years. One night, while dressing—and drinking—before one of the formal dances at the exclusive Dublin Lake Club we'd recently joined, I asked her about it. She explained that parties made her "a little nervous," that a few drinks calmed her down, and that she'd rather have them at home so that our friends wouldn't know. "But everyone drinks at parties," I said, "so who's to object if *you* do?" She replied she didn't want anyone to think of her as "a drinker."

Stupidly, I didn't understand. Sally was functioning effectively in our growing social world, transporting our two older boys from tennis lessons to golf lessons to sailing lessons (the three social sport requirements for country-club living and the three sports I was never exposed to during my own growing-up years in Vanceboro), as well as to Sunday school, Cub Scout meetings, Little League baseball games, even dancing classes. Besides all that, she was frequently putting on dinner and cocktail parties at our own home, was active in the Women's Club, the Garden Club, the Community Church (she'd slowly abandoned her Catholicism), and during the summer months she took on Fresh Air children from the slums of

New York City. With all that, who was I to say she shouldn't enjoy an occasional "pick-me-up" during her rare quiet moments at home?

Meanwhile, shortly after becoming managing editor, I had my own reason to be "a little nervous." For the first time I was asked to give a speech. The invitation came from a Young-at-Heart Club on Cape Cod, and even during my reading of the letter I could feel inner stirrings from the old monster which, had it not been for my mother, would have strangled me while I sang that lengthy song at the school play in Vanceboro so many years before.

They wanted me to speak for fifteen minutes on the subject of *The Old Farmer's Almanac.* I read through some of Robb's books on the subject, wrote a fifteen-minute history of the publication on yellow legal paper, and then practiced reading it to Sally, standing on our raised hearth while she sat on the sofa. She dozed off within the first five minutes of the first reading, but I chose to ignore the obvious message.

Typically in such affairs, following the chicken dinner at the Young-at-Heart Club there were a number of "acts" before mine. First, a twelve-piece banjo group played for a half hour. Following the completion of their repertoire, they accompanied the entire assemblage in a sing-along for which they handed out mimeographed sheets containing the words for *all* verses to such songs as "Down by the Old Mill Stream" and "If You Knew Susie." Then after a long introduction, an elderly man was brought to the microphone and given an award. His acceptance speech was of the long, rambling, stream-of-consciousness variety, but he received a nice hand at the end. Finally the president of the club rose to introduce "our featured speaker of the evening, who'll amuse you with his witty anecdotes about *The Old Farmer's Almanac.*"

Already I was in trouble. I couldn't recall having included a single "witty anecdote" in my prepared speech. I'd thought they wanted to hear about the *history* of the publication. A few seconds later he was saying my name and then, for the first time in my professional career, I was standing before an audience.

I hardly glanced at them. Without a single preliminary word I began reading my first dreary sentence: "Back when editor Robert B. Thomas brought out his initial edition of *The Old Farmer's Almanac* in the fall of 1792, George Washington was still President of the United States and the U.S. Constitution had been ratified just four

years earlier." By the time I reach the word "earlier," my voice had
reduced in volume to a near-whisper and I was reasonably certain
I'd either faint or die within the next minute. I couldn't swallow, I
felt a cold sweat, my legs were wobbly, and, perhaps the only en-
couraging sign insofar as survival was concerned, my heart was
pounding so hard it vibrated my entire body. "Originally a school-
master, farmer, and bookbinder, Robert B. Thomas lived all his life
in what's now West Boylston, Massachusetts," I croaked and then
risked a quick glance at my audience. Perhaps I unconsciously hoped
my mother would be in the third row center, beginning to speak the
words with me and pull me through.

But all I saw before me were strangers, very *old* strangers. Having already sat through a long evening and having been provided no
immediate reason to become attentive to what their "featured
speaker" was saying, many were dozing off into their cupped hands.
Several chins were resting on chests. Out of the corner of my eye,
I noticed a man slowly leaning to his right. Just when it looked as
though he'd surely fall off his chair, he righted himself with a violent
jerk. The only person who looked attentive was a handicapped man
in a wheelchair situated directly in front of me. He was staring at
me. Although he appeared to be almost ninety, he had a shock of
white hair and was dressed like a wealthy yachtsman—white pants,
dark blue blazer with gold buttons, a flashy red ascot tied around his
throat—and held an exceedingly long cigarette holder in his teeth,
straight up along his face, à la Franklin Roosevelt. There was a
lighted cigarette at the end of it. Unlike Roosevelt, however, he
didn't look at all jaunty. Something to do with his general condition
seemed to make him unconscious of the fact that the lighted end was
less than an inch from his white hair.

Perhaps it provided the distraction I needed. Instead of continuing to rivet my attention on my written words, I found myself
wondering what I should do or say if this man's hair caught fire.
Also, I found a certain comfort in the apparent fact he was the only
one in the room listening to me.

Slowly, ever so slowly, the monster withdrew, and I recovered
sufficiently to complete the reading. The momentary silence exactly
fifteen minutes later served to awaken everyone enough to give me
a short, polite round of applause. However, I was a little surprised
to note that my yachtsman friend didn't join in. He neither clapped

nor moved an inch. When people began to rise from their chairs to go home, a matronly middle-aged woman, perhaps his daughter, walked up to him, removed the cigarette holder from his teeth, doused the still-lighted stub, and wheeled him away. He continued to stare attentively.

A few weeks later, Robb said he'd be addressing the annual meeting of the New England Society in New York City, which was presenting him with their "New Englander of the Year" award. He wondered if I might want to go along, and I jumped at the opportunity. I was desperate to find some clue to keeping my monster at bay during public-speaking situations.

It was held in the ballroom of the old Biltmore Hotel. The men were in tuxedos, the women in long gowns. Robb was nowhere about during the cocktail hour. But as dinner began, I noticed him at the head table located on the stage. I was seated at a table near the rear of the hall.

The president of the Society began his introduction of Robb even before all the dessert dishes had been removed. He cited Robb's Harvard background, went on to say how Robb had saved *The Old Farmer's Almanac* from possible bankruptcy when he purchased it from Little, Brown in 1939, and ended by extolling various virtues of New England and New Englanders as reflected, he said solemnly, through the pages of Robb's original creation, *Yankee* magazine. "I give you now," he said, "a man wise in the ways of the beloved six-state region of all our ancestors—Mr. New England, Robb Sagendorph!" How, I wondered, would Robb ever live up to *that!*

Robb stepped to the microphone and calmly surveyed the assemblage. Dressed in a tuxedo, looking like a particularly craggy Abraham Lincoln, he was holding an almanac, a copy of *Yankee,* an old book with the leather cover coming off, several cards with notes scribbled on them, and a wasp nest on a stick.

After a polite round of applause following the introduction, everyone in the hall waited silently, expectantly. I could sense an electric feeling beginning to build, yet Robb remained silent while he slowly laid the items he was carrying onto the podium. He looked out at the audience once more and then opened the old leather book, as if he were going to read from it. Instantly a moth fluttered out from the pages, flew noisily upward for perhaps five feet above his head, and then dropped to the wooden stage, sounding metallic when it landed. It was, I realized, a windup mechanical moth.

The audience hesitated for a few seconds and then roared with laughter. Robb, unsmiling, turned to a different part of the book and blew on the pages. A great cloud of fake dust spewed forth, and the room continued to rock. When they quieted down a little, he began to speak his first words of the evening. "You know, as editor of this little yellow-covered publication," he said, holding his almanac aloft in one hand, "I get the silliest questions from people all over the country." He paused, waiting for the renewed laughter to subside. At this point, they'd have laughed if he'd coughed. "The other day," he went on, "a farmer in Texas called me to ask when would be the best time to castrate his bull"—laughter in waves throughout the room—"and I told him I guessed maybe he ought to try it when the bull's asleep!" Never has such a corny old joke received so much laughter and applause.

Then, while everyone was happily settling in for a comedy routine, Robb turned serious. With only occasional glances at his notes, he talked, sometimes rapidly and at other times slowly, about how an understanding of nature provides an insight into what the weather will be like months ahead. "When wasps build nests high off the ground, expect deep snows the following winter," he said, holding up the wasp nest while people near him shrank back worriedly. "Don't be alarmed," he said to them in an aside spoken loudly enough for everyone to hear, "the wasps that are in here are asleep for the winter and won't wake up 'til it's warm." Pause. "Boy," he said, pulling out a red "farmer" handkerchief and wiping his forehead, "it's a little warm in here, isn't it?" Laughter and scraping of chairs as some of the people at the head table moved back in mock terror.

Then, seriously again, "Bees, spiders, and ants—as well as certain plants—are useful as predictors, but nature, on the whole, is not easily understood, and birds and animals, who should know, are often as misled by her as is mankind." It was something he often said to people just when he'd convinced them weather could be accurately predicted by reading nature's "signs." As always, he loved to be totally unpredictable.

At the end, about a half hour later, he turned to one of his cards and read something he'd written for an almanac editorial the year before: "Tides, sunsets and moonrises, holidays- -as a maker of almanacs I find all these timetables useful in guiding us to what I like to call the edges of Creation. In arriving there, we must have plans and calculations and all manner of manmade data. But once there, the open sky, sea, canyon, mountain peak, or stillness of a pond takes over and regulates our lives and thoughts. In Nature's own house, we suddenly feel not care-worn, but cared for." The applause was long and enthusiastic, following which he was presented with a silver bowl, inscribed "New Englander of the Year."

In a half hour he'd come a long way from his fake dust and windup moth. In the process, he'd provided me with ten specific lessons in public speaking that I would never forget.* More important, although I wasn't aware of it at the time, he'd shown me the secret to taming my monster.

Robb wasn't, however, quite through for the evening. On his way back to his seat from the podium, he dropped the silver bowl. It clanged horribly when it hit the floor and I could see, even from the back of the hall, that it had been severely dented on one side. "Doesn't take much to make a New England antique," he said and the audience happily gave him one more round of applause. Was it an accident or the final part of the act? I've never been sure.

Several months later I found myself standing in front of a large audience in Rindge, New Hampshire. It was after a dinner of the Every Other Saturday Club, and I was once again "the featured speaker." I had brief notes on cards before me, I'd provided the club president with information for an introduction, and now with my monster lurking ominously along the dark edges of my consciousness, I was forcing myself to establish eye contact with everyone in the room before I began. Remembering how Robb had used his moth and dust to poke fun at his reputation as an old-time Yankee, I spontaneously thought to do the same. I would try poking fun at being "the nephew" and editorial heir apparent. Perhaps my doing

---

*(1) Be sure your introducer possesses the correct information with which to introduce you reasonably accurately. (2) Don't show up for social hour until the end—and then in time for only one drink. (3) Take time to establish eye contact with the audience. (4) Start with a self-deprecating joke. (5) Alternate humor with serious material. (6) Pause often. (7) Talk rapidly, then slowly; loudly, then softly. (8) Repeat important lines for emphasis. (9) Invite audience participation occasionally—ask questions, ask for a show of hands, etc. (10) End with an inspirational, provocative, serious thought—not a joke—and before you do, announce that it *will* be the ending (so people can prepare to clap following your "thank you"). P.S. If you wish questions at the end, be sure to say that well *before* you reach the end, so people will have time to think of some.

so would remove some of the negative connotations inherent in such a role.

"People sometimes ask me how I got to be an editor with *Yankee* magazine," I began. It was the first time I'd said anything to an audience without reading it. The monster, about to go into its strangling act, seemed momentarily confused. It hesitated, which allowed me to maintain a steady gaze out across the room. "I can answer that in just one word," I said, pausing briefly again. Then, with a smile I hoped wouldn't quiver, I delivered my punch line. "Nepotism!" The instantaneous roar of laughter almost physically pushed me back a step. What an incredibly lovely sound! And, miraculously, I could feel it blowing away the monster as if it were a fresh north breeze!

"They tell me it doesn't happen unless it happens in your mind," Robb wrote a classmate ill with cancer after returning from their forty-fifth reunion at Harvard in June of 1967. The classmate sent the letter to Trix three years later, after Robb had died. I wish I'd read it earlier. Perhaps I'd have had a head start in understanding Robb's apparent head-in-the-sand approach to his own cancer during the last two years of his life.

As it was, I felt only frustration and downright anger at his sudden embrace of Trix's Christian Science religion. How could he do that, I wondered, just when the pain he was experiencing in the area of his prostate, coupled with the continuously open sore on the lobe of his right ear, together shouted cancer! Medical science could save him if he acted *now*, I thought, and yet he'd talk only with a Christian Science practitioner—a healer—who'd come to his house to read from the works of Mary Baker Eddy. As his obvious discomfort and the open sore grew more severe, I was not reluctant to vent my feelings to him daily. "See a doctor," I'd say. Trow and other family members urged the same. His reply was always vague, noncommittal. "I'm gonna be fine," he'd say, "and, besides, who's to say doctors know what's really going on?"

One evening during the fall of 1968, I was present at a solemn family gathering in Robb's living room during which he asked us all to stop badgering him about "his health." Again he said he was "fine" and that whatever physical problems he did have could be dealt with through the spiritual sustenance derived from the teachings of Christian Science. "If by any remote chance I go down," he said with a finality that precluded any further discussion, "allow me to go down with my flags flying."

I went home that night and told Sally I thought Robb was going to die. "He wants to die with his Christian Science flags flying," I said, "so I guess there's nothing any of us can do." She agreed. We talked about people with problems refusing to accept available help. "First, I guess you have to acknowledge a problem exists," Sally said, looking over at me with a quiet smile. Suddenly I realized *she* was attempting to do exactly that!

I looked at her in surprise. I knew she was referring to her drinking, and I knew she didn't ordinarily like to talk about it.

"I'll admit a problem exists for me," she said, still smiling, but I could see she also was close to tears. "I don't want to 'go down' with or without my flags flying! Besides, I don't even *have* any flags."

Then she began to cry as she told me for the first time that she didn't drink merely to calm her nerves at parties. She drank, she said between sobs, to avoid "going insane."

Several months before, I'd been shocked to pick up her pocketbook and hear it gurgle. I didn't need to look inside to know she was now carrying a bottle with her everywhere she went. "I just like knowing it's there if I *might* need it," she had said then, casually. At night, sometimes at two or three in the morning, I'd been dimly aware of her sitting on the edge of our bed drinking from a full glass of vodka. No ice or mix. "One of these puts me right to sleep," she always said if she happened to notice I was awake, "and I've got a really busy day tomorrow." I'd mumble something about how she ought to begin worrying about her liver and then drift back off to sleep.

She had continued to appear to drink little or nothing at parties —seemingly content to nurse one mild scotch highball throughout the evening—but I had been noticing that lately she was often a little unsteady on her feet when we went home. On one occasion, when even her speech was slurred, she had admitted to me she'd "had a few" from her pocketbook in the guest bathroom. "But everyone thinks I'm a teetotaler," she murmured softly. I remember remarking that I didn't think they would for very much longer.

"The truth is," she said now, continuing to sob, "I'm hardly ever sober these days. I simply can't *risk* being sober."

Then she described her "panic attacks," as she called them. I instantly recognized my old monster and told her about it, explaining how its only apparent desire was to strangle me while I stood in front of an audience and how I'd recently learned to blow it away with laughter sprinkled with spontaneity and informality. Then she described hers, and I realized it was a variety of monster far more insidious and frightening. Unlike mine, hers struck at unpredictable times for no apparent reason. Waiting in the car for a red light to turn, for instance. While shopping in a store, perhaps. Sitting at a restaurant. Not always on those occasions, just sometimes.

"This thing stalks me always," she sobbed. "I never know when it will strike. I have to be always ready."

She described how, when it did strike, her heart would pound like a jackhammer, her breath would come in short gasps, sweat would pour from her face, and she'd struggle to find a private place, usually a stall in a ladies' room, before, as she put it, she went "permanently insane." Once there, the deliciously warm bite of the vodka from her pocketbook flask would bring physical as well as mental relief. She'd be in control again. "Lately," she said, "I've stayed 'prepared' all the time. That way I don't need to worry so much about it."

We ended our discussion that evening with the decision that she'd seek help from a doctor. Common sense indicated to us that when modern medicine, perhaps including tranquilizers, and professional psychiatric care ended her panic attacks, she would no longer feel the necessity or desire to drink more than "social" amounts of alcohol. After all, she wasn't—and we were both reluctant to even say the word—an "alcoholic." She was merely using alcohol as a relief from the unacceptable symptoms of a complex psychiatric problem. Much later we would both learn that naïveté and ignorance are sometimes disguised by the appealingly simple logic of what appears to be common sense.

So visits to a far-away psychiatrist began and continued over the next two years. First one, then another. When she failed to improve, she tried still another, even farther from home. (She dreaded meeting anyone she might know.)

As Robb was using faith, prayer, and a spiritual sense of fatalism, perhaps destiny, to deal with the cancer growing within him, Sally was tackling her trouble with the aid of alcohol and hour-long dis-

cussions about her childhood. Seldom have any psychiatrists heard
as bland a story, or so I would guess. She told them she loved and
respected her parents, enjoyed lots of friendships, attended good
schools she liked, and on and on. She'd allowed she probably had a
few "middle-child insecurities," she admitted she drank "a little" to
calm herself down every day. On the whole, however, she was
determined to surrender as little as possible of her inner heart and
soul to anyone. Besides, she wanted to keep the conversation simple.
Otherwise, the doctor might discern she'd come to the weekly session just this side of stone drunk.

Robb's condition was also worsening. Finally, one evening the
pain was so agonizing that even Trix didn't object when Trow,
who'd stopped by to check on him, called an ambulance. Once he
was in the hospital, an emergency prostate operation was performed,
authorized by the family. Robb returned to the office a month later
saying he was grateful he'd finally "gotten the operation over with,"
as if he'd expected it to be necessary sooner or later in spite of his
"flags." He seemed thinner, though, with a gaunt look that pro-
claimed to many of us that his ordeal was only beginning.

He walked as if he were limping on both legs, and pain was his
daily companion. As usual, he'd not speak of it—for reasons he
explained only in his writings. "Suffering out loud narrows life," he
wrote to one of several of his steady correspondents who returned
the letters to the family after Robb's death. In a sort of diary, actually
more a series of observations, he expanded on the thought by writing, "I try to maintain independence of mind, speak intelligently,
and suffer in silence."

"How are you feeling today, Robb?" I'd sometimes blurt out
cheerfully as he'd struggle into the office. I knew he didn't much like
the question, nor did I, but it would just pop out.

"Well, I've found something for my legs and they're feeling ever
so much better," he answered on one such occasion. I expected a
philosophical thought to follow, his zeal for Christian Science having
not in any way diminished since the emergency operation.

"What's that?" I asked.

"This," he answered, holding up a small bottle of Absorbine Jr.
Good Lord, I thought to myself, can he be serious? I wanted to
scream, "Cancer is treatable! Go see a doctor! Look how your opera-

tion helped you! Jesus!" But of course I didn't. As long as he continued flying his confounded "flags," what would be the use?

In spite of the ever-present pain in his legs and elsewhere he seemed calmer and less cantankerous, and he began to derive an almost childlike enjoyment out of purchasing radios, recorders, expensive tools for his island camp, and all manner of electronic gadgets. One noon hour, instead of lunching at the Dublin Inn, he went into nearby Keene and purchased a purple Lincoln Continental. It was as if he was determined to enjoy as many worldly possessions as he could, while he could.

There was another desire that took on a renewed urgency at this time, too. He'd always wanted to be a published book author. He'd written several book manuscripts over the course of his life, but they had either been rejected, as had one describing his years starting *Yankee,* or they had simply been squirreled away in his attic, more or less unfinished. To publish his own book himself—through *Yankee*—was a "vanity," as he often put it, in which he refused to indulge. In fact, he went so far as to instruct Mrs. Dupree to refuse all advertisements from printers who published people's books for a fee. "They're vultures," he'd say, "feeding on rotten literary garbage and human vanity."

One day during the summer of 1969, he mentioned to me the existence of a book manuscript he'd written some ten years earlier. It was, he said, about the history of almanac publishing in the United States. He indicated he felt that this one, among all those he'd written, had the best chance of being accepted by a reputable book publisher. "Trouble is," he said, "it's a mess." I told him I'd love to read it sometime, knowing he was hinting that I work on it right away.

An hour later, he limped into my office with his long arms wrapped around a thick bundle of loose manuscript pages.

"First thing you oughta do," he said, shuffling up to my desk, "is number the pages. But the whole thing needs reorganization." As he leaned over to dump the bundle in a heap in front of me, the middle section slipped out from the rest. As the sheets tumbled to the floor, some hit the corner of my desk, and all but several dozen of the top and bottom sheets followed close behind, some sailing this way and that before they landed. It was as if a trash barrel had been dumped over in a breeze. Papers were everywhere.

"You say you never numbered the pages?" I said quietly, looking up at him as he stood in front of me, still grasping perhaps fifty of the original three hundred or more pages.

"Well," he said, in an equally subdued, restrained tone of voice, "I told you it needed reorganization!" and then in one swift motion, he sailed the last few sheets out into the room. They fluttered like a flock of pigeons.

Then we laughed. It's one of the last hearty laughs with Robb I remember.

It required more than two solid weeks to reassemble and edit the manuscript. When we couldn't determine where a page should go, we'd either throw it out or write a couple of new sentences tying it into whatever portion of the book we happened to be working on. The finished product was not, we agreed, a potential best-seller, but a professional free-lance designer threw in some old woodcuts and made it look good. The important thing was that Little, Brown had agreed to publish it!

America and Her Almanacs didn't sell well, but Robb was never to know that. He held the first copy off the press in his hands one morning several months later and was as happy as when he'd bought his purple Lincoln. And by then, that's all there was of importance. I was so thankful to know there was little left he needed to accomplish.

Robb's final crisis began during a noon hour. Austin Stevens and I were walking back up the hill after lunch at the Dublin Inn when two workmen who were building yet another addition came running toward us. "Come quick!" they yelled while still some distance away. "The old man is down! The old man is down!"

We rushed up the hill and entered the back door of the office to find a group standing nervously next to the wide-open bathroom door. Inside, Trow was kneeling next to Robb, comforting him. Robb was lying on his back groaning, obviously in great pain. "Somebody call an ambulance," said Trow, and somebody did. Then, all any of us could do was wait, standing helplessly there outside the bathroom, until two orderlies came in with a stretcher, carefully placed him on it, and drove away with him. We all knew Robb's leg had broken at the thigh. It was obvious from the way it was positioned. But we assumed he'd fallen to cause the break, whereas, in truth, the break had caused the fall. He'd simply been standing and his right thigh had disintegrated beneath him. This became apparent later when x-rays revealed that the cancer had spread into his bones, specifically his right thigh bone. Those flags of his, I thought grimly when I heard the news, didn't seem to have much effect on a case of bone cancer. Nor did Absorbine Jr.

Following a few days in the hospital in neighboring Peterborough, Robb was transferred to Massachusetts General Hospital in Boston, where he stayed for several months. I often drove down to visit him there. Sometimes I went with Trow, sometimes with Trix, but usually we all went by ourselves so we'd spread out his visitors as much as possible.

The cancer slowly, insidiously progressed. Neither radiation nor chemotherapy treatments were undertaken (at this point, even the doctors believed that such treatments could serve no useful purpose), and although he looked more gaunt and hollow-eyed each time I saw him, he continued to talk about his condition as if he were suffering from a mild head cold. "Don't worry about me," he'd say brightly, "I'm feeling ever so much better today."

Trix was equally cheerful. During our occasional trips together to and from the hospital, she'd happily chatter on about skiing, perhaps her childhood in Chicago, ballroom dancing, her latest paintings, and how she was so looking forward to skating on Dublin Lake once it was frozen over. As to Robb, well, wasn't it wonderful how much better he seemed today and surely he'd be back home again before long. She'd leave my head spinning, and I began to wonder again whether the comment "The lights are on in all her windows, but nobody's home" had some truth to it.

Then one afternoon, after returning from Boston to the Sagendorphs' large Italian-style villa up on Beech Hill above Dublin Lake, she stepped out of the passenger side of Robb's purple Lincoln and stood there silently while I walked around from the driver's side and joined her, ready to escort her down the steep pathway to the house. But she continued to stand. I noticed she was gazing out across the sloping field where Robb, in other years, had kept an extensive garden. To the right, amongst tall pines, was the small octagonal "shanty," as the family called it, in which she and Robb together had begun *Yankee* magazine thirty-five years before. Beyond, rising majestically into a dark November sky, was Mount Monadnock. It was a gorgeous sight. I turned to say something about it to her, and that's when I noticed there were tears streaming down her face. I looked away, suddenly uncomfortable to be fleetingly exposed to the vulnerable human being always present behind her brightly lighted windows. And to think I almost doubted it!

She was right about his coming home. In plenty of time for Christmas, too. He was too weak to get about or climb stairs, so his bed was brought down from his second-storey room and placed in a small area off the living room. There during the winter of 1970, he worked diligently, every day, on the 1971 edition of *The Old Farmer's Almanac* while his once-massive body diminished to skeleton proportions and, as spring arrived, other bones began to break. In May he was again taken to the hospital in Peterborough, where the intensive care he required was more readily available.

From there on warm, sunny afternoons, accompanied by a nurse, sometimes two or three of them (women always enjoyed being around Robb, even when he was sick), he'd be taken for rides in his purple Lincoln. He'd invariably ask to have the car parked for long periods of time next to the lake or at some favorite spot with a view of Mount Monadnock. Everyone in town grew accustomed to seeing "Old Bob," as some of the natives called him, propped up with pillows in the back seat of his purple Lincoln, having his "last looks."

Eventually it became necessary for him to be lying on a bed or a stretcher. So instead of his purple Lincoln, an ambulance took him for his afternoon rides. For what turned out to be his last one, he was driven to the *Yankee* office. Everyone inside saw the ambulance sitting out there in the parking lot and the word went around that Robb was in it and would enjoy it if people would come out, one at a time. He'd like to say hello. Of course, as most realized, what he meant was that he'd like to say good-bye.

Austin Stevens told me later that upon climbing into the back of the ambulance and sitting down on a little jump seat next to Robb laid out on a stretcher, he found it difficult to think of anything appropriate to say. Robb didn't help either, staring over at Austin with the same squint-eyed suspicion he'd always enjoyed using on him.

"Hello, Mr. Sagendorph," Austin finally managed politely. And then, "How are you today?"

"That," Robb replied, "is one of the stupidest questions I've heard in a long, long time."

There was, said Austin, an awkward silent moment until Robb smiled, stretched out his hand and placed it on Austin's knee, and said, "You're a helluva designer, Austin Stevens, but . . ." and he paused. Then, with an even wider grin, he said, "But don't let *Yankee* get too *slick*, for Christ's sake," and, according to Austin, they laughed heartily and easily together for the first time. I guess Robb must have finally figured he'd put Austin through enough.

My own last meeting with Robb was four days before he died, but then he could no longer talk. I squeezed his hand, and he answered silently with a feeble squeeze of his own. Several weeks before that, Trow and I had sat at his bedside, and for the first time, at least in my presence, he talked as though he might soon be leaving us. He made it clear that I would become the editor of *Yankee* and *The Old Farmer's Almanac,* Trow the publisher and president of the corporation. He informed us he'd given us an equal number of shares in the business and that we'd be co-trustees of a trust holding the remaining shares in behalf of his two daughters, Lorna and Jane.

"But don't let *Yankee* grow any more, boys," he said. We asked why not. It was odd advice after all his own expansion efforts over the years.

"Well, because," he said slowly, "the plumbing won't take it!"

Good commonsense advice—but not Robb's last or most lasting contribution to my education. That was to be a lesson fully understandable only from a mountaintop, where the view goes on and on forever. And, in my youthful shortsightedness, I hadn't as yet climbed up to see it. Sally, through her own agony, would soon show me the way.

One afternoon, a few weeks after Robb died on July 4, 1970, I was sitting with Sally and her latest "far-away" doctor in his office. I'd begun accompanying her to her weekly sessions because she no longer trusted herself to drive safely. I didn't participate in their conversations, but I was surprised that neither of them discussed her drinking. He confined himself to asking questions about her feelings, particularly those in the past. For her part, Sally was obviously striving to say what she felt he wanted to hear. It was, I couldn't help thinking, a bizarre, hollow little dance going nowhere.

Then, on that particular afternoon, I interrupted them, more or less on an impulse: "Are you aware, doctor, that Sally carries a bottle of vodka in her pocketbook at all times?"

The doctor looked at me, surprised, and then turned to Sally. "Is that true?" he asked. She nodded, suddenly very close to tears.

"Alcohol is neither your problem nor the solution to your problem," he said firmly. "Now I want you to take that bottle out of your pocketbook and give it to Jud. Right now."

Obediently she fished it out and handed it to me.

"There," he said. "Now let's concentrate on your *real* problems," and he returned to the subject of her childhood. Sally and I exchanged quick, meaningful glances, and I noticed she was no longer particularly interested in answering his questions or discussing much of anything.

Today she describes that moment as the turning point of her life. "It was almost like a religious revelation," she says. "Yes, I was pretty drunk at the time, but all I can remember is being engulfed with the realization that no doctor could help me. No one in the world could. I was going to have to do it myself!" Ironically, she's grateful to that particular well-meaning psychiatrist. "A more skillful, less ignorant man might have strung me along for many more years," she says.

Afterward, as we walked to the parking lot outside, I handed the bottle back to her. I'd save her an extra trip to the liquor store. She silently placed it inside her pocketbook, and we continued on to the car. Once there, we sat silently for a few minutes contemplating, each in our own way, what had just transpired. Somehow I sensed something *bad*, although I couldn't for the life of me figure out what it might be. Sally knew.

"I'm an alcoholic," she said very quietly. The words sounded almost foreign to me—certainly disturbing and shocking. Not to her. She said later that uttering them was like opening dam gates to release floodwaters. The sense of relief that overwhelmed her was not dissimilar to the first mellow bite of warm, straight vodka running down her throat.

"I'm an alcoholic," she said again, this time louder and very clearly. Finally, after all her years of suffering, she was, as a favorite Alcoholics Anonymous expression puts it, "sick and tired of being sick and tired."

Over the next three weeks, I visited her every evening at Beech Hill, a rehabilitation and medical center for alcoholics situated atop the same mountain Robb and Trix had lived on, just above Dublin village. Sometimes I took J.D., Dan, or Chris up with me. One evening I ran into Sally's last doctor up there. He'd driven a long way to visit her and, as he said, to begin absorbing "how much we psychiatrists must learn about the disease of alcoholism." I told him we were indebted to him, but not exactly why. Nonetheless, his presence at the Beech Hill Rehabilitation Center that evening was, I thought, a credit to him and a bright sign for the future.

Sally began absorbing the spiritual side of the Alcoholics Anonymous program the way a person lost for days in the forest without food absorbs first nourishment following a rescue. She told me she was accepting the facts that she was powerless over alcohol and that alcohol had rendered her life unmanageable. "More than those panic attacks did?" I asked, realizing, as I said it, that it was a foolish question. "Nerves, anxieties, fears—even death—are an integral part of life, and life is difficult," she answered. How wise she sounded when she was sober! "In some ways, perhaps it will be more difficult for me without alcohol," she continued, "but I'll be *living* my life now, I'll be in *touch* with my life, I'll be *part* of life now." Was all this for real, I wondered.

One evening shortly before her scheduled release, while we sat together in the large common living room surrounded by windows looking east to Temple Mountain and south to Mount Monadnock and the hills of Massachusetts beyond, she said something about turning her will and her life over to the care of "a power greater than me." "You mean God?" I asked. I was still somewhat skeptical of what I considered to be the rather mindless slogans and religious pap I'd been hearing for the past three weeks.

Without replying, she opened a little black book: *The Twelve Steps to the Alcoholic's Way of Life.* On the page subtitled simply "Three," she showed me a line ending with ". . . turn our will and our lives over to the care of God, as we understand Him." Her finger was under the last four words.

"I must let go and let God," she said later, as I was leaving to go home, but I hardly heard her. Echoing about in my mind were those four little words she'd pointed to: *"as we understand Him."* How *key* they were to my or anyone's acceptance of the sort of spirituality that was now nourishing her life. They allowed for Rudolf Steiner's "cosmic life-giving force." They wouldn't exclude the teachings of Mary Baker Eddy. And surely the old-fashioned Yankee God of the Holy Bible was more than welcome. Anything. But *something*. Why, perhaps they'd even acknowledge the existence of a guardian angel or two!

After driving the babysitter home, I sat alone on our screened-in porch later that night, contemplating the dark, dim outline of Monadnock. "Let go and let God." I'd barely heard Sally say those words as I'd left her much earlier, but now they drifted back. I thought of Robb and the spiritual flags he'd flown before and after he "went down." If only my father had been able to see as clearly —and as far.

It was almost midnight when I walked into the house and wrote a brief tribute to Robb to be included in the first issue of *Yankee* for which I'd officially be the editor. I had a number of his quotes I wanted to use, taken from past articles and editorials, but one in particular. It was from something he'd written on the occasion of *Yankee*'s twenty-fifth anniversary in 1960. "We have done, for whatever its lowly value, our best," he wrote in the last paragraph, "and if it be God's wish that we keep on for another twenty-five years, so be it. The Good Lord, we feel, has more to do with life than most of us can ever realize or be brought to admit."

When I finished typing it, I went to bed and slept as soundly as if I were Juddie again, in a tent on Star Island with Sunny lying at the foot of my cot.

At thirty-seven years of age, I was dimly aware my education was over . . . and that it was just beginning.

Epilogue

Since Robb Sagendorph died, the old maple outside my office window has turned to bright orange seventeen times. Yankee Publishing Incorporated now has eight magazines, as well as other enterprises. With a monthly circulation of one million, *Yankee,* now a *real* magazine, has become the third largest regional in the country (after *Southern Living* and *Sunset*), while *The Old Farmer's Almanac* has been appearing every late fall and early winter on the *New York Times* list of best-sellers.

Our three sons, J.D., Dan, and Chris, have grown up, moved away from home, and made us proud. Patsy, with her schoolteacher husband, Whit, lives on a beautiful farm in northern Vermont. She's a professional photographer, rides her horses, and hunts deer every fall (though she never did with my father). Their three children are also adults. When I visit Patsy these days, the smells and sounds in their big old barn full of heifers, a cow, and horses, all with pet names, take me back to the days of Sunrise Farm forty years ago. And I'm still not much help with the chores.

As Sally predicted, her life without alcohol (or any other mind-altering drug, such as tranquilizers) has had its difficulties. "But," she says firmly today, without hesitation, "my decision to become sober was the best decision of my life."

I saw Robb's purple Lincoln the other day. I knew it from certain little marks, though I've never seen another *purple* Lincoln. It was sitting with a "For Sale" sign on its windshield on a lawn off Route 202 just south of the village of Hillsborough, New Hampshire.

We don't have lunches at the Dublin Inn anymore—it's become a drug rehabilitation center called Marathon House. Besides, lunch with the 250 or so people now working for Yankee Publishing wouldn't be quite the same as it was in the *"Yankee* round table" days. And though we still live in our Dublin house overlooking Mount Monadnock, Sally and I no longer participate in the active summer social life in town. Our spring, summer, and fall weekends (except for Octobers, when I now travel the country talking about the latest edition of *The Old Farmer's Almanac* on radio and television shows) are spent on an island on Lake Winnipesaukee, where we're usually joined by one or more of our boys along with their many wonderful friends. The antlers of that bull moose my father and I shot in the fall of 1944 hang there, over the glass doors facing west.

Since leaving Vanceboro in 1947, I have returned just once—out of a combination of curiosity and nostalgia, I guess. It was late spring of 1974, and I wish I hadn't gone. It was such a sad experience for me. The population of the town is less than half what it was in the days of Sunrise Farm, some of the houses are abandoned, many are in poor repair, and, well, they've even torn down the steam-engine roundhouse and half the railroad station.

I pitched a pup tent out on Alice May Point for one night and wandered around my old childhood haunts from there. All I could find of the outdoor stage built for my mother's lavish production of *Cinderella* was a half dozen boards rotting in thick undergrowth. The Mainewoods School is gone—there's only forest there now, as if it had never existed—and so are the laboratory and the majority of the other Sunrise Farm buildings.

Our family house on the hill overlooking the duck ponds has been cut in half. The half no longer there is a home for someone in the village. With permission of the owner of what's left, I wandered through. The shapes and arrangements of the rooms were familiar, although obviously the place had endured hard living and few repairs. On one wall in what was once our living room, I noticed the fancy silver wallpaper, now stained and torn, that my mother had purchased long ago in New York City.

On my second morning in Vanceboro, I rented an old outboard motorboat from a man living about where my father's two lumber mills were once located (there was no sign of either of them) and drove it up the ten miles of Spednic Lake into Palfry Lake and on to Star Island next to the north shore. I remembered perfectly the tricky, twisting channel through the thoroughfare separating the two lakes. After all, I'd dreamt about it often enough!

Someone at the store in town had told me Star Island was owned by the dean of Dartmouth College, Carroll W. Brewster, but no one was there that morning, so I didn't land my boat. From the water, as I slowly cruised around the island, I could see that most of the log cabins, originally built by our old guide, Sid, and his four sons, looked to be in reasonably good shape. The huge birch tree on the north end of the island, under which my dog, Sunny, and I would lie for hours while I played my harmonica and she snapped at flies, was still there. But our elaborate wooden dock and float were no more.

Beyond the island, on the east mainland shore, I noticed what appeared to be a pile of rotting boards amongst the dry kye (driftwood), some of them obviously having once been painted white. I hadn't remembered a cabin there, let alone a white one. On closer inspection, however, it turned out to be the remains of our wonderful, faithful cabin cruiser, the *Milky Way*. I can't imagine how or why she had ended up along the shore.

The drive home to New Hampshire that evening and into the morning took more than nine hours. A little less than when my mother drove me to High Mowing School in September 1942. But not much. Distances don't change and, northeast of Bangor, neither do the roads.

Drake is still at the *Sonnenhof* in Arlesheim. He still speaks only German, he still feels more comfortable with his hands inside his sleeves, and he still lives in the same fifth-floor bedroom he's been in since 1930. He's sixty years old now, about forty years older than any of the other patients there. As always, he goes to concerts, the theater, and art exhibits, he takes occasional boat rides on the Rhine, and he's read to by his nurse every day.

Seldom does more than a year go by without either Patsy, my mother, or me flying over (or in the case of my mother, sailing) to see him for a few days. There have been occasional two-year intervals. Eleven years ago, I was accompanied by my then sixteen-year-old son J.D., who loves ice cream with about the same passion as Drake does. Smiling at each other in a sort of conspiratorial manner, they ate dish after dish of it together during our afternoons in Arlesheim. When Drake's nurse would tell him "*Genug, Drake, genug!* (Enough, Drake, enough!),*" I noticed J.D. slipping him more when she wasn't looking.

As for my mother, she enrolled as a freshman at Emerson College in Boston following my father's death, endured freshman "hazing" (wearing a funny hat, she had to stop motorists on Commonwealth Avenue and ask for a dime), and received her Bachelor of Arts degree four years later, in June 1967. Naturally we were all in attendance for the grand ceremony.

After her graduation, she tried living near us in neighboring Peterborough ("There's nothing for me to *do* here") and then briefly in New York. Finally she settled in an apartment outside Washington, D.C., for a few years. There she worked as a volunteer with an organization attempting to raise funds for a hospital for retarded children. It was spearheaded by Mrs. Hubert Humphrey, and naturally my mother came to know her reasonably well. When Hubert Humphrey died and Muriel Humphrey returned to Minnesota, however, my mother decided she, too, would come home—to New England. "I've come to brink after brink of doing something worthwhile with my life," she often reflected later, "but I can't seem to push past those *brinks.*"

She settled again in Marblehead, but this time it was in a small house on the town side of the harbor, almost directly across the water from the elegant house on the Neck in which my father had died. That house, incidentally, had been sold by the banks within weeks, maybe days, of his death. While visiting my mother during the 1970s and early '80s, I'd sometimes find myself staring across the harbor at it. It always looked eerie to me.

While we all hoped a new man would come into her life sometime during those years, he never did. ("The men I meet either can't hear, can't see, can't walk, or are about to have an operation.") She has remained alone since 1963.

Today she resides in Peterborough once again ("There's still nothing for me to *do* here") within five minutes' drive of Sally and me. She also has a small apartment on Beacon Street in Boston. In both places, much of her time is spent attempting to deal with the problems and frustrations of advancing age.

When I mentioned to her a year and a half ago that I was

beginning to write a book about our family experiences at Sunrise Farm, my early years with her brother at *Yankee,* and so forth, she looked surprised.

"You mean you're writing your autobiography?" she asked.

I allowed that it was, in a way, an autobiography, although I suddenly disliked the pompous sound of the word.

"You're too *young* to be writing your autobiography, Butch," she said, looking me straight in the eye with that self-assurance she's never lost.

"Oh, Mom!" is about all I could manage for a reply. I was, of course, slightly irritated to be reminded once again that, when it came to certain basics, my mother was almost always right.

October 1986